RAISING PHILADELPHIA

RAISING PHILADELPHIA

The Making of America's First Great City, 1750–1775

JUSTIN MCHENRY

BROOKLINE
books
Havertown, Pennsylvania

Brookline Books is an imprint of Casemate Publishers

Published in the United States of America and Great Britain in 2024 by
BROOKLINE BOOKS
1950 Lawrence Road, Havertown, PA 19083, USA
and
47 Church Street, Barnsley, S70 2AS, UK

Hardcover Edition: ISBN 978-1-955041-20-1
Digital Edition: ISBN 978-1-955041-21-8

A CIP record for this book is available from the British Library

Printed and bound in the United Kingdom by CPI Group (UK) Ltd, Croydon, CR0 4YY
Typeset in India by DiTech Publishing Services

For a complete list of Casemate titles, please contact:

CASEMATE PUBLISHERS (US)
Telephone (610) 853-9131
Fax (610) 853-9146
Email: casemate@casematepublishers.com
www.casematepublishers.com

CASEMATE PUBLISHERS (UK)
Telephone (0)1226 734350
Email: casemate@casemateuk.com
www.casemateuk.com

Front cover images: (from left) A portait of Olaudah Equiano (Royal Albert Memorial Museum and Art Gallery, and Exeter City Council); A portrait of Elizabeth Graeme (Wikimedia Commons); A painting of Benjamin Franklin from 1778 (Wikimedia Commons)
Back cover image: A view of Philadelphia from across the Delaware river (*Philadelphia: A History of the City and its People*)

For Rick and Gail and all Pennsylvanians.

Contents

Introduction: The City and the Boy

You were 10 once. Awkward. And everything seemed so big. So scary. Imagine yourself left alone at 10 in the middle of the biggest city in all of America. The people. More people than you ever could have imagined living, let alone living all together in one place, moving all around you. The horses pulling wagons down the street. Your senses overloaded with the sights. The smells. A mixture of Market Street, the produce, the meat, the dung. The sounds. The hammering at the docks, the shouts from the streets. It's overwhelming. And for Robert Johnston that is the situation he found himself in. Dropped off in the middle of Philadelphia in 1760 at the age of 10. A boy in the city.

Johnston came from the western counties, which were the battleground of the Seven Years' War. The random explosions of violence had the entire west of Pennsylvania on edge, forcing entire communities to shelter in and around the string of Western forts. Those that could afford it would move their family or just their children to the safety of Philadelphia.

Robert Johnston was born into a large, prosperous family in Cumberland County (what is now Franklin County) near the border of Pennsylvania and Maryland.

A view of Philadelphia from across the Delaware river showing the busy port and the city's skyline as it appeared throughout the late colonial period. (*Philadelphia: A History of the City and its People*)

Johnston's father immigrated from Ireland and amassed a considerable amount of land in Antrim Township and the surrounding areas. And as hostilities increased between the white European settlers and the Indigenous peoples in the late 1750s, violent raids frequented the land around the Johnstons. The decision was made to ship the youngest son, Robert, to Philadelphia to continue his education.

There he found himself, alone and on the doorstep of the relatively new College of Philadelphia under the leadership of Provost William Smith, one of the most controversial and consequential figures of the period. And on Robert's graduation in 1763, the leading members of the Philadelphia Society, including Benjamin Franklin, would quiz the 13-year-old Johnston in Latin and Greek.

Johnston would go on to earn his master's degree at the college, working as an instructor at the academy while enrolled in graduate school, all the while living through the most tumultuous period in the colonial era. The Paxton Boys scare of the winter of 1764; the following political maelstrom; the Stamp Act crisis. He followed in the same footsteps as other young doctors and traveled to England and Scotland to further his education. He may have even attended the first medical lectures of William Shippen, Jr. and made the rounds at the Pennsylvania Hospital.

He was there a witness to the grand expansion of Philadelphia as it became the largest city in British North America, filled with such vibrancy and imbued with spirit by the likes of other young transplants to the city: Robert Morris, William Smith, Anthony Benezet, Charles Thomson, and so many others who along with Benjamin Franklin helped to shape and mold Philadelphia into their image. Along the way, their actions and battles, good deeds and bad, gave Philadelphia an identity.

A long history existed of political and religious freedoms that made the city a haven for a diverse representation of white European cultures. As this unique mixture kneaded together, histories and beliefs were shared and debated in the taverns and in the coffee houses, at the market and the college, and in the newspapers and across the broadsheets and the pamphlets. This cultural blending created the foundations for Philadelphia to blossom and explode, economically, culturally, intellectually, and in terms of population.

Yet despite those unique advantages enjoyed by the more well-off white population, there existed an unfree, subservient one of enslaved Africans and indentured servants that provided much of the labor necessary for the unprecedented growth of Philadelphia. Enslaved peoples were an essential and original part of Philadelphia's history, arriving there prior to the Penns and with some of the first white European settlers to the area. They were owned throughout the city by all classes from Franklin on down to white sailors, being employed in many different trades. The history of Philadelphia is one of enslavement and unfree labor, but there also grew there through the influence of some Quakers the first efforts to overturn the brutal institution.

The late colonial era saw an increase in opportunities for women. Philadelphian women, whether they were single, married or widowed, provided for themselves and their families no matter the challenges that faced them because of their sex. Women held a number of unique positions and accounted for large portions of the city's tavernkeepers, wholesalers, and small shop owners. They took ownership of their sexuality and challenged the norms.

Several women expressed themselves through their writing. Writers like Elizabeth Graeme and Hannah Griffitts produced impressive, ambitious works fitting in with the burgeoning cultural scene of Philadelphia. At Graeme's salons, writers, artists, and musicians mingled with politicians, merchants, and religious leaders, creating an atmosphere in the community that established the free discourse of ideas and art; developments which led to the first concerts and written plays in America.

The inquisitive environment led to many advancements in the scientific world. Benjamin Franklin's experiments with electricity set the tone, occurring with the aid of a number of other citizen-scientists of Philadelphia. His discoveries represented just one of the areas where Philadelphians made key scientific advancements. Others included John Bartram's seed-hunting travels and the botanical garden he built at his home on the banks of the Schuylkill, and David Rittenhouse's technological and astronomical achievements with his orrery and the work he put into the grand scientific event of the era, the Transit of Venus. These efforts were guided by a number of organizations like the Library Company and the American Philosophical Society.

All of this was made possible by a spirit of education. Robert Johnston benefited from this emphasis on learning as it spread through to higher education and the beginnings of a proper medical training establishment in the city. In the process, this created a population that was highly literate and intellectually engaged.

Underlying all of this was the unprecedented economic growth and expansion in the city. Spurred on by wartime spending during the Seven Years' War, all aspects of the city's economy prospered and though dips occurred after the hostilities died away, it would still be healthy and experienced incredible growth that sustained the growing population. Philadelphia would be the preferred destination for many immigrating Europeans, which caused the population to balloon till it became the largest in the British Empire.

However large in population it became, Philadelphia was geographically small. The city proper only constituted eight blocks north by south and 22 blocks east by west, with most of the business and residential areas concentrated in a 20-block section centering around High (or Market) Street. A traveler by sea coming up the Delaware would notice how busy the port of Philadelphia was. Ships of all sizes, merchantmen, sloops, pleasure cruisers, barges, and ferries, patrolled the Delaware, docking at one of the dozens of docks owned and operated by the city's merchants. There, any number of specialty workers would begin the job of unloading the cargo: some human, enslaved and free, and some finished goods from England or foodstuffs from around the Atlantic world. Stevedores and shipwrights, sailmakers and ropemakers and many more would work to outfit the ship for its next journey,

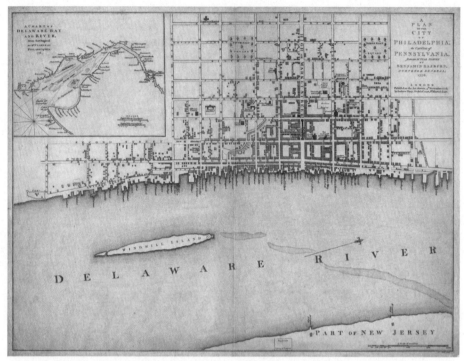

A 1776 survey map of Philadelphia showing the streets and locations of major institutions around the city and the waterfront at the time of the Declaration of Independence. (Library of Congress)

while the sailors would go and spend their pay in one of the many taverns lining Front Street that ran the length of the two-mile waterfront spreading from the Northern Liberties down into Southwark.

There on the southernmost edge of the city as it merged into Southwark was Plumsted's Warehouse which would house the first theater company to come through the city. Across the street, Lewis Hallam and the American Company would build Philadelphia's first permanent theater.

In between the two would be one of the busiest docks in all of Philadelphia, owned and operated by Willing and Son and then Willing and Morris. Thomas Willing and Robert Morris formed a successful mercantile business that saw them become two of the wealthiest men in the city. As the Revolution came, Morris played a crucial role in securing trade routes for the continental cause, and their warehouse was of such importance that armed guards were stationed there at all times.

Further along Front Street the traveler would arrive at the nerve center of the city, the intersection of Front and Market. There on the corner stood the London Coffee House, one of the most public meeting places in all of Philadelphia. Every morning merchants gathered at the Coffee House to discuss their most recent shipments, set prices, make deals, establish partnerships, insure one another's voyages—conduct any number of business transactions in order to secure their own personal success and that of the city.

For inbound captains and supercargoes, the London Coffee House would be their first stop once in Philadelphia to meet with their bosses. Outside its door, public auctions were held to sell off the newly arrived enslaved Africans. Announcements were made in the city's multiple newspapers and those from all over Pennsylvania and the surrounding colonies would come to purchase these enslaved peoples. Families were torn apart. Some would stay in Philadelphia where they would work any and every job that there was to do, from domestic to tailor.

A quick walk down Market Street would soon reveal why it was called that. Stalls lined the middle of the street. Two full markets were held each week where vendors would fill their stalls as residents browsed and visitors from all over came to sell and buy goods and supplies. Carts arrived filled with produce from the western counties to be scooped up by merchants to fill their outgoing ships.

Small businesses occupied the buildings on Market Street, whether dry goods or specialty item shops such as the silversmith. This was where you would also find the offices of Franklin's printing press where he produced his *Poor Richard's Almanack* and the newspaper, *Pennsylvania Gazette*. Behind the press on Chestnut between Second and Third is where Franklin would build his home.

View of Market Street, the hub of the city with the City Courthouse and the market stalls stretching off behind. This spot would serve as the primary public congregating area for the many of the city's residents on a daily basis. (*The Historic Mansions and Buildings of Philadelphia*)

Further down Market and onto North Fourth Street stood the Academy and College of Philadelphia, where Robert Johnston spent his formative years along with hundreds of other young men under the dark visage of William Smith. Smith ruled over the schools for close to half a century, an outspoken proponent of Pennsylvania's proprietors, which would land him in jail and make himself a mortal enemy of Franklin.

The Assembly met at the State House across Market on Chestnut between Fifth and Sixth streets. The impressive structure served as the center of many political battles of the late colonial era and witnessed the political rise of luminaries like John Dickinson and Charles Thomson. Its rooms would house the Library Company's collection and host William Shippen, Jr.'s first medical lectures. And, of course, it would host the Second Continental Congress, where the Declaration of Independence was signed. In its courtyard stood a large wooden platform built in 1769 to house telescopes to document the Transit of Venus, and there it remained in July of 1776 when the Declaration of Independence was first read publicly to a crowd gathered around. On the corner of the lot stood Carpenters Hall where the First Continental Congress met, and beginnings of a trans-colonial movement began. Out on its own, just a couple blocks away, was the large multi-winged Pennsylvania Hospital and Bettering House.

These close quarters created a vibrant atmosphere. Right across the street from the Shippen house, where William Shippen, Jr.'s early dissections caused riots, stood the merchant Willings family's house with abolitionist Anthony Benezet's home and his school just around the corner. All these different characters with different perspectives, from different classes, races, and countries, lived and worked around one another. Maybe their relationships never reached the levels of brotherly love for which William Penn had hoped, but there was a sort of begrudging sibling respect for one another's abilities and intellectual capabilities.

And it is exactly these characters that were instrumental in building Philadelphia, raising the city to be a shining example of American excellence for Great Britain and the whole of Europe to take notice. They applied their talents to Philadelphia and in turn Philadelphia provided a creative, expansive work and living environment. Scores would be left behind, struggling economically in this same environment, but even then, Philadelphia stood above the rest in addressing these issues, from providing free inoculations to building an almshouse and hospital to care for the impoverished. It may not have been enough, but these efforts were indicative of the spirit of the age which rested upon reason and belief in steadfastness to overcome any obstacle. Trying new solutions; opposing established viewpoints; pushing one another. Creating an energizing friction that raised Philadelphia up to become America's first great city.

CHAPTER ONE

The Franklin that Philadelphia Built

This book has a problem. A Benjamin Franklin-sized problem.

Philadelphia is famously monikered "the city that Franklin built." The merit is all there, too. Franklin, the man and the character, crafted much of the tenor of Philadelphia.

But which came first, the city or the man? Did Franklin make Philadelphia, or did Philadelphia make him? As you read, you will see that it is a little bit of both. The elements put in place by the Penns—the Assembly, the solid economic foundations, geographic advantages, and the intellectual atmosphere—helped to develop the young Franklin, and he, in turn, shaped all of that. Rattling the politics of Penn's colony. Creating thriving businesses. Lobbying for political appointments that sent him around the rest of British North America. Possessing innate curiosity that fostered scientific, artistic, and educational advancements over the late colonial period. Franklin was Philadelphia, as much as Philadelphia was Franklin. He is a figure that looms large in the history of colonial America, the Revolution, and Philadelphia.

None were so keenly aware as Franklin was of being American, of being Pennsylvanian, and especially of being Philadelphian. For 84 years he walked this earth, and for nearly 70 of those years, he represented not only the best of what America had to offer but also what Philadelphia could offer to the world. His Americanness allowed him to represent America to his colonial overlords and the rest of the Western world. He made himself (or at least exploited others and relationships to make himself), which, in time, became the basis of the American Dream. He showed how a self-made person, through hard work, dedication, and their own irascible ingenuity, could pull themselves up to look the kings of the day in the eye and thumb their noses at belligerent Parliaments.

You can't have Philadelphia without Franklin, and you can't have Franklin without Philadelphia. For better or worse, the two were made for one another. Yet despite the love between them, there were equal amounts of scorn and bitterness, too. Contention between Franklin and many different factions and people in Philadelphia helped to define this relationship.

Throughout his formidable years of becoming the leading printer in America, its most original writer and humorist, a leading scientist, statesman, postmaster, and diplomat, Franklin also had his fingerprints all over Philadelphia society. By leading, championing, or lending his support and clout, he managed to shape the city, raising Philadelphia to be the leading cultural center in the American colonies and its economic and educational heart.

Yet despite all of that, this book does have a Franklin problem. Not so much Franklin himself, although he erred personally, professionally, and politically throughout his long career and life. No, the problem lies in that the two, Philadelphia and Franklin, have become near inseparable from one another and with good cause. The straightforward narrative hoists up Benjamin Franklin, the example from this age, and it is not wrong because as you make your way through the rise of Philadelphia, at each juncture, there's good ol' Ben Franklin sticking his bifocals into the debate. Franklin's spirit was never far away. Even where he did not play a direct role, he would be there off-stage, offering words of encouragement, a letter of introduction, or his blessing and acquiescence—a power broker.

There were others, though; lots of them. Supporting Franklin, combating Franklin, hating him, respecting him. Many, many others, as we will see throughout this book, played their part in this urban transformation of the city. For over half of the years covered by this book, Franklin was away doing business in London as the Pennsylvania Assembly's agent, lobbying the proprietors or Parliament, and doing a rather poor job at it. This time away did not mean that he was still not a significant voice in Philadelphia, writing and publishing articles in London to support Philadelphia's causes or belittle the proprietors. However, the distance allowed others to blossom and bloom out from under the star power that Franklin exuded.

To understand how Philadelphia rose to become the center of the colonial American world, Franklin needs to be included in the equation, as does the spirit of the Enlightenment, which imbued him and many other philosophers, scientists, and revolutionaries of this time. Franklin is the center of that center.

If there ever was a Person of Reason in the Age of Reason, it was Franklin. He embodied its dedication to progress, the power of education and science, fitting things into reasoned laws, mistrust of orthodoxy and traditional authority, along with pragmatism and organization. As the Enlightenment historian Henry Steele Commager put it, Franklin "had a tidy mind and hated to see anything go to waste time, energy, money, or the opportunity for happiness. He liked to organize everything—even morals. He saw no reason why Philadelphia should not be tidied up and organized or why the whole of humankind should not be similarly tidied up and organized along sensible lines."[1]

A grouch though he was, John Adams was astute and provided some of the best observations about people from the colonial, revolutionary, and early American periods. He also spent a lot of time with Franklin and witnessed the astronomical pull that the celebrity Benjamin Franklin played upon, remarking on the Philadelphian's universal appeal:

> His reputation was more universal than that of Leibnitz or Newton, Frederick or Voltaire, and his character more beloved and esteemed than any or all of them ... Franklin's fame was universal. His name was familiar to government and people, to kings, courtiers, nobility, clergy and philosophers as well as plebeians to such a degree that there was scarcely a peasant or a citizen, a valet de chambre, coachman or footman, a lady's chambermaid or a scullion in a kitchen who was not familiar with it and who did not consider him a friend to human kind. When they spoke of him, they seemed to think he was to restore the golden age ... He was considered as a citizen of the world, a friend of all men and an enemy to none.[2]

When French peasants, German philosophers, and British nobility all sing your praises, you know you have achieved a new level of notoriety.

Benjamin Franklin was a man of constant invention and reinvention, fully aware of himself and how he projected out to the world around him, and careful to control that narrative. Having risen from the burgeoning American middle class, he would forever remain a champion to the "middling peoples," and his vision of America rested on a national identity based on these middle-class values.

He was born January 17, 1706, in Boston to Josiah Franklin and Abiah Folger. Josiah was a candle and soap maker who had emigrated from England in 1683 with his first wife, Anne. Following her death in 1689, Josiah quickly remarried to Abiah, and the two would go on to have 10 children together. Along with the previous five Josiah had with his first wife they made for one crowded household.

Never much for sentimentality, Franklin provided a straightforward description of his father in his *Autobiography*:

> He had an excellent Constitution of Body, was of middle Stature, but well set and very strong. He was ingenious, could draw prettily, was skill'd a little in Music and had a clear pleasing Voice, so that when he play'd Psalm Tunes on his Violin and sung withal as he sometimes did in an Evening after the Business of the Day was over, it was extremely agreeable to hear. He had a mechanical Genius too, and on occasion was very handy in the Use of other Tradesmen's Tools. But his great Excellence lay in a sound Understanding, and solid Judgment in prudential Matters, both in private and publick Affairs.[3]

It was that sound judgment and prudence that made Josiah a sought-after arbitrator. Though Franklin's father never held public office, he counseled many people in Boston, helping them make personal and professional decisions. Franklin believed this trait was passed down to him, and maybe there was some projection going on there, but he was not far off. Benjamin counseled business associates, political allies, and rivals and had a fondness for assisting young people of promise through letters of introduction.

Josiah was just one of the many tradesmen and merchants in Boston. Early 18th-century Boston was a bustling port in the American colonies, housing around 11,000 to 12,000 people, most of whom were English Puritans. They made Boston in their image, fostering a society deeply rooted in their strict religious principles. The Puritan influence shaped daily life, social norms, and governance, impacting the city's moral and legal codes. Economically, Boston was a thriving commercial center whose lifeblood rested upon the maritime trade. Shipbuilding, fishing, and trade dominated the economy with merchants directing most of that trade and contributing to the city's prosperity; industries such as ropemaking and printing became major economic drivers.[4]

At age eight, Josiah enrolled young Benjamin in Boston's Latin School in preparation for his eventual attendance at Harvard, and he excelled there, managing to skip a grade. Despite that success, Josiah pulled him out of school after only two years after not being able to afford tuition and needing the extra pair of hands for Josiah's candlemaking business, which would be the only formal education Franklin would receive. This led him to be put into working full-time at Josiah's candle and soap store, which he detested: "But my Dislike to the Trade continuing, my Father was under Apprehensions that if he did not find one for me more agreeable, I should break away and get to Sea."[5]

Josiah took Ben on long walks around Boston to visit other craftsmen to see if he would find any of their trades more suitable. These workshops, stores, and the people who occupied them left an indelible impact on the young Franklin and would foster his lifelong appreciation for artisans and tradespeople:

> It has ever since been a Pleasure to me to see good Workmen handle their Tools; and it has been useful to me, having learnt so much by it, as to be able to do little Jobs my self in my House, when a Workman could not readily be got; and to construct little Machines for my Experiments while the Intention of making the Experiment was fresh and warm in my Mind.[6]

Franklin spent two years working for his father, being ferried around Boston, getting a taste for other trades. Despite all of that, at the age of 12, his family ended up signing his indenture papers with his 21-year-old brother James, a printer who published *The Boston Gazette*. When James lost the contract to print that newspaper, he took the unheard-of step of creating his own weekly independent newspaper, *New England Courant*, in 1721. The *Courant* earned a reputation as being America's first independent and anti-establishment paper. It wore its irreverence on its pages, being openly and proudly defiant against the Puritan Boston establishment, exemplified by the powerful Mather clan, who since Richard Mather in the early 17th century and followed by his son, Increase Mather, and grandson, Cotton Mather, had held significant religious and political sway in Boston and Massachusetts. The *Courant* happily thumbed its nose at the clergy, Harvard elites, the rich of all sorts, and all of Massachusetts' elites.[7]

The *Courant* not only allowed Franklin to get firsthand experience in the printing business but also provided him the opportunity to write, publishing the first works of his career. These took the form of a series of letters from his literary creation, Silence Dogood, a middle-aged widow with a lot of opinions. She was very much inspired by the English models from *The Spectator* and the satires being published by his brother, like Abigail Afterwit and Timothy Turnstone satirical literary creations used as stand-ins for stereotypical Bostonians, and other *Courant* writers. They helped carry on the paper's satirical style of lambasting the religious, moral, and political atmosphere of Massachusetts in 1722.[8]

Silence Dogood was the first in a long line of pithy, humorous literary characters Franklin created to lampoon society and himself. It was in the pages of the *Courant* where he began to hone his literary style of direct, conversational, easy-going prose. The Dogood essays offered a mix of folksy tales paired with observational humor:

> I find it a very difficult Matter to reprove Women separate from the Men; for what Vice is there in which the Men have not as great a Share as the Women? and in some have they not a far greater, as in Drunkenness, Swearing, &c.? And if they have, then it follows, that when a Vice is to be reproved, Men, who are most culpable, deserve the most Reprehension, and certainly therefore, ought to have it. But we will wave this Point at present and proceed to a particular Consideration of what my Correspondent calls Female Vice.[9]

Five productive years were spent in his brother James's print shop, where Benjamin worked on his writing craft and learned the ins and outs of the printing business. Though he was indentured to James until age 21, Benjamin did not stick around that long.

James and the paper had gotten into legal trouble for publishing content that had made a mockery of religion. Where at the time deeply ingrained Puritan beliefs controlled Boston, fostering a strict religious environment centered around Calvinist principles that dominated life in the city. Thanks to a court order, each issue of the *Courant* needed to be submitted for approval to the Massachusetts provincial government before printing. Failure to do so threatened the existence of the newspaper and the livelihood of not only James but Benjamin as a result. The court held the power to forbid the publication of the *Courant*.

As a means around this setup, James handed over control of the paper to Benjamin, who signed an official discharge from his indenture to take over the new role as sole printer and editor. A secret apprentice agreement was agreed to between the brothers Franklin. Not too much time elapsed before James took back control of the paper, and Benjamin, not wanting to be back under his brother's yoke and figuring a secret agreement wasn't enforceable, decided to run away. He would end up in Philadelphia.[10]

Franklin, at 17, was muscular with a barrel chest, standing nearly six feet tall. No matter the situation or the company, he felt at ease, from hardscrabble tradespeople to the governor and everyone in between. Franklin was quick to make acquaintances. Even at this young age, he was a charmer who drew people to him;

Benjamin making amends with his brother and fellow printer, James. Franklin had broken his indenture with his brother and fled Boston to settle down in Philadelphia. (*The Life of Benjamin Franklin*)

a gregarious personality who was anything but shy and always on the hunt for a well-placed friend or the more lucrative wealthy patron.[11]

He unleashed a charm offensive that showcased a self-deprecating and unpretentious humor and a pleasing, welcoming manner, which served his calculated means in advancing his career and life. He applied this at once upon his arrival in Philadelphia, and Samuel Keimer gave him a job in his print shop. Franklin, though, with an ever-wandering eye, stepped out on Keimer after working for him for five months and gained the patronage of Pennsylvania's governor at the time, William Keith.

Keith convinced Franklin to set up his own print shop with the promise that he would supply the funds needed. With those assurances, Franklin set sail on his first trip to London to buy the necessary printing equipment. Once there, though, Franklin quickly learned that Keith's mouth ran ahead of his purse, and the promised funds were never forthcoming from the hapless and broke Keith. The governor's promises were made in an effort just to be loved.[12]

Franklin spent two years in London working at various print shops while still spreading that Franklin charm, the lack of funds along with the allure of the city keeping him there. He made new friends and acquaintances that he would rely on in the years and decades to come. Returning to Philadelphia in 1726, he found himself once again at Keimer's print shop. And once again, his time there would be short-lived as he and another worker there, Hugh Meredith, secured the supplies needed to begin their own print shop. At the age of 22, Franklin became his own boss.[13]

Franklin wasted no time embedding himself in the life and culture of 1720s Philadelphia. In 1727, he started what would be the first of many clubs he would be associated with, the Junto, an association of young tradesmen and artisans that met at local taverns to discuss what was going on around the city, work on improving themselves, and create a network to enhance their careers. Initiation into the group included having to lay your hand on your heart and correctly answer these questions: "Do you have disrespect for any current member? Do you love humanity in general, regardless of religion or profession? Do you feel people should ever be punished because of their opinions or mode of worship? Do you love and pursue truth for its own sake?"[14]

The Junto served as a means to test his service-minded ideas, to help the public in general and himself in the process. Later, the Junto organized a library that would become The Library Company of Philadelphia in 1731, the first subscription library in America. It remains an institution dedicated to promoting the study of American history and culture while maintaining a research library that houses rare books and other historical records.[15]

Franklin proved to be astute at business. In the span of a decade, he built a media empire in the colonies that included franchised printers in other cities, as well as a wide range of newspapers, magazines, almanacs, and book publishing endeavors. He created the content and owned the means of production, too.

The *Pennsylvania Gazette* became the showcase of his regular writing contributions, with the first issue coming out in October 1729. Almost immediately, the *Gazette* became the leading newspaper in the city and the colonies by publishing Franklin's writings, true crime stories, and the usual fare of announcements and letters.

In 1730, he entered into a common-law marriage arrangement with Deborah Read. At the time, she was technically still married to John Rogers, who had run away to the West Indies, and there were reports that he had died. So, to avoid any claims of bigamy, they were never officially married but lived together or were together for the next 40 years. It was an odd pairing, as Deborah was a homebody, and Franklin jumped at any chance he got to travel, so they would spend large chunks of time apart. And he would be away

Deborah Read Franklin (1708–74), Franklin's common-law wife, who bore the brunt of hostilities at the Franklin home during the Stamp Act crisis. (*The Many Sided Franklin*)

from her when she died in 1774. There was affection there of a sort that at times bordered on friendly companionship rather than anything romantic.

As has been widely noted by many, Franklin was a keen flirt and adulterer who had quite a fascination with nearly all women. Some of his closest friends and consorts were women like Catharine Ray, Margaret Stevenson, and Ann-Louise Brillon de Jouy. While he let male friends and acquaintances come and go, female ones he held on to for most of his life. He had been known to frequent prostitutes and take advantage of vulnerable women like maids and cooks, one of whom he had allegedly impregnated and who gave birth to his son William. He would end up taking care of William, taking him under his tutelage and bringing him along to London, and even working hard behind the scenes to secure William's education and

a royal appointment. They shared a close relationship up until a split thanks to the Revolution.

By the end of 1732, he published his first *Poor Richard's Almanack,* which would be published yearly for the next quarter of a century. The *Almanack* was Franklin's way of injecting humor into explorations of virtue for the masses who bought and read the yearly book. It supplied practical information like weather forecasts and agricultural advice but also imparted Franklin's wit and wisdom through proverbs and aphorisms ("Lost time is never found again").

The Junto and Library Company were just the first of many public service-related associations and organizations Franklin was involved in, from organizing the Union Fire Company to becoming the clerk to the Pennsylvania Assembly and then serving as postmaster of Philadelphia. He created an independent Pennsylvania militia, and also organized the American Philosophical Society in 1743, which he envisioned to be a larger

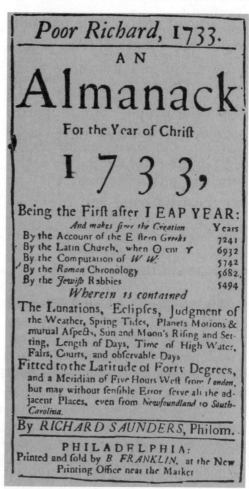

Title page of the first Poor Richard's Almanack. (*The Many Sided Franklin*)

version of the Junto that encompassed all of the American colonies and a means to connect like-minded individuals. These baby steps laid the foundation for an American identity based on American thought leaders.

And then, in 1748, Franklin retired rather unexpectedly from the printing business at the age of 42. The printing business was handed over to his supervisor. At the same time, he pocketed a tidy sum from his printing empire every year to live comfortably and pursue even more passions, like scientific experiments and inventions, and furthering his outreach with even more civic endeavors.[16]

His writings, publishing house, and *Poor Richard's Almanack* provided name recognition throughout the colonies. But his experiments with electricity would bring him fame throughout Europe on his way to becoming the first truly American celebrity.

The first known portrait of a youthful Franklin, by the artist Robert Feke, dates from 1746, right around his retirement from the publishing business and the start of a more active political life. (*The Many Sided Franklin*)

As a result of his various experiments, he introduced terminology still used today, proposing the existence of two types of electrical charges: positive and negative. Ever the pragmatist, he applied this knowledge to practical use by inventing the lightning rod in 1752. Franklin's rod protected buildings and ships from lightning strikes and the resulting fires by providing a conduit to discharge the electricity into the ground safely. It would have significant ramifications for public safety and the protection of property. These would garner international acclaim and make him a prominent scientific figure. With his letters and publications on electricity being widely read and translated, he helped to disseminate his scientific knowledge across the globe and inspired subsequent scientists like Michael Faraday and Alessandro Volta.[17]

His lightning rod was quickly adopted throughout Europe and the colonies, earning him accolades on both continents. To many, he had tamed lightning. It no longer remained a mystery as he had definitively proven that it was a form of electricity. And he had provided the means for lessening its destructive power. German philosopher Immanuel Kant called Franklin the "new Prometheus," a thief of fire from the heavens. He became the most celebrated scientist on the American continent and in Europe, the equivalent of an overnight celebrity in that day and age. He had become a true American folk hero.[18]

Education had always had a special place in Franklin's heart, and for a time, he believed that Philadelphia needed its own college. Retirement allowed him the opportunity to pursue the founding of a new, secular college. In 1749, he published the pamphlet *Proposals Relating to the Education of Youth in Pennsylvania*, laying out the reasons for an academy, what its curriculum should encompass, and even a means for funding the new institution. Fundraising efforts soon followed, and over the next two years, he secured the use of the Great Hall located at Fourth and Arch Street. The Great Hall had been built in 1740 to serve as a tabernacle for George Whitefield's roving evangelical sermonry, but lack of funds kept it from ever being fully completed. Sitting there unused in 1749 the Hall became the first home of the Academy of Philadelphia, which eventually became the University of Pennsylvania.[19]

At the same time, he was also involved in fundraising for a new hospital. Founded in 1751 by Dr. Thomas Bond and himself, the Pennsylvania Hospital in Philadelphia became one of the earliest medical institutions in America where the sick and mentally ill could receive some sort of healthcare. In order to fund the enterprise, Franklin cleverly devised the first known government matching grant in the world with the Assembly agreeing to match private funds in order to begin construction on the new hospital in the year it was founded.

Along with fellow American publisher William Hunter, Franklin served as the deputy postmaster general of British North America from 1753 to 1774. The two men greatly improved postal service in the colonies by implementing efficiencies that helped to expand the system. Franklin introduced innovations such as standardized rates based on weight and distance, streamlined postal operations and improved mail delivery times, and made the postal service financially self-sustaining.[20]

Though retired from business, he stayed active and accepted a seat in the Pennsylvania Assembly, his first official foray into politics. He found himself at odds with the Penns, their governors, and eventually the British government. While in the Assembly and later as its agent in London, he bristled at the proprietors' control over taxes and their encroachment on government affairs. Being a proprietary colony meant that Pennsylvania was governed by a private family—the Penns—who owned and controlled all of the unsettled lands in the colony. Charles II had granted the original charter to William Penn in 1681 to repay a debt, and it would stay in the Penn family up to the Revolution. Most colonies began life as proprietaries, though by the 1720s, many had been converted to royal colonies overseen by the king and his ministers. Just Pennsylvania, Maryland, and Delaware fell under the rule of their proprietors until the American Revolution. This relationship would cause Franklin and the ruling party in the Assembly great consternation throughout the late colonial period.

In 1754 a conference was called at Albany, New York, to gain from the Iroquois Confederation a reaffirmation of their allegiance. As one of the delegates, when talk shifted towards having a more unified defense system in place, Franklin took the opportunity to sketch out a cooperation plan for the colonies to unite around shared purposes. This included a congress comprised of delegates from the colonies with representation proportional to taxes paid from each colony. The delegation would meet regularly on a rotational basis around the various colonial capitals so that delegates could gain a greater appreciation of the challenges the other colonies faced. There would be an executive president general; the king would appoint that position. This scheme provided the basics of a federal system and followed Franklin's ideals of being balanced, enlightened, and orderly. The plan would be rejected by all the colonial assemblies and by Parliament. No one was ready to give up so much power at the moment.[21]

With the outbreak of the Seven Years' War in 1754, Franklin took an active role in preparing the defense of Pennsylvania. Known commonly as the French and Indian War in America, the Seven Years' War was a global conflict involving major European powers, primarily Britain and France, that was fought on multiple continents and seas with many major battles fought in North America. He pushed through a bill that created an all-voluntary militia with the democratic election of officers. He was elected colonel and spent several weeks in camps all over western Pennsylvania. After his return to Philadelphia, the Assembly became fed up with the proprietors' handling of hostilities as well as their general antagonism; it voted to send Franklin to London to appeal directly to the proprietors to get better accommodations for taxation and other matters. If that approach failed, he would go directly to the British government.[22]

He landed in London in the summer of 1757 as a loyalist to the Crown and enthusiastic supporter of the empire—an empire where America played a crucial role while its citizens were afforded the rights of any other British subject. This included the right to elect assemblies that had the power to legislate their internal affairs and held the power to tax, much like Parliament. The Penns did not see matters that way. Still, Franklin believed he could convince the British ministers to partner with him to pressure the Penns into loosening their autocratic grip on Pennsylvania. He received a rude awakening upon learning how the leaders in the British government viewed Americans and he immediately antagonized the Penns.

Some months passed in London while he settled into his room at the house of Mrs. Margaret Stevenson on Craven Street, and when he was good and ready, he presented the Assembly's "Heads of Complaint" to the proprietor, Thomas Penn, listing its grievances. Next came the waiting. Franklin and the Assembly endured a year and a half of it to hear the official response from the Penns. And much like you would expect from a year and a half of ignoring the complaint, the response was a complete dismissal of the grievances, followed by a refusal to deal directly with Franklin. Access is vital in lobbying, and with that access denied, Franklin did not make way for another agent to try their hand at negotiating or return to Philadelphia. Instead, he recommended to leaders of the Assembly to petition the king directly with a plan to make Pennsylvania a royal colony to pull an end around the Penns and take Pennsylvania away from them. Throughout the late colonial period, the Assembly leadership made this effort to strip the Penns of their control of Pennsylvania and hand it over to the King, one of the most controversial internal issues that Pennsylvania dealt with. Opponents stressed that switching the type of government would threaten the very dear liberties at the heart of the Pennsylvania Charter, the highest of which were the strict religious freedoms and the general freedoms provided for the Assembly. Not until well into Parliament's series of taxation efforts on the colonies, beginning with the Stamp Act, and their punitive measures following the colonial response did the issue of a royal government quietly die within Pennsylvania.

Franklin's first—but not last—proposal for the royal government was met with the same response as the list of grievances to the Penns. Dead in the water. To the British government, the American colonists were expected to be subservient politically and economically to Great Britain and for Pennsylvanians, the Penns. And no change in government could modify that. Attempts by the Assembly and Franklin to circumvent their current political establishment were not taken very seriously in Parliament or by the Crown. The Penns still wielded a considerable amount of influence.

From 1757 to 1762, Franklin spent his time in England making acquaintances, traveling around, and receiving various honors and degrees from universities and institutions all over Europe. Upon his return to Philadelphia, his stay at home would be relatively short, but during this time he continued to fulfill his duties as colonial postmaster, visiting and inspecting routes all over the colonies. His role as a colony-wide publisher and then as postmaster for the colonies allowed him the unique vantage point of taking in all of the colonies—something that very few Americans had the opportunity to do. This enabled him to see America not as individual colonies but as a collective whole working in concert and towards similar goals and shared interests.[23]

Over the winter of 1763–4, news of the Paxton Boys affair seized Philadelphia. A mob of men from Paxton, PA, ambushed and murdered a group of Native Americans

Portrait of Franklin's son, William Franklin, who was a frequent traveling companion of Franklin on his trips to London and would become the governor of New Jersey. Their relationship would fray and break with the coming of the American Revolution. (*The Many Sided Franklin*)

from the Susquehannock Tribe. The "Paxton Boys" claimed that the government was doing nothing to protect the frontier from possible raids by Native Americans. Their anger was directed towards the Assembly's failure to provide adequate funding for Western defenses during the Seven Years' War. During those years, the Assembly engaged in a constant struggle with the Penns over taxation of their lands that delayed the necessary funding to help secure the Pennsylvania frontier. That the Assembly was led by the Quaker Party only helped to fuel the predominantly Scots-Irish Paxton Boys in their protests and murderous ways. As a result, some residents of Paxton turned vigilante and massacred a peaceful and friendly community of Indigenous peoples. Other communities of Native Americans began to fear for their lives and appealed to the governor and Assembly to take them in and protect them from the gathering mob in Paxton. Troops were duly sent to escort this group of Native Americans to Philadelphia. They were a bit of a hot potato, and with no good place for them to be lodged, they were placed on Province Island while the governor and Assembly tried to relocate them to New Jersey or New York.[24]

The situation in Paxton worsened as leaders of the rabble-rousers began threatening a march on Philadelphia to forcibly seize the group of Native Americans, who they claimed were responsible for murder or for abetting a murderer of white, Pennsylvanian settlers. They were out for their own form of justice. By February 1764, hundreds of them had made their way to Germantown and were knocking on the door of Philadelphia. The city went on high alert, and the new governor, John Penn, was in over his head and teamed up with Franklin to quell the unrest. Franklin worked to prepare the city's defenses, led a delegation out to Germantown to meet with the Paxton leaders, and negotiated a cease to the march and the breakup of their movement.[25]

As the Paxton Boys affair subsided, it showed the opponents of the proprietors the negligence and impotence of their leadership, and a new push was made by Franklin and the leaders in the Assembly to try again to obtain a royal government. This kicked off a flurry of pamphlet writing throughout the summer and fall of 1764, with Franklin joining in with a few of his political tracts. For the Assembly, he authored a "necklace" of resolutions that proposed an end to the proprietary government, calling them tyrannical and inhuman in their handling of affairs and using the threat from Native Americans as a means of extending their hold and infringing on the liberties of the people of Pennsylvania and the Assembly. He called for a new petition to be presented to the king to take over the Pennsylvania government and place the colony under his protection. These new resolves went nowhere and were generally not well received, with the likes of John Dickinson making impassioned pleas against such actions. They proved so unpopular that Franklin lost his seat in the Assembly.

However, the Quaker Party, so named because Quakers made up the major political faction in the city and in Pennsylvania, with which Franklin was affiliated, remained in power in the Assembly. They voted to submit the petition to British ministers and selected Franklin to act once again as an agent, which was met with much consternation around Philadelphia; many claimed he would be ineffectual. For the second time, he sailed for London as an agent of the Assembly early in 1765 and arrived just in time for Parliament to pass the much despised Stamp Act, imposing internal taxes on the colonies who had no representation of their own in Parliament. This was seen as a violation of the American colonist's rights and freedoms as a British subject.

As news of the first massive internal tax on the American colonies spread across the Atlantic, it created a vortex of scorn and activity even before the Act was set to take effect. For his part, Franklin thought that Parliament did reserve the right to levy external taxes in the form of tariffs or duties to regulate trade. Internal taxes, though, he saw as taxation without representation in Parliament, which bordered on unconstitutional in his mind. Despite those thoughts, he did not outwardly oppose the Stamp Act as it was debated in Parliament. He and other colonial agents lobbied Prime Minister George Grenville in February 1765 to offer alternatives to an internal tax placed upon the people of America. Grenville stressed to the agents that the high cost of the Seven Years' War, which was primarily fought in British North America, made the tax necessary. Franklin argued that the tax went counter to some colonies, like Pennsylvania, having the power of their assemblies to tax their own.[26]

In the wake of the Stamp Act's passage, Franklin made a pragmatic decision to accept the Act's existence and find the best ways to deal with it, rather than to continue the fight for its repeal. He clearly underestimated the intensity of disdain for the Act back home. While tax collectors in other parts of the colonies were being harassed regularly, and their homes torn down board by board, he went so far as to recommend a close acquaintance for the position of tax collector of Philadelphia. This threat of violence also existed in Philadelphia, where Franklin's wife, Deborah, faced the ire of many Philadelphians for her husband's perceived transgressions in the wake of the Stamp Act fiasco. This resulted in a mob-like atmosphere that was planning to march on Franklin's home and tear it down. She later wrote to Benjamin:

> Toward night I said he [cousin Davenport] should fetch a gun or two, as we had none. I sent to ask my brother to come and bring his gun. Also we made one room the magazine. I ordered some sort of defense upstairs as I could manage myself. I said when I was advised to remove that I was very sure you had done nothing to hurt anybody, nor I had not given any offense to any person at all. Nor would I be made uneasy by anybody. Nor would I stir.[27]

Franklin managed to find redemption in February of 1766 when he appeared before Parliament and provided the American rebuttal to the Stamp Act directly on the floor of Parliament. He was calm in the face of questioning from friend and foe alike, keeping the focus on the realities that existed in America and, in the process, becoming the de facto spokesperson for the American colonies. The following month on March 18, 1766, Parliament repealed the Stamp Act. Shortly thereafter Georgia, New Jersey, and Massachusetts all named him their agent in England.[28]

For the remainder of his nine additional years in London, Franklin primarily focused on colonial matters, providing the American response to Parliament's increasing encroachment into internal colonial affairs. Whether penning essays against the Townshend Acts or trying to fashion some compromise to remain loyal to the king (but out from under the thumb of Parliament), year after year, amid the increasing tensions between the colonies and England, Franklin became more and more radicalized to the American cause. During these days, he began writing his *Autobiography*, which would become the first classic in American literature.

Though fraught politically, he enjoyed an agreeable existence in Britain, with his London life supplemented by summer travels around the British Isles and Europe. In addition, when he required a retreat from city life, he was always welcome at the homes of the Shipleys in Hampshire and the Dashwoods at West Wycombe Park. But politics were never quite so far away. It was not too long after the repeal of the Stamp Act that the chancellor of the Exchequer, Charles Townshend, introduced duties on glass, paint, paper and tea, igniting a new furor. Always quite adept at gauging the political temperature, Franklin described to Lord Kames the situation as he saw it: "Things daily wear a worse Aspect, and tend more to a breach and final separation."[29]

It was now a game of escalation: every British government action caused an equal and opposite reaction in the colonies, with Massachusetts reacting the most vociferously culminating with the Boston Tea Party. When word of the Tea Party reached London right before Franklin's appearance before the Privy Council it led to heightened tensions in London and the passage of a series of retaliatory and punitive acts against Boston, known as the Intolerable Acts. For many in the American colonies, these Acts brought them together to act collectively against British policies in a way they had never done before.

Franklin's increasing radicalization culminated with his appearance before the Privy Council in the Cockpit on January 29, 1774, which would serve as a pivotal moment in the lead-up to the American Revolution. The Privy Council, a group of advisors to the king typically culled from the Houses of Commons and Lords, called on him to respond to accusations made by Massachusetts Governor Thomas Hutchinson with regard to Franklin acquiring and sending confidential letters to the colonies, known as the Hutchinson letters. These letters revealed that British officials in the colonies were advocating for a more authoritarian rule and suggested the use of military force to quell colonial unrest. Franklin admitted to procuring the letters but argued that he did so in the public interest, believing that their contents were detrimental to the colonies' relationship with Britain. The solicitor general, Alexander Wedderburn, was the most aggressive in his attacks on Franklin, accusing him of theft and betrayal, designing to intimidate and disgrace him. The council met him with much vitriol, but Franklin would not betray himself and did not meet the opposition's emotions with any of his own. Instead, he remained calm and primarily silent, showing a contemptuous and condescending manner that no doubt further ruffled the already ruffled feathers.[30]

If there was still a straw left, this proved to be the last of them as Franklin's relationship with the British government cratered. Word spread to the colonies of his treatment, which only furthered the growing resentment toward the perceived general disregard shown for colonial rights.

The affair with the Hutchinson letters resulted in the loss of his position as colonial postmaster, and with the disintegration of relations and the dramatic increase in acrimony between the colonies and Parliament, Franklin, the statesman, had no official duties to attend to. He remained in England with nothing really left to do. Deborah was at home on her deathbed (she would pass away in 1774), and he was a political pariah in London, but still he remained. For his remaining days in England, he worked back channels, meeting with Admiral Howe and former prime minister Lord Chatham to try to stave off any military actions and come to some peace. But war had come, and Franklin set sail for America in the spring of 1775.

He arrived back home in Philadelphia on the eve of the Second Continental Congress and was quickly selected as a member the day after returning home. At 70, he was by far the oldest member, and his age showed as many other members of Congress noted his regular naps during debates. In those early months of the Second Continental Congress, Franklin mostly remained quiet, avoided debates, kept mainly to himself, and attended congressional sessions and committee meetings. Franklin described his days: "My time was never more fully employed. In the morning at 6, I am at the committee of safety, appointed by the assembly to put the province in a state of defense; which committee holds till near 9, when I am at the congress, and that sits till after 4 in the afternoon."[31]

Throughout the remainder of 1775, Franklin held various committee responsibilities, from munitions and gunpowder to promoting trade with England's enemies and, in 1776, traveling to Quebec to meet with the colonial forces led by Benedict Arnold there. He made it back to Philadelphia in time to help edit the Declaration of Independence. This culminated with Congress tapping Franklin to travel to France to act as an envoy in an attempt to get some sort of French support for the colonial cause.

For the next nine years, he remained in Paris, basking in the adulation of the French and eventually securing their support, which was invaluable to the American victory and gaining American independence. He returned to America in 1785 and was second only to George Washington as the most celebrated of Americans. Though nearly 80 and in declining health, he continued to serve in public office. He was elected as president of the Supreme Council of Pennsylvania and served there for three years. Benjamin Franklin died shortly before his 85th birthday in January of 1790.

~

From the day he stepped onto Philadelphia soil in 1723 to his death 70-some years later, not much happened in the city without Franklin's planning, blessing, or comment. He had relationships, good and contentious, with all of the characters who will be making an appearance in this book and helped shape Philadelphia: Robert Morris, William Smith, John Morgan, William Shippen, Elizabeth Graeme, Anthony Benezet, David Rittenhouse, Joseph Galloway, John Dickinson, and more.

In the late 18th century when Philadelphia was still a comparatively small city where everyone knew one another, Franklin lived in the epicenter, helping create the atmosphere that allowed Philadelphia to grow and blossom. It was through the relationships among these individuals and the groups and associations they formed together, their exertions, and their works and passions, that Philadelphia was brought to the forefront of the American colonies.

With William Smith, Franklin helped to create the academy and brought a more formal educational foundation to Philadelphia. Through his connections in England and Scotland he helped to introduce many of the future Philadelphia doctors like John Morgan, William Shippen, Jr., and Benjamin Rush when they

Illustration from *The Life of Benjamin Franklin* of Franklin conducting his famous kite experiment. The Leyden jar in his hand collected the electrical charge of lightning, which Franklin would use to prove that lightning contained electricity. (*The Life of Benjamin Franklin*)

flocked to England to continue their medical education. His son William would entertain an engagement with Elizabeth Graeme. Charles Thomson would revive the Junto. Franklin's political partnership with Joseph Galloway, despite its ups and downs, defined the Pennsylvania political landscape of the last quarter century of the colonial era.

Though he was heralded as one of the scientific geniuses of his time thanks to his experiments with electricity and the invention of the lightning rod, it was his effort to create an atmosphere that supported scientific inquiry that had a long-lasting impact on the city and America. As one of the co-founders of the American Philosophical Society, he helped to create with John Bartram a sense of American intellectual identity

Portrait of a late middle-aged Franklin after the one painted by Jean-Baptiste Greuze. (National Gallery of Art)

that was not present yet anywhere in British North America. His dedication to education, despite his constant battling over the academy he helped to create, is still felt to this day. Politics shared his distinctive stamp through his newspapers, pamphlets, and printing press, as well as direct involvement in the Pennsylvania Assembly, all of which shaped and influenced the tone and tenor of Philadelphia, as did his commitment to civil engagement through the creation of organizations that served to better the public good. Through the Junto, or the first subscription library, or the Pennsylvania Hospital, or through fire companies, Franklin helped to improve Philadelphia and gave it the foundation on which it could build itself into being the leading city in the colonies.

The emphasis on Franklin's contributions is not meant to diminish the hard work put in by many others, for the day-to-day toil needed to bring these projects to fruition often lay upon the overburdened shoulders of multitudes of American men and women. But one common thread was Franklin and his ideas and support. Those ideas were fostered by the spirit of the age and encompassed this era known as the Enlightenment. Through Franklin, the Enlightenment had no brighter-shining figure in America. And no other place in the colonies exhibited the ideals of the Enlightenment quite like Philadelphia. It was the city of the Enlightenment, built up by its beliefs, where all of those chords would come together to form a melody. A living experiment, playing out in nearly every aspect of life.

CHAPTER TWO

King Credit and the Merchants of Bloom

History allows us to step back and contextualize existence in a way that those living in the moment are not afforded. It is one thing centuries later to make connections, but 18th-century Philadelphians did not live with such luxuries. While Franklin and Enlightenment ideals helped fuel Philadelphia's ascendence, it was the people of the city and its meteoric economic rise that helped make it all possible.

No one quite embodies the Philadelphia experience like Robert Morris: a pull-yourself-up-by-the-bootstraps man—with a little assist from his father—who worked, worked, and worked his way up the Philadelphia mercantile ladder until he became one of the most prominent and most successful businesspersons in British North America. That he was just another young British emigré into the city who had to work as an apprentice during his formative years was a shared experience with thousands of others who stepped off European ships and onto Philadelphia's docks looking for a new start, a new life, in this new world.

These life experiences led Morris toward becoming the financier of the Revolution. Without the network of connections he established in the years prior to the Revolution and the acumen he acquired, Morris wouldn't have been able to create the financial infrastructure necessary to keep the war effort going.

He was born in Liverpool on the last day of January in 1734. After the death of his mother and his father's move to America, young Robert was left in the care of his grandparents. Morris's grandfather, Andrew Morris, was a mariner who trawled up and down the English coast, exposing Robert early to the nautical life but meaning he was primarily raised by his grandmother.

Portrait of Robert Morris, successful Philadelphia merchant and financier of the Revolution. (*Philadelphia: A History of the City and its People*)

His father, Robert Morris, Sr., had moved to Oxford, Maryland, on Chesapeake Bay to work as an agent for the tobacco merchant firm Foster, Cunliffe, and Sons of Liverpool. The elder Robert handled purchasing shipments of baled tobacco leaves from the Southern states and shipping them back to Great Britain. When the junior Robert turned 13 in 1747, he was deemed old enough to travel across the ocean to America to join his father. His grandparents threw him on an American-bound ship of his father's boss, and he was off to live with his father. On arrival his father quickly shipped him off to Philadelphia to a business acquaintance and friend, Robert Greenway, to get an education. Greenway then apprenticed Robert off at the Philadelphia mercantile house of Charles Willing and Son.[1]

Charles Willing created his firm in 1726 and systematically built it into a thriving institution in Philadelphia. He sent his son Thomas to England for an education, where he developed business shrewdness—one that he shared with Morris, who was three years his junior. Returning to Philadelphia, Thomas Willing became a partner in his father's merchant business and worked alongside the young Robert Morris. Soon after the passing of his father in 1757, Thomas assumed complete control of the company.[2]

Not long after he arrived in Philadelphia, Morris was orphaned when his father died in a freak saluting accident. In 1750, he visited a ship at port in Chesapeake Bay. As was the custom at the time, the ship fired a salute at the departure of a guest. Members of the crew of the ship mistook the signal to fire (an errant handkerchief drop or itchy nose may have spurred the confusion), so the shot was premature and ripped through the pinnace of the boat transporting Morris, Sr. It struck him and shattered his arm above the elbow. Without proper medical attention, he developed blood poisoning and died, leaving Morris, Jr. with a small inheritance.[3]

Morris started his business career in the counting room and showed a remarkable adeptness for business, beginning his rapid rise in the Willing firm. He routinely demonstrated keen business decision-making powers. Left alone at the office while Willing was away, Morris learned from a ship entering the harbor that the price of flour in foreign markets had skyrocketed. With this knowledge, he took it upon himself to act quickly before other merchants could and procured on the firm's account all the flour within his grasp. And when the elder Willing returned, he was met by a flurry of furious Philadelphia merchants complaining about how Morris managed to corner the market himself, leaving them to foot the bill for higher flour fees.[4]

The young Morris's natural resourcefulness earned the trust of Willing enough that he was named supercargo, the agent on the boat and in the port tasked with making the best deals and ensuring the success of a voyage, on several trade ships to the West Indies. Morris would travel on the ships to the West Indies and Europe, and on one such voyage during the Seven Years' War, French privateers took him captive. They treated him rather roughly and put him ashore with no money, a long, long way from home. But he was able to repair a watch, get some money for it, and make his way back home to Philadelphia.[5]

These qualities impressed Charles Willing, who in 1754 made the 17-year-old a partner in his firm. Three years later, following the death of Charles, Thomas Willing and Morris founded the merchant firm Willing and Morris. In 10 years, he had gone from apprentice to clerk to partner.

Though the name Willing carried weight, business and credit, the heart of any business success at the time, needed something additional. Businesses were built on reputations. It was not a given that Charles Willing's reputation carried over to his son. Charles's long career included the nurturing of relationships in Philadelphia, around Pennsylvania, the mid-Atlantic colonies, and British holdings throughout the Atlantic world. With his death, these relationships had to be re-established and new ones forged. Having Morris by his side helped this transition go much smoother for Thomas.

Many responsibilities were thrust upon Morris, as Thomas had to care for his father's young and large family. Willing and Morris were more than just business partners; they were very affectionate personal friends. Willing's letters to Morris demonstrate this genuine fondness for one another; he wished Morris a safe journey to the West Indies and back again, "where my house shall be your home and myself your friend." During the occupation of Philadelphia, he would write to Morris, "I hope still to be happy in the esteem and friendship of the Man in the World I love most, and for whom I have every feeling of affection and regard."[6]

Theirs would be a very successful personal and professional partnership. They built up the firm so that they were both wealthy men and when the Revolution came around, the firm was in a position to leverage its contacts and knowledge of the trans-Atlantic trade business to assist the newly independent country. Willing and Morris focused their trade on Great Britain, Ireland, Portugal, Spain, and the West Indies, establishing close, mutually beneficial contacts and trading in the ingredients needed in each location.

Portrait of Thomas Willing, business partner and friend of Robert Morris. (Met Museum)

To Ireland and Great Britain went grain and flour, while dry goods came the other way; lumber and provisions went to the West Indies with rum and molasses in return; Portugal and Spain provided wine, lemons, and salt. They acted as correspondents for other merchants, handled their goods, drew on bills of exchange, and headed their own insurance group. This was done on a relatively small but near-constant scale, with individual enterprises seldom topping £1,000. The firm owned up to three vessels to facilitate this trade, while other merchants were left to buy into a ship or lease space on one to carry their goods.[7]

Willing and Morris expanded their operations outside of Philadelphia and Pennsylvania, investing in an orange plantation in Mississippi that enslaved over 100 people. Early in the partnership, Willing was the dominant partner as his share on many voyages was triple that of Morris. He was the one issuing the orders to the captains and supercargoes. However, this began to shift over the latter years of the colonial era, and Morris took on a more active role. By 1775, he was managing the affairs of the company, and on the eve of the Revolution, Willing and Morris was one of the city's largest firms, if not the largest.[8]

The two men would both take active roles in the mercantile community during the growing tensions of the era, starting with the Stamp Act but followed closely by the Townshend Acts. The two merchants supported the colonial side throughout the various controversies, lending their signatures to non-importation resolutions and the petition opposing the Stamp Act from the Philadelphia Committee of Merchants.

Morris would be a part of the delegation of prominent Philadelphians that sought out John Hughes, the Stamp Act collector for Philadelphia, to warn him about enforcing the Stamp Act that doing so would cause potential harm to him as the populace was itching to tear down his house. After he was non-committal, Morris returned to his house to get him to issue a statement saying he wouldn't enforce the Act unless the other colonies started to. This seemed to appease the masses. Morris received his first taste of public service when Governor John Penn in 1766 made him a member of the Board of Port Wardens.[9]

He was no revolutionary, though. Not one for independence, he still held out hope for some reconciliation, with many of Philadelphia's elite holding similar beliefs. In 1775, when he looked at himself in the mirror, Morris saw a wealthy and respected 41-year-old, married for six years, with four children, three sons and one daughter, and the active partner in one of the largest mercantile houses in Philadelphia, which made it one of the largest in America and the West Indies. John Adams described him upon meeting him at the Continental Congress:

> I think he has a masterly Understanding, an open Temper and an honest Heart; and if he does not always vote for what you and I should think proper, it is because he believes that a large Body of People remains, who are not yet of his Mind. He has vast designs in the mercantile way. And no doubt pursues mercantile ends, which are always gain.[10]

Morris had 20 years of experience in trade and, maybe most importantly, had spent 20 years building a sterling business reputation with contacts all over the Atlantic world and a wealth of credit to cash in on.

~

Merchants and the mercantile arts drove the city forward. They performed many essential roles not only to keep Philadelphia running but to ensure their own financial growth and, as a consequence, the city's growth. The wealth they acquired created colonial Philadelphia, and this merchant-aristocratic class came to rule the city. They would collude to keep prices high and discourage peddlers who came in from the country. Merchants controlled critical economic phases, including production, distribution, capital, assumption of marketing risks, and finding new markets around the empire. They held many roles, including banker, insurance underwriter, and shipowner, and would serve others in those roles.[11] Merchants were often ship captains and trained their sons to be captains as well. And this wealth trickled down to shopkeepers and tradespeople: those who built the ships and houses of the merchants, and furnished them.[12]

Philadelphia merchants helped arrange markets throughout the week where locally made goods like linens, shalloons (wool lining), flannels, and ink-powder would be sold. This local manufacturing employed nearly two hundred impoverished women in spinning flax for fabric. They also dealt with shopkeepers who would bring the goods to customers. Philadelphia had hundreds of small shopkeepers, many of whom were women who served as arbiters of taste by picking and choosing the best British goods and clothing to retail in their stores before the importation ban. During the Stamp Act crisis and under pressure from the other colonies, Philadelphia merchants agreed to a non-importation agreement in January 1766 to last until May 1766, when another meeting was set up to decide whether they should keep it going. Four hundred Philadelphia merchants and traders signed the agreement, and a committee was appointed to ensure the community members adhered to the ban.[13] In this way merchants began gaining a semblance of political acumen and come to be leaders in the various political crises that swamped the colonies following the Seven Years' War.

If an aspiring merchant had no close relatives, then they would gain experience at a firm. They were on a near-constant hunt for the credit necessary to fund and fuel their mercantile missions. Merchants often sent advance payments to ensure goods would be shipped to them from abroad and write letters of recommendation to relay some of their trust in others to third parties. Getting together at the local coffee house, they would exchange gossip and news and pass along prices and information related to the quality of items or other merchants abroad while monitoring one another's reputations. They would enter into agreements with one another to share space on vessels or even charter a piece of a vessel for a particular voyage.

View of Market Street showing the market stalls that ran along the middle of the street, which twice a week would be full of vendors selling their produce or manufactured goods. (*The Life of Benjamin Franklin*)

During this whole process, or in preparing just one shipment, a merchant had an incredible number of duties to attend to. They drafted orders and receipts to city laborers and retailers, and the shipwrights, teamsters, and various artisans who all contributed either goods or services to make the voyage successful. Each would submit bills and receive payments in the form of work orders, proof of delivery, and notes on deliveries. The merchant would make a series of pragmatic decisions utilizing the local vernacular and understanding the peculiarities of the intimate financial obligations that ran the city, and work within the hyper-localized framework of their shop or warehouse and the people directly around them to eke out a living in an ever-changing world.[14]

Once a new shipment of cargo arrived, the merchant would place an advertisement in a newspaper to let prospective buyers know of the new items up for sale, which they could buy in wholesale quantities for cash or credit. Retailers were the most likely to buy wholesale. This included not only the many Philadelphia retailers but also those in the country towns of Pennsylvania, Delaware, and West Jersey, and even as far away as North Carolina. Supply and demand determined prices so that when certain goods were scarce, they would fetch astronomical prices, while other times they would go for a loss. Merchants also complained about retailers comparing prices and returning to haggle with the merchants.[15]

They were in a state of constant hustle, trying to stay within the bounds of royal decrees and the Navigation Acts and navigating the local networks of merchants and creditors and debtors, playing off on their excellent reputation and figuring out the reputations of others to gain that extra sliver of credit needed to be able to compete and survive in the trans-Atlantic trade game. It was all unstable and in constant flux. And while total mastery wasn't attainable, one could become good enough to move around this complex system of interpersonal affairs and relationships that made up the Philadelphia trade industry.

Merchants offered many different types of services beyond selling and purchasing goods. They managed to make money from storing goods in warehouses owned by them, remitting bills, providing insurance, being paid commissions, negotiating bills, and recovering losses on insurance. Merchants typically did not specialize in one thing but offered a wide range of services and dealt in a whole slew of goods, selling anything from nails and anchors to silk handkerchiefs and sails. Whatever they could get their hands on and think they could sell quickly and for a profit. They had agents scattered around, keeping them up to date on customers and credit in ports elsewhere.[16]

Merchants represented a crucial piece in an economic engine that included the entire social makeup of Philadelphia. An impressive and intricate commercial structure laid the foundation for the city's growth and created the atmosphere for social and political engagement and changes. Without this robust economy and the diverse population, Philadelphia would not have blossomed as it did. Population and economy were two driving, motivating, and harsh factors that competed and complemented one another. They rested under the hood of the city, powering its meteoric rise.

~

Philadelphia is humming. Bristling with activity, coming and going. Every day, cartloads from the farms from the west rumble into the city. Wheat, flour, and meat are taken off carts and placed in the waiting ships to set sail for England, Ireland, and the West Indies. Those same ships off-load their cargo. Some of it is in the form of goods: molasses from the West Indies, wine from Portugal. A lot of it in the form of people—family members crossing over to reunite with a husband or father who came over before; indentured servants who would have their lives and work owned by another. And enslaved people coming from the West Indies or directly from Africa, to be shuffled off in front of the London Coffee House where they will stand and be auctioned off. Watching their families broken apart. Some who are bought will leave and go to live and work elsewhere. Some will stay in the city and be put to work in the homes and various trades found throughout bustling colonial Philadelphia.

Eighteenth-century Philadelphia was a close-knit community with a population that did not rise above 35,000 people before the Revolution. It had its class distinctions, but it still functioned as a solidified community built upon relationships. Relationships sat at the heart of it all. Familial relations, bringing over family from the old country to the new. Ethnic relations. Forming business partnerships or trusts based upon a shared heritage, where the economic engine ran on credit and credit was only doled out based on your word's strength and the relationships you fostered. Religious relations. Political relations. All building personal and public networks that became the city as the people became Philadelphians.

In the waning years of the colonial period, America was experiencing unprecedented population growth, spurred on by immigration from Europe and the importation of enslaved people, but also by strong birth-to-death ratios. While in Europe, deaths surpassed births, in America, there were twice as many births as deaths. And on top of that, childhood death rates were lower, meaning those children who were born in America were expected to live. They also lived longer lives as the average life expectancy in Europe was 32 years, while in America it was 45 years.[17]

Abundant harvests propped up healthy diets, and the new land's largeness helped keep population densities lower to stave off the spread of potentially deadly diseases.

Scene from Birch's *Views of Philadelphia* of the busy waterfront of Philadelphia, with workers unloading cargo from ships and sailors venturing off to local taverns in the background. (Library of Congress)

A typical white resident of America was enjoying the highest standard of living in the modern world.[18]

This high standard served as a siren song to the economically depressed in Europe, primarily those from Germany and Ireland. Over the century prior to the Revolution, over 100,000 German-speaking immigrants came to America. Philadelphia served as the chief point of entry for many of those who would either stay in the city or go out into Pennsylvania and populate the western counties. The Irish similarly came in large numbers, with over 1,000 a year pouring into Philadelphia over the last two decades of the colonial era.[19]

Philadelphia was at the center of this influx of humanity and served as the hub for immigration to the American colonies. As it became more and more the shipping and trading center of British North America, Philadelphia ships would set out with wheat, wood, and the raw materials needed around the Atlantic world. They would return filled with people paying passage to Philadelphia or promising a certain number of years of their lives as indentured servants or enslaved people.

Along with the rest of the colonial world, Philadelphia's population multiplied many times in the generations leading up to the Revolution. Most of the early growth had immigration to thank. Still, after 1760, incredibly high birth rates fueled by the youth of the average Philadelphian led to a natural increase in the population.[20]

By 1750, Philadelphia overtook New York as the largest city in America. Soon, the city witnessed extraordinary population growth that saw nearly 1,000 new inhabitants every year. By the time of the Revolution it was double the size of Boston.

Average Population Totals in Philadelphia[21]	
1751	13,478
1756	15,539
1760	17,909
1767	24,637
1769	25,739
1772	28,873
1774	31,166
1775	32,350

Before mass transportation, the most valued property was within walking distance of the commercial centers, where the rich located their city dwellings—while also maintaining country estates to retire to during the sweltering summer months. Southwark was the poorest of the suburbs, where sailors and dock workers often lived and transients bedded down for a while. Immigrants fresh from Germany tended to live in the north of the city, in the Northern Liberties, or completely outside of it in Germantown.

Philadelphia's growing population was diverse for the time, and thanks to the city's generous religious freedoms, many different religious denominations could be found there, including Quakers (Society of Friends), the Church of England (Episcopalians), the Presbyterians, German Lutherans, German Reformed Church, and Swedish Lutherans.

Quakers were typically wealthier than any other religious denomination or group, residing almost wholly in the upper or middle classes. The Anglicans represented a broader social spectrum including merchants, artisans, and people experiencing poverty. On the eve of the Revolution, they would account for around 18 percent of the population. Presbyterians tended to be more attached to their particular church. The Swedish Lutheran Church of Philadelphia, Gloria Dei, had nearly fallen off the face of the Earth when, in 1750, the king of Sweden stepped in to send a missionary to Philadelphia to re-establish the church for the small congregation.[22]

All Philadelphians fell within five primary occupational groups: upper class— well-to-do merchants, professionals, and gentlemen (landed gentry); middle class—artisans (primarily working in construction and shipbuilding); lower middle class—less skilled workers (shoemakers, tailors, coopers); lower class—unskilled laborers and the poor (who did not pay any taxes); and unknown—too poor to be bothered by tax collectors.

In a busy port city like Philadelphia, there would be many artisans, merchants, and common laborers. "Merchant" was a broad catch-all term that encompassed everyone from storekeepers to the wealthier shipowners. Along the same lines, "artisan" was also used to cover a wide swath of activities from those requiring minimal skills like coopers, tailors, shoemakers, and weavers to more elite craftspersons such as silversmiths. Unskilled laborers filled out the rest of the ranks of the male workforce. Artisans were primarily responsible for making and fashioning materials, mostly for local consumption and not for export. They were usually self-employed and worked either out of their homes or on a job site. They made significant investments in their tools and materials, and like most small business owners, they were responsible for their own time and for their accounts. Most became well-off enough to own property, which meant they were able to vote in local and colonial elections. An artisan would often take on an apprentice or indentured youth and would sign a long-term contract to provide room and board, education, and training in return for their labor, usually until they reached the age of 21. Artisan careers covered a wide spectrum: stocking weaver, weaver, tailor, hatter, dyer, cordwainer, tanner, saddlemaker, skinner, butcher, miller, baker, blacksmith, coachmaker, bookbinder, painter, printer, cooper, mason, carpenter, joiner, clockmaker, and wheelwright.[23]

Philadelphia also had a special class of marine-based occupations. In 1774, mariners made up 9 percent of the city's workforce and another 5 percent were directly involved in the shipping industry as ship carpenters, ropemakers, sailmakers, caulkers, joiners, etc. Shipbuilding facilities were extensive in Philadelphia. When building a ship, a shipwright regularly contracted out the specialized work to local craftspersons. Wages were high, but the work was seasonal, with little to no work being done on building ships in the winter months. The rising number of artisans represented a significant political stratum in the colonies, and they would play a much more substantial role in public affairs than in any other place in the world.[24]

~

This great movement and thrust of humanity into the city worked in concert with the expansion of Philadelphia's economy, both growing simultaneously and because of one another. And the economy ran on the trading business.

Throughout the colonial era, the American colonies were expected to serve and provide the necessary materials for all of England. Parliament did this by placing regulations on colonial trade that dictated conditions on who the American colonies could and could not sell their goods to. The benefit of these restrictions for Great Britain was that it also limited competition from those other countries. In addition, they protected English craftspersons and manufacturers through protective Acts that limited colonial economic activity. While this did curb the production for export of certain goods it did not deter the production of goods for local markets.

Nor could it deter the primary strength of the American economy: that of its bountiful agricultural production. These foodstuffs not only helped spur consumption within the colonies but were so plentiful that they created massive surpluses that could be sold and shipped across the Atlantic back to Great Britain. And by 1750, the colonies no longer depended upon Great Britain for survival. They could produce the necessities for life and started to produce goods that rivaled British goods. So, when the Parliamentary taxes were pushed through following the Seven Years' War this would be just one of the many areas that caused resentment amongst the colonists.[25]

Because of Pennsylvania's rich agricultural hinterland, Philadelphia would be a major export facility. This first took the shape of active grain trade with Caribbean islands and southern Europe, but soon would build to a network that came to include Great Britain. Bread and flour, wheat, beef and pork, iron, potash, and more were being shipped to Great Britain, ports around the Caribbean, and the Mediterranean. At the same time, those ships would return bearing rum, sugar, molasses, wine, salt, and enslaved people. Merchants helped pay for this and their trade deficit with Great Britain and West Indies locales by providing shipping and financial services. Philadelphia served as a major port and busy commercial center. When merchants, retailers, and suppliers are included, at any one time, up to 35 percent of the workforce was employed directly in shipping or shipbuilding.[26]

Over the period, Philadelphia became an entrepôt for finished goods from England that were then sent to storekeepers in town and around the countryside, helping to lead to the amassing of great wealth by many of the city's merchants. The total tonnage of goods traveling through Philadelphia would soon dwarf any other port in the Americas.[27]

The Seven Years' War supercharged the transformation of Philadelphia's economy as the British government poured money into Pennsylvania in unprecedented amounts. Big military contracts meant that Philadelphia's merchants and builders had to scale up their operations. Shipbuilding skyrocketed so much that by 1770, the city produced all that it required to meet its shipping needs. It also caused many merchants to think more expansively about newer markets and new trade routes, and as such, the city became a magnet from other parts of the colonies to act as their market town of choice. It became the busiest seaport in America.[28]

This growth was built upon credit that ran the extensive Atlantic trade and colonial economic spheres. King Credit was the fuel that powered the economy. Philadelphia's economy, British America's economy, and the larger British realm's economy. The majority of wealth was held in the form of obligations that others owed to them. These series of credits and debts created connections amongst various groups and through the commercial activities they promoted. Locally, credit provided bonds that tied merchants to the community at large, making individual connections along the way.[29]

The inner workings of a mercantile business. A merchant wore many hats and performed many roles from clerk to insurer, mailman, enslaver, middleman, and much, much more. (*The Life of Benjamin Franklin*)

Credit was a necessity for the colonies and Philadelphia in large part because there was no banking system in America, and the only form of currency came in either foreign gold and silver coins or colonial paper money issued by the various colonial assemblies, that served as currency in that colony but would not be recognized in foreign countries, Great Britain, or possibly even other colonies. Despite this, the system worked well enough to support the economic growth of the colonies. Parliament barred the export of English coins to the American colonies, nor did it allow the establishment of a mint there. However, the supply appeared to meet the demand, with credit stepping in and filling in the gaps resulting from the lack of money.

Credit came to be used for everyday consumer purchases as well as day-to-day business activities. This was achieved by interpersonal lending and tabulating in books and accounts. Credit, though, relies upon trust; without that trust, the system would falter and crumble, so it was trust that allowed customers to take out goods and be the recipient of services with the promise of paying later. Credit became synonymous with a person's reputation built upon an individualized assessment of their moral, social, and economic standing.[30]

This trust was gained through associations: either personal, knowing a person and then doing business with them, or through groups and networks revolving around shared religious, ethnic or other similarities. It was an imperfect system reliant upon secondhand knowledge about other individuals that left itself open to exploitation by unsavory characters. To grant credit to someone was often a fraught experience. Networks helped to alleviate some of this anxiety. They also helped those new to the business world build their own reputations on the path toward opening up credit for themselves and their business endeavors. These networks were constructed upon kinship, religion, occupation, and friendships.[31]

For example, the St. Andrew's Society of Philadelphia, an organization established by and for Philadelphia's Scottish population (only men allowed, though), used membership to provide secured lines of credit to members. It was a built-in means to provide that step that allowed the members to prosper and, at the same time, build connections between the members and through the members. It also helped to tie ethnicity and religion to financial worth. And in a city where between a third and a half of all men belonged to some sort of club or society, it provided ample means for these formal and informal relationships to grow and be used to secure, extend, and obtain credit. These networks provided debt relief, social capital, and small capital loans, establishing a reputation for independence, honesty, and virtue.[32]

Towards the latter part of the colonial period, when Parliament began leveling new taxes upon American goods and services, British merchants started loudly complaining about the competition they received from colonial merchants and colonial goods just as Philadelphia witnessed a great increase in its shipping industry. Year after year, more and more colonial-owned and operated vessels entered into service in direct competition with their British counterparts, who very much viewed this as their purview. By the 1770s, colonial business factions owned, operated, and constructed one third of the shipping for the entire British Empire, with as much as 20 percent of this belonging to ships from Philadelphia. So nearly 7 percent of all British trade throughout the entire empire was controlled by Philadelphians in the years just prior to the Revolution. These American-owned vessels posed a major threat to British shipping and diplomacy as they began trading directly with continental entities like Portugal or any number of nations lining the Mediterranean. Discussions in Parliament began about placing discriminatory taxes on colonial ships or even banning them outright from the trans-Atlantic trade. This threatened the prosperity that the colonies had built up over decades.[33]

~

In general, the white residents of Philadelphia were doing better than their counterparts in England. And that goes for all white colonists as they enjoyed a substantially higher standard of living than their European relatives. They had more disposable income and paid lower taxes, as much as 75 percent below what was being paid in England.[34]

For the average family, those of lower artisans and laborers, food for the year would cost the family around £31, while rent would be anywhere between £10 and £22, heating costs around £5, clothes £8.5, and taxes would be around £2 or £3. The total budget for the year hovered around £60, which is at the upper end.[35] And for the most part, jobs would pay at least around that total, or if not due to the seasonal nature of the work workers would supplement their wages with part-time gigs. The lower classes lived right on the poverty line. Any kind of illness or injury and loss of income stream would easily mean falling below that line.

Most of the people in the city were individual entrepreneurs. They were solo artisans or tradespersons hiring themselves out or running a small shop. The typical artisan or shopkeeper lived a comfortably frugal life as long as their health allowed them to keep working. Plentiful, cheap food helped to make ends meet and the rise in trade meant regular work and good earnings to be made.[36]

Families lived the tiny-house life with the average artisan or shopkeeper residing in a narrow story-and a-half building of about 800 sq ft. The home was occupied by a large work area, fireplace for cooking and heating, a few beds made of straw, a couple of chairs or stools made of barrels, candles or whale oil lamps for lighting, and no indoor plumbing. No upholstered furniture. No carpets. Whitewashed walls and a sand-scrubbed floor. Winter garments consisted of a couple of woolen items and a pair of shoes. Most ate from wooden bowls, but middle-class families did have earthenware, and the upper class ate from china. The fireplace or stove only partially heated the home, making the rooms quite drafty. Wood and coal in the winter would become a major household expense.[37]

The hectic home life of a middle-class colonial Philadelphia family that included babies, children, horns, knitting, dogs barking, and kettle whistling all in the same room together. (*The Life of Benjamin Franklin*)

The smallness of the houses and their use for trades and stores meant people lived a lot of their lives out on the streets. This encouraged a public, social life. A robust coffee house, tavern, and inn scene grew out of this and became central to the city's communications system. In these places residents could sit and hear the news of the day by having newspapers read out and discussed. The most prominent was the London Coffee House, on the corner of Front and Market streets, which was established in 1754 and run by newspaper publisher William Bradford. For many years, merchants gathered there at noon to discuss prices and do business. These conversations and business dealings served as the foundations for future insurance companies and banks. The Coffee House was often the first stop for incoming ship captains and other travelers, where they left messages and auction notices. When Paul Revere arrived with news of the closing of Boston's port, revolutionary committees met at the taverns and held banquets and balls throughout the Revolution, entertaining the dignitaries who came through the city.[38]

Philadelphia's prosperity showed in the increasingly luxurious items that the wealthy purchased, and artisans sprang up to manufacture those items. This increasing affluence that started during the 1750s had Pennsylvania thinking of itself as "the best poor man's country in the world." There was a strong belief that a person could get ahead and get above the drowning poverty of the old world.[39]

While Philadelphia had a reputation for being a city of nearly endless economic possibilities in the colonial era, following the flush years of the Seven Years' War, the population experienced an economic recession that was exacerbated by an increase in immigration to Philadelphia that overwhelmed the leaders of the state, the city, and the benevolent factions looking to control the rampant poverty that was crippling a large swath of the population. The lower classes in Philadelphia lived an unpredictable existence that was jeopardized by illness, seasonal unemployment, and general economic slowdowns.[40]

Prior to 1760, poverty rates in Philadelphia remained low; roughly 1 percent received some sort of relief from the Overseers of the Poor. However, this does not include servants, enslaved people, and children, with the actual number being nearly double that. Philadelphia's poor consisted of people with disabilities, older adults, and those abandoned. A familial-style social system looked after them; while not entirely effective, it was still the most comprehensive and robust welfare program in the colonies. At the time, poverty was not viewed as a critical problem; when it did arise, it was seen as coming about as the result of circumstances. Families often were the ones providing safety nets, but it was those without that kinship network that tended to slip into impoverishment: elderly with no relatives around to care for them, widows and orphans with no roots in the city, or those with mental illnesses who were abandoned by their family.[41]

Beginning in the 1750s, the increasing population and number of poor had civic leaders seeking out alternatives to address poverty without having to constantly hike the poor tax. The solution at the time was the building of the Pennsylvania Hospital for the Sick Poor. While altruistic, it should also be seen as a move to counter the rising poor rates, which upset the upper and middle classes. And part of the reasoning around the hospital's creation revolved around the idea held by its champions that providing medical care for a sick worker would not only mean they would eventually rejoin the workforce but that their potentially widowed wife or orphaned children wouldn't become wards of the city. There was also a firm belief among the upper class, who led the effort to get the hospital built, that it would inspire patients "with proper love and reverence towards their superiors and by consequence promote that harmony and subordination in which the peace and happiness of society consists."[42] Those receiving assistance should be grateful for the help their betters so graciously provided. Most of the patients were mariners or from the maritime trades, demonstrating the dangers and diseases involved in the seagoing businesses. The care provided by the hospital did allow workers to return to work and provide for their families, making it a success that benefited the laborers and the middle-class taxpayers alike.[43]

The primary economic event during this late colonial period was the Seven Years' War (1756–63). The war fueled the economic ascendancy of Philadelphia but this was erased with the peace that fell after the fighting stopped on the continent with the fall of Montreal in 1760. It left an economy in which there was a lack of bills of exchange to pay back debts to British financiers and a lack of any kind of adequate currency. And on a macro level Great Britain was all but broke, spurring Parliament to act and pass a series of infamous internal taxation bills that caused great consternation in the colonies. The end of the war had a far-reaching, global economic impact. The war brought about inflation and speculation fueled by cheap money and a huge demand. When the demand dried up, economic collapse in Europe and North America soon followed.[44]

For merchants, the Seven Years' War was a time when sales of goods exceeded those at any previous time in the city's history. Helping this business along were English merchants extending credit quite liberally and often indiscriminately. In a world where connections, familial and personal and professional, were often the only means of securing any kind of credit for a merchant, the war opened up that world to lowly clerks, supercargoes, and retailers with dreams of casting away on their own. Credit allowed them to secure their stock of goods and begin the trading game.

Imports increased exponentially, going from £168,246 in 1757 to £260,953 in 1758 and £498,161 in 1759 before reaching an all-time peak of £707,998 in 1760. Merchants were recording that they had cotton goods in the city equal to three years' consumption. Day after day, goods were imported by gleeful merchants who showed little worry by the glut of products accumulating. Helping this importation was an exchange rate that was actually declining at the same time.[45]

But over the course of just a few months in the summer and into the fall of 1760, the bubble burst. One Philadelphia merchant observed during that period, "Times have changed much within these few months that we apprehend many of the importers of European goods must feel the Alteration very sensibly had they continued as they have for two or three years past."[46]

This would lead to an economic depression engulfing the city, brought about by huge debts accrued by retailers to Philadelphia merchants and the merchants to their English counterparts, exacerbated by the sharp decline in war spending. Great Britain shifted its military focus away from North America and to the West Indies, which meant not as many war funds were being spent in America. This coupled with a decline in illicit trade and smuggling, which had kept prices low. The means of the merchants to pay back their creditors declined just at the time when they wanted to start being paid back.[47]

Daniel Clark, a Philadelphia merchant, described that situation:

> The present time the most distressful the Philadelphians have ever met in the way of business, at least the modern part of them. We owe heavy sums in England. Sales dull. Goods high and scarce at home [England], here plenty, money prodigious scarce and not easily Collected from the Inhabitants. These circumstances have reduced the trading part of us to a most Tragick condition and the merchants of London am affraid will participate of

this our generall calamity. I have the misfortune to be one of a number of those that own money in London and other parts of England and to remit at 180 (which the exchange is now risen to) vexes my soul.[48]

The shrinking credit and economy caused a trickle-down, shake-down effect throughout the economic system, where British creditors began pressuring Philadelphia merchants, who in turn put pressure on their customers to pay their debts. There were few ways to pay back these debts without acceptable British currency available in the colonies, and merchants were unable to pay in the paper currency of Pennsylvania. Bills of exchange were often one of the only ways to do so. They served as the colonies' primary financial instruments, acting as a form of credit that allowed merchants to defer payment for goods or services. This often took the form of written orders for the transfer of funds between parties, promoting economic transactions across the Atlantic world. The lack of these bills drove up the exchange rate, making an already perilous situation even more dire. As the firm James and Drinker put it, "There are very few Bills of Exchange to be had at any rate, and the greatest part of them spoken for. Our Silver and Gold sent away within these 8 months last, what little is left the people in Trade are collecting as fast as they can to send to England and we see no way of being supplied from any Trade we can carry on."[49]

With no means of making remittance or it being unbearably expensive, added to overstuffed shelves, lack of sales, and customers unable to pay off their debts, merchants had little choice but to go into delinquency. A large number of Philadelphia merchants went bankrupt or failed in 1763. When merchants stayed in business, the cost of goods they were selling kept increasing due to the exchange rate situation.[50]

When the final peace was announced by the Treaty of Paris in 1763, merchants hoped that this would lead to the market calming down, prices beginning to lower, and transportation becoming less expensive and dangerous, since the seas were no longer a battlefield and specie could once again start to be shipped safely. But all hopes were dashed in the colonies when Parliament began implementing new trade regulations and revenue "measures," starting in 1764 and carrying over to 1765, to help pay off the costs accumulated during seven years of war. This would reach a climax in the colonies with the passing of the Stamp Act in 1765, which kicked off a political maelstrom.

Throughout the war years, a tremendous amount of money was made from war contracts and other war means (privateering and trade), creating the first push for country estate building outside of the city. Wealthy merchants made even wealthier by the war began constructing elegant country estates outside of the city. Contractors like Joseph Fox and John Baynton received lucrative building contracts. John MacPherson profited handsomely from privateering ventures. Indentured servants took the opportunity to break their indentures and sign up to serve in the military. For most of the citizens of Philadelphia, the war meant prosperity.[51]

This wartime boom provided full employment in Philadelphia, which came to a near-sudden halt in 1760. The city swelled as veterans began returning. Making matters worse, ships carrying immigrants began landing in Philadelphia once again after a hiatus during much of the war.

Compounding their situation was inflation caused by the war, the lack of currency, a recession that left many out of work, and then the brutal winter of 1761–2, which put many of the city's poor in a perilous situation. The price of fuel to heat homes became astronomical, and many could not afford firewood. The Overseers of the Poor coordinated the relief effort. They were appointed officials responsible for managing poor relief that operated through a combination of public assistance, including almshouses and outdoor relief, and private charity to supply aid to the indigent. During this crisis, the Overseers of the Poor were overwhelmed with the amount of relief needed. A group of Quaker merchants banded together to form a "Committee to Alleviate the Miseries of the Poor" that raised funds by going door to door to help fill in some of the gaps needed to purchase firewood for those impoverished.[52]

Scene from Birch's *Views of Philadelphia* that shows the vibrant shipbuilding industry of the city. (Library of Congress)

After this winter, many pleas and petitions were submitted to the Pennsylvania Assembly to provide additional assistance and come to the aid of the city and its poor. However, nothing would be done. Years went by. The only solution was for the overseers to raise the poor tax. At the same time, the almshouse was overflowing with people.

Then, in 1766, Quaker merchants again came together to propose building a new, larger almshouse/workhouse, which would come to be known by the rather ominous name "Bettering House." The idea behind the Bettering House was for the aged and disabled to reside in the almshouse portion. At the same time, destitute but able-bodied souls would work in the workhouse portion, where they would make and manufacture items and contribute to their upkeep and the upkeep of the entire house. This would eliminate the distribution of relief, as all of those receiving any kind of relief would be found in the Bettering House. In theory, this would cut down on costs and be funded by private sources, the work of the residents, and, if need be, additional poor taxes. The Assembly approved the setup.[53]

While the Bettering House has received much praise as a philanthropic endeavor, it was still done with an eye toward reducing costs and the tax burden upon the upper and middle classes. And it was implemented with the notion of scaring people off the dole with the prospect of having to leave their homes and do hard labor in the workhouse. It was set up as a kind of incentive to find employment or get support elsewhere.

There was also the beginning of a shift in the way people experiencing poverty were viewed. Blame started to be hefted upon them for their plight. As poverty rates increased there was no lowering in the poor taxes (even though the population was growing steadily, tax revenue remained relatively static over the same time); in fact, there had been an increase in the tax. Even the rising taxes were not enough to meet the financial need. The city and civic and moral leaders failed to recognize that those in poverty were not at fault but rather a systemic issue which depressed the labor market was causing the poverty situation. Insecurity became the new reality. The percentage of those not taxed, meaning they did not have any taxable property, was around 6 percent in 1750 but had nearly doubled to 11 percent by the time of the Revolution. The programs so lauded as examples of the Age of Benevolence and the Age of Reason, the hospital, the Bettering House, and the almshouse, all failed in their mission of driving poverty out of the city. Twenty-five percent of the free male population was at or below the poverty line. The hard work and frugal ethos of the likes of Franklin just wasn't cutting it. It was the elites like Franklin who were pushing these ideas, placing the blame onto the poor and then, disproportionately, the cost of their schemes onto the middle and lower classes.[54]

~

Merchants performed many roles in the city. They facilitated trade from outside the city and the sale of goods within it, creating the economic conditions that supported most of white Philadelphia. The economic growth experienced by Philadelphia since 1750 fueled the personal wealth of many and expanded the economy to make the city a destination for tens of thousands in the decades prior to the Revolution, pulling in people from across Pennsylvania and from across the Atlantic. At the same time, the atmosphere brought about an increase in the number of enslaved individuals in the city. The dynamic nature of the economy, with its mixture of commerce, manufacturing, and agriculture, helped shape the nature of slavery in the city. Philadelphians actively sought out the labor of enslaved peoples to meet their workforce requirements, but this period also saw the first burgeoning groups of white Philadelphians dedicating themselves to eradicating the scourge of slavery in the city.

CHAPTER THREE

Fear of a Free City

From top: *Pennsylvania Gazette*, October 13, 1763, 3; *Pennsylvania Gazette*, March 10, 1763, 3; *Pennsylvania Gazette*, September 23, 1762, 3; *Pennsylvania Gazette*, July 8, 1762, 4; *Pennsylvania Gazette*, July 9, 1761, 4; *Pennsylvania Gazette*, August 13, 1761, 4; *Pennsylvania Gazette*, May 7, 1761, 3. (Newspapers.com)

These are but a sample of the advertisements placed in Philadelphia newspapers showing the normalcy of enslavement in the city, how institutionalized it was, the diverse forms that it took, and how the leading citizens participated in the slave trade and the perpetuation of the enslavement of Black peoples in the American colonies. The enslaved peoples of Philadelphia and those enslaved peoples who reached America through the port of Philadelphia were just as instrumental in the building of the city as those who kept them in bondage, either directly through the exploitation of their labor and lives or indirectly through the consumption of products made through the labor of enslaved peoples, which covered the entire spectrum of consumer products from baked goods to leather goods. The enslavement of Blacks in Philadelphia affected every segment and class of the population.

With scant evidence surviving of the thoughts and feelings, hearts and minds of enslaved Philadelphians in the colonial period, it makes a work like Olaudah Equiano's narrative of his time as an enslaved person, *The Life of Olaudah Equiano, or Gustavus Vassa, The African*, all the more remarkable and valuable. Even though a Philadelphia Quaker merchant, Robert King, purchased Equiano, he spent most of his time in captivity living and working in the West Indies. But his retelling of his initial capture, what conditions were like on the slave ship across the Atlantic, and other personal insights, including recollections of his visits to Philadelphia as an enslaved person aboard one of King's ships, tell an important story and lend insight into the life of an enslaved person. And though there is but this one source you get to peer into the thoughts of those who were enslaved at the time.

The front page of Olaudah Equiano's memoir showing what is thought to be the only known portrait of Equiano. (*The Interesting Narrative of the Life of Olaudah Equiano, or Gustavus Vassa, the African*)

Equiano's home in Africa was in a small farming community. A happy life was disrupted by his capture one night by a rival tribe, who transported him a long way from his home. He passed through a series of hands as the contraband of multiple other African peoples until he was ultimately sold to white enslavers:

The first object which saluted my eyes when I arrived on the coast, was the sea, and a slave ship, which was then riding at anchor, and waiting for its cargo. These filled me with astonishment, which was soon converted into terror, when I was carried on board. I was immediately handled, and tossed up to see if I were sound, by some of the crew; and I was now persuaded that I had gotten into a world of bad spirits, and that they were going to kill me. Their complexions, too, differing so much from ours, their long hair, and the language they spoke, (which was very different from any I had ever heard) united to confirm me in this belief. Indeed, such were the horrors of my views and fears at the moment, that, if ten thousand worlds had been my own, I would have freely parted with them all to have exchanged my condition with that of the meanest slave in my own country. When I looked round the ship too, and saw a large furnace of copper boiling, and a multitude of black people of every description chained together, every one of their countenances expressing dejection and sorrow, I no longer doubted of my fate; and, quite overpowered with horror and anguish, I fell motionless on the deck and fainted ... I was soon put down under the decks, and there I received such a salutation in my nostrils as I had never experienced in my life: so that, with the loathsomeness of the stench, and crying together, I became so sick and low that I was not able to eat, nor had I the least desire to taste any thing. I now wished for the last friend, death, to relieve me.[1]

Elsewhere, Equiano describes the intensely wretched conditions below deck in the hold of the ship:

The stench of the hold while we were on the coast was so intolerably loathsome, that it was dangerous to remain there for any time, and some of us had been permitted to stay on the deck for the fresh air; but now that the whole ship's cargo were confined together, it became absolutely pestilential. The closeness of the place, and the heat of the climate, added to the number in the ship, which was so crowded that each had scarcely room to turn himself, almost suffocated us. This produced copious perspirations, so that the air soon became unfit for respiration, from a variety of loathsome smells, and brought on a sickness among the slaves, of which many died—thus falling victims to the improvident avarice, as I may call it, of their purchasers. This wretched situation was again aggravated by the galling of the chains, now became insupportable; and the filth of the necessary tubs, into which the children often fell, and were almost suffocated. The shrieks of the women, and the groans of the dying, rendered the whole a scene of horror almost inconceivable.[2]

During the passage, Equiano faced beatings for not eating and was forced to eat. He witnessed the crew throw fish back into the ocean instead of offering them to the starving enslaved people, and experienced the deaths of many below decks. Then, upon reaching the island of Barbados, he was put into the auction:

Many merchants and planters now came on board, though it was in the evening. They put us in separate parcels, and examined us attentively. They also made us jump, and pointed to the land, signifying we were to go there. We thought by this, we should be eaten by these ugly men, as they appeared to us; and, when soon after we were all put down under the deck again, there was much dread and trembling among us, and nothing but bitter cries to be heard all the night from these apprehensions, insomuch, that at last the white people got some old slaves from the land to pacify us. They told us we were not to be eaten, but to work, and were soon to go on land, where we should see many of our country people. This report eased us much. And sure enough, soon after we were landed, there came to us Africans of all languages ... On a signal given, (as the beat of a drum,) the buyers rush at once into the yard where the slaves are confined, and make choice of that parcel they like best. The noise and clamor with which this is attended, and the eagerness visible in the countenances of the buyers, serve not a little to increase the apprehension of terrified Africans, who may well be supposed to consider them as the ministers of that destruction to which they think themselves devoted. In this manner, without scruple, are relations and friends separated, most of them never to see each other again. I remember, in the vessel in which I was brought over, in the men's apartment, there were several brothers, who, in the sale, were sold in different lots: and it was very moving on this occasion, to see and hear their cries at parting.[3]

Throughout his enslavement, Equiano tells of being given many names, from Jacob to Michael and finally Gustavus. With each change in enslaver, he received a new name, and he settled into the life of working aboard multiple ships. The crew would terrorize him, telling him that they were going to kill and eat him, and had him living in constant fear. Still a boy not even in his teens, only 10–12 years old, he would be forced to fight other boys for the pleasure and entertainment of the rest of the crew.

Robert King, a Quaker merchant from Philadelphia, would be the next to purchase Equiano at age 13. At that time, King asked the teen what he could do: "I told him I knew something of seamanship, and could shave and dress hair pretty well; and I could refine wines, which I had learned on shipboard, where I had often done it; and that I could write, and understood arithmetic tolerably well, as far as the Rule of Three."[4] King immediately began treating Equiano better than anyone previously had, and hired him out where he generally earned more than other enslaved peoples. He performed several different jobs, from clerking to receiving and delivering cargo, tending to store, delivering goods, shaving and dressing King, taking care of horses, and working aboard many different vessels. At one point, King remarked that Equiano saved him £100 a year.

Equiano made a deal with King, where he agreed to a price of £40 for Equiano's freedom. He went about gathering goods while in the West Indies and then selling them whilst in other ports on business for King. Over the course of a few years, Equiano was able to acquire the necessary funds to purchase his freedom, and his joy was palpable:

I could scarcely believe I was awake. Heavens! who could do justice to my feelings at this moment! Not conquering heroes themselves, in the midst of a triumph—Not the tender mother who has just regained her long lost infant, and presses it to her heart;—Not the weary, hungry mariner, at the sight of the desired friendly port—Not the lover, when he once more embraces his beloved mistress, after she has been ravished from his arms! All within my breast was tumult, wildness, and delirium! My feet scarcely touched the ground, for they were winged with joy; and, like Elijah, as he rose to Heaven, they "were with lightning sped as I went on." Every one I met I told of my happiness, and blazed about the virtue of my amiable master and captain.[5]

Following his emancipation in 1766, Equiano lived a varied and interesting life that reflected his many talents and included a dedication to social causes. He continued working as a sailor, traveling back and forth across the Atlantic, and even served on a voyage to the Arctic. He collected these experiences in his autobiography, published in 1789. His narrative became a tool for the abolitionist movement and contributed significantly to the discourse against the slave trade.

~

The history of colonial Philadelphia has always included slavery. As soon as Europeans settled in an area, enslaved Black people were soon to follow. William Penn, the founder of Pennsylvania and the city of brotherly love, enslaved people. Slavery grew and developed organically, with laws coming after the fact to control or shape its impact.

Three years after the arrival of the Penns in December of 1684, a ship landed in Philadelphia bearing 150 enslaved Africans. The Quaker settlers quickly bought them and put them to work clearing the land and building some of the first structures in Philadelphia. They paid with what little specie was available in the colony to purchase these people. Philadelphia had only 2,000 residents at the time, making an influx of 150 enslaved peoples a significant increase in the town.[6]

Pennsylvania was not suited to the plantation-style agriculture of the South, which meant enslaved people were instead used in more industrial and specialized settings. Due to the harsh nature of Pennsylvania's winters, the upkeep of enslaved people,

Title page of Olaudah Equiano's memoir, *The Interesting Narrative of the Life of Olaudah Equiano, or Gustavus Vassa, the African.* (*The Interesting Narrative of the Life of Olaudah Equiano, or Gustavus Vassa, the African*)

accounting for clothing and lodging, came at a higher cost than in the southern colonies; food and clothing alone accounted annually for around a quarter of the enslaved person's value.

Beginning in 1700, the first laws were passed in Pennsylvania regulating the slave trade when a duty upon the importation of enslaved Black people was put into effect. Starting at around £2 per person, over the next couple of decades it rose to £20. However, these internal taxes passed by the Pennsylvania Assembly would routinely be vetoed by the British lords of trade, thanks to the lucrative influence of the heavily ensconced African Company, the primary organization in the trans-Atlantic slave conglomeration.

The 1700 legislation would kick off a string of Acts passed by the Assembly based around controlling the growing Black population. For example, Black people were to be tried in special jury-less courts, a law that stayed on the books until the Revolution. Other laws throughout the 18th century placed strict restrictions on Black people's movement and ability to congregate.[7]

A typical regulation like the 1726 "Act for the Better Regulating of Negroes in this Province" would also try to regulate the integrity of those enslaved peoples being brought into Pennsylvania by levying steep fines against enslavers whose enslaved peoples committed misdemeanors or other petty offenses. Consequently though, enslavers would be compensated if those they enslaved committed a capital crime that resulted in the execution of the enslaved person.[8] White fears and prejudices toward Blacks began to be seen in the state Assembly as they passed a set of Black Codes: "'tis found by experience that free negroes are an idle, slothful people and often prove burdensome to the neighborhood and afford ill examples to other negroes [slaves]." The new law put into place bonds to be paid by those who were freeing their slaves, £30, to cover any costs that might occur if the newly freed person needed public assistance. The law also established the practice of indenturing "slothful" free Black adults and children to any willing employers until males reached the age of 24, or 21 years old for females. And it levied fines on free Black people who harbored runaway slaves or consorted with slaves without their master's consent. But the most significant penalties were left for those who entered into biracial sexual relationships. For Black-and-white sexual relationships, the white participant faced the typical punishment given out for fornication or adultery, while the Black partner faced up to seven years of servitude. An interracial marriage led to seven years of servitude or a £30 fine for the white partner, with the Black partner being re-enslaved. And any children produced as a result of these relationships were bound out until the age of 31.[9]

After Parliament forbade the Assembly's duties placed on newly arrived enslaved peoples, Philadelphia received a relative, short-term boom in the number of enslaved people entering the colony. However, by the end of the 1730s, the importing of enslaved people dwindled and was replaced by a significant increase in white, European indentured servants. From 1732 to 1754, even though indentured servitude probably cost more on the whole, it was preferred to Black slavery by Philadelphians. With the onset of the Seven Years' War, the preference flip-flopped. The British recruited large numbers of indentured servants from Philadelphia into military service, which dried up the labor market, and many enslaved persons were brought in to perform that missing labor. The situation became so bad that the Pennsylvania Assembly sent a stern warning to the governor: "If the Possession of a bought Servant … is … rendered precarious … the Purchase, and Of Course the Importation, of Servants will be discouraged, and the People driven to the Necessity of providing themselves with Negroe Slaves, as the Property in them and their Service seems at present more secure."[10]

This brought about a nine-year period where more enslaved people entered Philadelphia and Pennsylvania than in any other period of its history. Throughout the

1740s, there were, on average, 20 enslaved people imported a year, while in the early 1750s, it rose to around 30. After the start of the war, the numbers quickly rose to 100, peaking in 1762 with as many as 500 enslaved persons arriving in the city in a year. This became the greatest infusion of African culture in the city's history. One of the city's enslavers commented on the labor shortage brought on by the war: "All importation of white servants is ruined by enlisting them, and we must make more general use of Slaves." Most arrived directly from Africa. However, as soon as peace settled upon America, servants and soldiers returned to Philadelphia, along with a whole new influx of indentured servants and immigrants who began pouring into Philadelphia.[11]

This marked a steady decline in the importation of enslaved peoples, so much so that between 1768 and 1770, fewer than 30 enslaved people entered the city per year. And by the time of the Revolution, the forceful trade of enslaved persons in Philadelphia had all but stopped, with the abolitionist Anthony Benezet commenting that by 1773, Philadelphia was exporting more enslaved people than it was importing.[12]

The number of enslaved people represented a significant minority of Philadelphia's total population. By 1767 an estimated 1,400 enslaved persons lived in Philadelphia, nearly 9 percent of the total. This number and percentage dropped precipitously throughout the remaining years of colonial rule until 1775, when around 672 enslaved people resided in the city. Pennsylvania, in general, had a smaller proportion of enslaved people than its neighbors, New York and Maryland. The reason for the decline mostly fell upon the lack of natural reproduction from the enslaved population. While importation slowed to a halt, enslaved peoples were not having children in sufficient numbers to replenish the Black population. Enslaved females past the age of fertility were not replaced by younger women. Even though there were roughly the same number of enslaved men as enslaved women, in a Northern city like Philadelphia enslaved Black people were often isolated in a white family, making the formation of families difficult. When children of an enslaved woman were born, they were often sold or bound out to rural areas outside of Philadelphia or to a Southern colony. One contemporary said, "In this city, negroes just born, are considered an encumbrance only."[13]

Most enslavers owned and kept one or two enslaved persons, with most of those enslaved not residing in households where an enslaved couple lived and could procreate. This disruption to families added to low fertility amongst enslaved women, along with high infant mortality rates and the selling of children enslaved people out of the city, leaving the nature of the enslaved population of Philadelphia to be dominated by adolescents and young adults.[14]

Towards the end of the 1760s, about a quarter of all white residents were enslaving a Black Philadelphian. Add to that the number of residents who owned and employed indentured servants, and Philadelphia was a society defined by this subservient culture.

White masters still preferred to employ white servants over enslaved Black people even though slavery meant complete, lifetime control over a person, and enslaved people were less likely to run away than white servants. But white servants were typically cheaper, being purchased for about half the cost of an enslaved person; they were also familiar with the language, the climate, and the diseases. But maybe most important and telling, white servants were the most like their masters. The white owners felt more of a kinship with their white servants, believing that their goals and beliefs in the society at large were much in the same. At the same time, enslaved Black people were regarded as alien to white society and placed upon the fringes. White servants were believed to be a part of the community and expected to protect it and share in making sure it continued to exist; they were enlisted in militias and were active participants in the fights against the king's enemies. Enslaved Black people were not trusted with weapons.[15]

However, there was no clear distinction between Black enslaved persons and white indentured servants besides the color of their skin and how they were treated and viewed. Both performed the same work and tasks. They would work right alongside one another and would even run off together.[16]

Slaveholding became a status symbol in the city where there existed a direct correlation between wealth and being an enslaver. Many of the leading citizens of the city bought and kept slaves. Throughout his life, Benjamin Franklin purchased and enslaved multiple people starting as early as the 1730s, and by the 1750s, he kept four slaves (Peter, Jemime, King, and Othello), with King being his personal attendant while stationed in London. There existed an elite society where some of the most prominent people enslaved others. But it was not limited to the wealthy class as artisans, mariners, tradesmen, and those in the food industry also enslaved people. Half were owned by aristocrats, but the middle and working classes owned the other half. All occupations in Philadelphia were represented by slave ownership. Southwark ropemaker John Phillips owned 13 enslaved people, and presumably most of them worked splicing and making rope. And John Peter, a biscuit maker, at one time enslaved over 30 women. Almost 10 percent of enslavers were captains or mariners, who presumably bought enslaved people to work on the ships, meaning the American merchant marine had a substantial Black workforce. To increase their share of the profits on voyages, mariners, who generally were part of the lower class, used what available capital they had to purchase enslaved people.[17] Robert Ellis was one such seaman who enslaved a person, Cojoe, while he served aboard the ship *Catherine*. Cojoe was regarded as "a Young able fellow fit for any Business." Whenever Cojoe sailed, Ellis was careful to insure him as well as the cargo and vessel, usually asking that Cojoe be insured for between £40 and £50. More than his services while at sea, Cojoe sometimes purchased goods for Ellis in other ports. A correspondent at Lewes was once told to "Order my

Negroe Cojoe to get me them trees that I Spoke of for he is to Come up in the Sloop [*Charming Sally*]."[18]

Many enslavers decided to invest in slavery rather than purchasing land or property. They put what liquid capital they owned into purchasing an enslaved person and renting their home. Or they decided to purchase an enslaved person to continue or expand their craft or small-scale home industry. One in six households contained at least one enslaved person in 1767. By 1772, 10 percent of craftspeople enslaved people, and a more significant proportion held indentured servants; by 1775, the number of enslaved people and indentured servants in the city equaled the number of free laborers.

Enslaved Black people could receive specialized training from their enslavers to assist with their businesses. Many were employed in the sailmaking industry; others became master craftsmen, bakers, masons, carpenters, shoemakers, butchers, tailors, and millers. Artisans put them to work as hatters, skinners, brush makers, sugar boilers, distillers, candlers, coopers, clockmakers, joiners, barbers, brewers, painters, harness makers, stonecutters, and even chocolate grinders. Robert Warren, an enslaved person in Philadelphia, hired himself out as a fiddler. Though the diversity of work they performed was high, the majority of enslaved people fell under the umbrella of household servants.[19]

Younger Black people were called boys and girls instead of men and women, and they received preference over older enslaved Black people. When someone was in the market for an enslaved person, they wanted a person between the ages of 14 and 20, as they were perceived to be more active and able to master new tasks better while also having a longer potential life span under enslavement. When bringing in new enslaved people, it was not so important that they were fully grown or able to perform hard labor. More consideration was placed on their ability to be trained in some skill that fit the specific needs of Philadelphian enslavers. Younger enslaved people also faced reduced risk of dying from disease. However, newly imported enslaved people were susceptible to New World diseases and ill-prepared for Pennsylvania's climate. And while whites were on the lookout for enslaved people who exhibited honesty, sobriety, and diligence, enslaved Black people fell to the same habits as their white masters in imbibing spirits and shirking their duties.[20]

Prior to the 1730s, Pennsylvania was importing what was called "refuse": enslaved people from the Caribbean who were regarded as low quality or undesirable, because of illness, physical defects, or being accused of criminal activities in the West Indies. And there was a genuine suspicion that grew up around all enslaved Black people being shipped to Philadelphia for sale. While the commonly held notion is that premiums were placed on "seasoned" enslaved people, those who had resided in other parts of the Atlantic world, particularly the West Indies, the opposite was true. Enslaved persons from the West Indies or other colonies were considered objectionable workers. They had attached to them notions of criminality and belligerence, and were considered to be old and infirm, which reduced their value. As one Philadelphia merchant, Isaac Norris, put it:

> I am thus particular because thous mentions thy Spouse's purpose of Sending more Neagroes, to Shew they are a Sort of Maze Hazardous & rarely profitably [*sic*] to ye owner, and seldom pleasing to factors here, because tis Troublesome & hard to make ye Sale beneficiall to ye Imployer People who would buy being Jealous They are Criminalls or otherwise of Little worth who are So Transported.[21]

There was a genuine fear that "seasoned slaves" from the West Indies or the South were generally more rebellious and obstinate than those coming directly from Africa.[22]

This led to there being a preference in Philadelphia and Pennsylvania for enslaved people directly imported from Africa. However, there was never a sophisticated understanding of the differences between the regions of Africa from where they came amongst enslavers and potential enslavers (though abolitionists like Benezet had a firm grasp on this knowledge). This led to claims such as, "It is generally allowed that the Gambia Slaves are much more robust and tractable than any other slaves from the Coast

Title page of Benezet's *A Short Account of that Part of Africa, Inhabited by the Negroes* that details the regions of Africa where many of the city's enslaved persons arrived from. (*A Short Account of that Part of Africa, Inhabited by the Negroes*)

of Guinea, and more capable of undergoing the Severity of the Winter Seasons in the North-American Colonies, which occasions their being Vastly more esteemed and coveted in this Province and those to the Northward, than any other Slaves whatsoever."[23] The make-up of the enslaved Philadelphians was diverse, coming from the nations and kingdoms of West Africa like Benin, Senegal, Goree, Guinea, Gambia, Fida, and more. They represented many ethnicities: Mandingo and Fuli, Akan, and others. "In the West-India Islands, where Slaves are best known, those of the Gold Coast are in much great Esteem, and higher valued than any others, on Account of their natural good Dispositions, and being better capable of hard Labour."[24]

To accommodate this importation directly from Africa, enslavers tried to organize shipments of enslaved people between April and September to avoid exposure to extreme cold. The late fall and winter months also saw the coming of more and more respiratory diseases, which increased the death rates among enslaved people.[25]

The diet of enslaved people also did not help. It consisted primarily of grains, rye or corn, and meat broths, and verged on being just bread and water. Very rarely were vegetables or any cut of meat added to it, and often, the food was dirty, stale, or spoiled. This diet failed to provide the vitamins and proteins needed. At the same time, white indentured servants would receive greater variety and balance in their meals. On average, an enslaved person received 1,000 fewer calories a day than a resident of the Philadelphia workhouse received. To supplement this, enslaved people had Sundays off and would typically hire themselves out to gain additional monies to pay for necessities like food and clothing. In a few instances, masters gave enslaved people a small plot of land to grow vegetables. This disparity was even more acute in enslaved Black women, whose diet was poorer than the men's and stunted their growth.[26]

Enslaved people commonly slept in outhouses such as stables, barns, cellars, and attics, but kitchens were the most common locations. Kitchens often stood separate from the main house due to the smoke and heat they produced, the smells of garbage and the butchering of animals. This led to enslaved people being called the "kitchen family." Residing in the kitchen did provide a semblance of independence, out from under the thumb of their masters. But the living conditions were harsh. It was a drafty and smoky room, which only exacerbated respiratory problems, worsened by their sleeping directly on the damp and chilled floor.[27]

Accounts of white attitudes toward their domestic enslaved persons are scarce, but Fanny Saltar's account offers a little perspective:

> Hired English and bought Africans, many of whom were dead and gone before my time, but of Daddy Caesar, I have a vivid recollection. He was a prince in his native country and as a mark of that distinction his forehead and cheeks were deeply slashed with lines. He was low of stature, bandy-legged, his skin very black, his wool tightly knotted, his nose flat, lips thick, mouth wide, but his teeth wide and even. In his dialect there was as much African as English, and when a child I liked to hear his talk as he sat in the old fashioned chimney corner; and no Italian music is now so Sweet to my ears as were then his African songs. Whether his manners were princely or not I cannot determine, as he was the only member of royalty I have ever seen, but this I do know—that there was a gentleness, a tenderness, and I think I may say, a dellicacy in his manner that made me greatly prefer him to Daddy Jack, Samuel, Manuel or any of the colored population of the kitchen. Yet Mammy Katy, a little hump-backed mulato Cook was also a great favorite. I loved to sit in her lap as she ate her breakfast and get a sip of her strong coffee from her blue dragon cup and saucer. I liked the smoke too of her old pipe, until one evening, as I sat on her knee, she dropped asleep and her short pipe with its very contents fell into my bosom; from that time I have never liked tobacco in any form. But this accident did not cool my love for Mammy Katy, for when I was being weaned, nothing could console me the first night of mother's absence, until Molly carried me into her chamber, where the kind little woman and her son changed my cries of distress into merry laughter by exerting their skill in alternately blowing out a lighted candle and blowing it in again, and to crown all, Manny put a lighted candle into his mouth, the light shining curiously through his black cheeks.[28]

Enslaved people were seen as below the lowest whites in society but slightly above non-productive animals, often equating them to horses or dogs. Enslavers would bestow upon their enslaved peoples the same names they would give their work animals. This attitude towards the enslaved led to beatings, and little to no care given to the clothing that they were provided. Enslaved persons were usually forced to wear inadequate clothing, with the justification being it would discourage running away.[29]

A constant fear of being sold off filled enslaved people, which would lead to resistance on the part of some, like when Bernard Gratz, a merchant in Philadelphia, dispatched an enslaved person, George, to Reading to be sold there. The overseer in charge of the sale, though, reported back George's behavior:

> I took your Negroe George some time ago home, thinking I might be the better able to Sell him: who after beening with me a night behaved himself in such an Insolent manner I immediately remanded back to the Gaol. About a Week since I put him up at Public Sale at Christopher Witman's Tavern, where there was a Number of Persons who inclined to Purchase him. But he protested publickly that he would not be sold, and if Any one should purchase him he wou'd be the Death of him and Words to the like purpose which deter'd the people from biding. I then sent him back again wth Directions to the Gouler to keep him at Hard Labour which he refuses to do & goes on in such An Insolent Manner that's impossible to get a Master for him here.[30]

This led George to be brought back to Philadelphia where he was "almost Naked ... Chain'd & Hand Cuff'd."[31]

Resistance took a few forms for enslaved peoples. They might simply slow down the rate of work they were performing, not producing the expected output, or produce shoddy work. But the most effective form of resistance was running away. Time was a tangible asset that the enslaved had control over. Running away meant that loss of time for their enslavers—weeks, months, or even years until they could be recaptured—was not something they could recoup. Philadelphia's newspapers are full of announcements seeking the return of runaway enslaved persons. A diverse range of subterfuges was used by the enslaved to leave their masters. One person carried a bridle and when approached, he simply said he was out looking for his enslaver's runaway horse. Another with light enough skin to pass for white simply slipped away to begin life as a white man. One of the most popular avenues for escape was the ships that entered and left the city's docks on a daily basis. Captains weren't too inquisitive when it came to the background of their crew.[32]

Philadelphia enjoyed no slave insurrections or plots to launch one, and experienced no panics. Tensions were relieved by the city's white mechanics securing the inclusion of language in the 1726 "Act for the Better Regulating of Negroes in this Province" that forbade enslavers or enslaved people from hiring themselves out.[33]

In the late colonial period, roughly 15 percent of Philadelphia's working male population was enslaved, while enslaved people performed 20 percent of domestic work. Since so many enslaved people had daily, direct contact with the white family

Illustration of the London Coffee House with an auction of enslaved people taking place in front of the establishment. (*Philadelphia: A History of the City and its People*)

that owned them, this helped them to become accustomed to European customs and culture. They toiled right alongside their enslavers, acquiring the same skills while performing the same duties.

Philadelphia was a physically compact area, with all of the enslaved people living within about 20 blocks of developed space. Its dense population area meant everything was within walking distance, and public spaces were used by the Black inhabitants for social interaction, such as the Court House on the corner of Second and High Street. Whites used the exact locations, so both commingled and socialized with or at least near one another.

The cosmopolitan setting also allowed enslaved people freer access to socializing, greater access to intellectual stimulation, and additional opportunities to hire themselves to earn extra funds to attempt to pay for their freedom. The city atmosphere allowed for social network development and a semblance of family life. Enslaved people enjoyed meeting on Sundays, holidays, and fair days to dance together, and these days offered them the opportunity to talk and sing in their native dialects from Africa. This socializing and congregating after the day's work was over sparked complaints by the city's white residents, which led to restrictions being placed upon the number of Blacks allowed to gather together.[34]

However, due to the small-scale nature of ownership in the city, enslavers held, on average, 2.4 enslaved people, so often those who entered into relationships with one another lived apart in separate households. While most Black women and men did not live together which posed relationship and socializing challenges, the city's close nature allowed for visitation as most residences were never more than a few blocks away. But it also meant that children of enslaved people grew up without both parents being a substantial part of their lives, and even they were often sold off or hired out when they were old enough, typically 10 or 12 years of age. With the expense of raising a child being so great, a common practice was to hire out the children of enslaved people to other families.[35] These slave families were not immune to one of the members being sold off out of the colony to Delaware or Maryland or to a larger agriculture center in the counties west of Philadelphia.[36]

Many enslaved people would take to evangelical Christianity in part thanks to the Great Awakening and the preaching of popular preachers like George Whitefield, who offered up ideas of personal liberation. The Anglican Church would become the leader in opening schools to teach Black children, and Christ Church would record enslaved persons' and free Black marriages and many baptisms.[37]

Black enslaved women in colonial Philadelphia performed housework, cooking, cleaning, washing, ironing, maintaining the fires, gardening, looking after the children, and serving as maids. They would also sew and make clothing. They became versatile members of the household. Black women lived in the house, sleeping in the kitchen or a room off the kitchen. Merchants and others in the professional class would occasionally hire enslaved women by the year or through indenture. Women would also be lent or hired out for a short period to help with the sick, work in the gardens, or work special parties or soirées. Younger Black women could also be apprenticed to gain a trade such as housewifery or spinning. After freedom, Black women still worked in domestic settings as servants and laundrywomen.[38]

Equiano also provides a vivid glimpse into the brutal treatment of enslaved women, who routinely faced degradations and sexual abuse from their captors or enslavers. The number of mixed-race children, listed amongst the rolls, wills, and inventories of enslavers, attests to that:

> While I was thus employed by my master, I was often a witness to cruelties of every kind, which were exercised on my unhappy fellow slaves. I used frequently to have different cargoes of new negroes in my care for sale; and it was almost a constant practice with our clerks, and other whites, to commit violent depredations on the chastity of the female slaves; and these I was, though with reluctance, obliged to submit to at all times, being unable to help them. When we have had some of these slaves on board my master's vessels, to carry them to other islands, or to America, I have known our mates to commit these acts most shame-fully, to the disgrace, not of Christians only, but of men. I have even known them gratify their brutal passion with females not ten years old; and these abominations, some of them practiced to such scandalous excess, that one of our captains discharged the mate and others on that account. And yet in Montserrat I have seen a negro man staked to the ground, and cut most shockingly, and then his ears cut off bit by bit, because he had been connected with a white woman, who was a common prostitute. As if it were no crime in the whites to rob an innocent African girl of her virtue; but most heinous in a black man only to gratify a passion of nature,

where the temptation was offered by one of a different color, though the most abandoned woman of her species.[39]

There were a few successful free Black women in Philadelphia, like Jane Row, who, when she passed away in 1766, had real estate on Fourth Street and in Southwark while owning two enslaved people, who she requested in her will be sold to good and reasonable masters. She lived with Henry Hainy, though they never married, and had two sons together. She had two other sons, William Row and John Miller, who were mixed-race.[40]

Throughout the period, a major factor in determining the demand for enslaved people at any given time was the status and number of indentured servants available. The Seven Years' War significantly affected this supply and demand, having a two-pronged impact. First, the need for soldiers outweighed the need for labor, and indentured servants were allowed to serve their king in exchange for getting out of their indenture. The other factor limiting indentured servants was the drying-up of cargo ships full of new immigrants to the colony, thanks to the hostilities on the seas.

The end of those hostilities paved the way for a legion of Scots, Irish and Germans to sign indentures in an effort to secure employment and provide their families with a semblance of economic relief. For those shipping them, it became a numbers game: seeing how many indentured servants they could cram onto a ship and then sell off in the New World. Once in America, the new masters of these indentured servants and their ethnic makeup created some tensions and led to reports of abusive behavior amongst the masters and a spike in runaways. And for servants, the trade-off of years of indenture for the hope of prosperous futures never quite materialized like they planned as Philadelphia's economy underwent massive changes following the Seven Years' War.[41]

The city could no longer provide for the constant influx of freed servants and immigrants, and there was scarcely a job to be had for them. And the social and economic mobility that once existed evaporated, taking with it the notions of the need for unfree labor. A new reality made itself known where hiring short-term help became more practical than keeping and maintaining an unfree workforce. Wages were also dropping below the cost of unfree labor, further encouraging a flexible labor system, particularly in a favorable labor market. Labor practices in the city began to change towards relying on free workers.[42]

During the late colonial period, manumission, while increasing slightly over time, never really accounted for much of the reduction in the number of enslaved people in the city. Over a 20-year period from the Stamp Act protests in 1765 to the end of the Revolution in 1783, the city's Black population flip-flopped from containing about 100 free Blacks and 1,400 enslaved people to 400 enslaved people and over 1,000 free Blacks.[43]

During this period, as the free Black population increased, the lives they lived were much like those of new immigrants who flocked to the city. Subject to the same fluctuations in the labor market, they experienced their own prejudices along the way, both socially and legally. While free in nature, they still operated under the onerous laws that aimed to separate Black and white in the world. It was a continual struggle for free Black people to make a life for themselves. However, as their numbers grew, a rich and diverse community of free Black people grew in Philadelphia in the post-war period.[44]

The increase in the number of free Black people was precipitated by a concerted effort by a select few of the city's white population who fought against the institution of slavery. They included revolutionary luminaries like Benjamin Rush and Thomas Paine, but it would be the concentrated efforts of Anthony Benezet that would define the late colonial push to abolish slavery in the province of Pennsylvania. In the process, Philadelphia became the center of the anti-slavery movement in the New World.

George Fox, the founder of Quakerism, was an early advocate against slavery in the mid-to-late 17th century. He argued all men were equal before God and urged his fellow Quakers to:

> consider with yourselves, if you were in the same condition as the Blacks are—who came strangers to you, and were sold to you as slaves. I say if this should be the condition of you or yours, you would think it hard measure. Yea and very great bondage and cruelty. And therefore, consider seriously of this, and do you for them, as you would have them, or any other, to do unto you, were you in the like slavish condition.[45]

This sentiment would bear fruit in Pennsylvania when Quakers in Germantown lodged a protest petition at a Monthly Meeting in 1688 that called into question slavery, saying that it violated the Golden Rule, "do unto others as you would have done unto yourself," and that the inhumane treatment of Blacks not only caused embarrassment to Quakers but would cause the enslaved people to violently revolt. By 1696, the Yearly Meeting, where all of the regional Quaker congregations gathered together once a year to plan and address issues arising in the area, began to urge its members to stop the importation of enslaved people, and they started a "Quarterly Meeting for Negroes" to address the Black Quakers of the area. This began the strain of antislavery that ran through specific segments of Quakers; however, it did not discourage many Quakers from enslaving people.[46]

From 1688 on to the 1750s, there remained a steady stream of Quakers who spoke out against the practice of slavery, from William Sotheby and Cadwalder Morgan to Ralph Sandiford and the incredibly weird and devout Benjamin Lay. However, nearly all of these efforts were confined to writing pamphlets and lodging complaints and protests at Quaker Monthly Meetings. Albeit Lay would employ theatrics in his steadfast dedication to the abolitionist cause, showing up to one meeting dressed in a military uniform complete with a sword, which he used to great effect when railing against the evils of slavery and using the sword to stab a Bible filled with a bladder of blood-like juice that went flying across the typically sedate Quaker meeting. He also kidnapped a child to prove a point about slavery and to show people how it feels to lose a child even for an afternoon.

Quakers did not hold the monopoly on showing concern for the plight of Black residents and enslaved people of the city. During the economic downturn following the end of the Seven Years' War, a charity sermon "in Favour of the distressed Black Inhabitants" was preached across most of the city's churches on Sunday, August 4, 1763. This was followed by a door-to-door canvassing to raise funds for Black relief efforts.[47]

America's greatest anti-slavery voice in the colonial period made his appearance in 1754 when Anthony Benezet promoted the letter of a fellow Quaker, John Woolman, "Epistle of Caution and Advice," at that year's Philadelphia Meeting. The epistle called on Quakers to act against the buying and selling of human beings into bondage. Benezet followed this with a dramatic performance of his own at the 1758 Philadelphia Meeting when he rose before those gathered, tears streaming down his face, and recited from the Book of Psalms, "Ethiopia shall soon stretch out her hands unto God." He connected that the children of Africa were also God's children and worthy.[48]

Eccentric abolitionist Benjamin Lay. (National Portrait Gallery, Smithsonian Institution; this acquisition was made possible by a generous contribution from the James Smithson Society)

Benezet set out to write his own views on slavery in a series of influential pamphlets and books:

An Epistle of Caution and Advice, Concerning the Buying and Keeping of enslaved people, 1754

A short account of that part of Africa inhabited by the negroes, 1762

A Caution and Warning to Great Britain and her Colonies, in a short representation of the calamitous state of the enslaved negroes in the British Dominions. Collected from various authors, etc., 1767

Some Historical Account of Guinea ... With an inquiry into the rise and progress of the slave-trade ... Also a republication of the sentiments of several authors of note on this interesting subject; particularly an extract of a treatise by Granville Sharp, 1771

The potent enemies of America laid open: being some account of the baneful effects attending the use of distilled spirituous liquors, and the slavery of the Negroes: to which is added, The happiness attending life, when dedicated to the honour of God, and good of mankind, in the sentiments of some persons of eminence near the close of their lives, viz. the Earl of Essex, Count Oxcistern, H. Grotius, D. Brainard, John Lock, &c., 1774

Through these works, he presented a new philosophy that showed his frustrations at the slow progress of the antislavery movement and used moral discourse to challenge the economic motives behind slavery. Also, it had him beginning to think beyond the boundaries of Pennsylvania and North America and hoping to affect change in Great Britain. This began his mission to present a counter-narrative to the one that suggested that Black people were inferior and savage, arguing that if they were savage, then so were whites, and if whites were human, then so too were Black people. He saw that: "Africans were the human equals of the Europeans: that they were honest, hardworking people whose tranquility and traditional morality were disrupted by European depredations."[49]

Through his efforts, Anthony Benezet became the leading abolitionist in the Western world. In America and in Europe, he led the charge in the pre-revolutionary colonies and afterward to shine a light on the plight of enslaved people in America and the slave trade. He worked to bring about

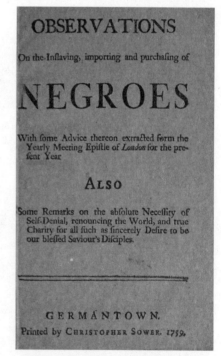

Title page of Benezet's *Observations on the Inslaving, Importing and Purchasing of Negroes.* One of the first anti-enslavement tracts produced in America. (*Observations on the Inslaving, Importing and Purchasing of Negroes*)

more understanding towards Africa and the areas where the slaves of Philadelphia were originating from, and made legitimate claims of equality between Blacks and whites when at the time European white males expressed their superiority in all things. Through his efforts, he helped to create an atmosphere where the first abolition legislation in North America was passed in Pennsylvania in 1780. He helped to link the profits derived from slavery to killing the soul of America, the souls of both white and Black.

Benezet was born in France to Huguenot parents on January 31, 1713. The persecution of the Huguenots in France and elsewhere brought about several moves while Benezet was growing up, and ingrained itself in Benezet. His family's fight against religious persecution became a source of pride for him. They had settled in London for several years, where they likely converted to Quakerism, and in 1731, they immigrated to Philadelphia.

Benezet was a small man but an animated one; ugly to a noticeable degree, so much so that he declined to sit for a portrait, saying, "Oh, no, no! my ugly face shall not go down to posterity." After a few years, Benezet became a naturalized British subject and married Joyce Marriott. While they were childless—their two children died as infants—their house at 115 Chestnut Street was often a hive of activity owing to Benezet's endeavors as an educator or his efforts in the abolitionist movement.

He was a student of science, a voracious reader who owned over a hundred science and medicine works and read extensively in medical journals and books to improve his frail health. That ultimately led him and Joyce to become vegetarians, much like their friend and fellow abolitionist Benjamin Lay. Benezet also had philosophical and ethical reasons for foregoing meat, saying he did not wish to eat anything that may have been tied to slave labor, not believing that any life, even that of an animal, should be taken to feed another living being. He could often be seen feeding rats and other animals and would be a source of merriment for his students. His physician, Benjamin Rush, even claimed that his vegetarianism ultimately brought about his death: he contracted stomach and bowel illnesses that produced the disease of which he finally died.[50]

Benezet was a lifelong teacher and educator. He briefly tried to follow in his father's footsteps as a merchant, but the pursuit of profits disagreed with his religious beliefs, and he quickly pivoted to becoming a teacher in Philadelphia in the 1730s. From 1742 to 1754, he ran the William Penn Charter School, then retired and took over a girls' school, where he stayed for nearly 20 years. In 1750, he began teaching young Black adults and children in his home in the evenings. This came to be known as Benezet's School. He stated, "Having observed the many disadvantages these afflicted people labor under in point of education and otherwise, a tender care has taken place to promote their instruction in school learning, and also their religious and temporal welfare, to qualify them for becoming reputable members of society."[51]

Benezet instructing colored children.
ANTHONY BENEZET.

Anthony Benezet instructing children. There are no known portraits or likenesses of Benezet who once said, "Oh, no, no! My ugly face shall not go down to posterity." (*Historical, Poetical and Pictorial American Scenes*)

Benezet ran this impromptu school out of his house for the next 20 years before he put forth a plan to the Monthly Meeting of Quakers in January 1770 to create an official school for Black students. This led to the creation of the African Free School that became a division of the Penn Charter School.

Benezet's school was the first concerted effort to provide education to Black children. A small number of Black children over the years had been admitted to the Friends' Public School, but no plans existed to specifically provide education to the Black children of Philadelphia as a whole. Benjamin Franklin, in 1758, lobbied businessmen around London about providing education for the Black population in Philadelphia. As a result, this led Christ Church Reverend William Sturgeon to hire a schoolmistress to teach 30 young Black people in sewing, knitting, reading, and other skills. The following year, the number of pupils rose to 60, with 36 boys and 24 girls. This setup thrived until the eve of the Revolution.[52]

The African Free School opened on June 28, 1770, and by 1775 at least 250 Black children had been students. Their success helped to bolster Benezet's ideas of Black equality. Benezet worked hard to see that students became prepared as productive members of society, giving them backgrounds in reading, writing, and arithmetic—as well as sewing and knitting for girls—but also providing vocational education so that the Black children could be prepared to join the workforce upon leaving the school. The *Pennsylvania Gazette* would praise Benezet's work, saying he "devoted his attention considerable to the educations of Negroe and Mulattoe children, from a desire that they might thereafter prove valuable members of society and worthy of that freedom to which the humane and righteous law of this commonwealth, passed in 1780, has restored them."[53] Upon his death in 1784, he bequeathed most of his estate to the school, which helped keep it afloat for several more years.

These pamphlets and his letter-writing campaigns to acquaintances, politicians, and power brokers aimed to build an antislavery network throughout the Atlantic world. Piece by piece, one letter, pamphlet, and petition at a time. Chipping away. He perfected the use of mass petitioning. His social network helped to spread antislavery messages and works across the colonies, around England, and to the rest of Europe.[54]

Despite Benezet's efforts, the enslavement of people in Philadelphia would last well into the 19th century, but each year brought about a gradual decline in the number of enslaved people. This period of Philadelphia's history is marked by the pervasive and deeply entrenched institution of slavery. The city's rise was intricately tied to selling and maintaining enslaved people. Every sector of the economy exploited the labor of those enslaved, from working in the homes of their enslavers to various jobs related to the shipping industry. Not an area was spared from the specter of slavery. And those toiling under this oppressive system forged ahead, creating lives for themselves or being lost to history. While the beginnings of an antislavery and abolition movement arose that would result in the first abolition legislation in America, their struggles form an essential part of the city's narrative.

CHAPTER FOUR

Hope. Doubt. Solitude. Adversity.

Running alongside the rapid increase in population, growth of the economy, and spread of Enlightenment sentiment and experiencing them in the same circumstances as their male counterparts, but under very different conditions placed upon them by societal norms, were the women of Philadelphia. Women filled significant roles around the city, working in many different facets of the economy and in the home. Women were often in charge of the household, either theirs or someone else's. They owned their own businesses and found employment in every segment of the city. And as Philadelphia grew, there developed a uniquely Philadelphian pleasure culture where nonmarital sex became a part of city life. In the process, gender roles became malleable, and women asserted their autonomy more and more over the decades. This change in sexual morals and gender dynamics was helped along by the Enlightenment ideas of scientific rationalism that shattered belief in a fixed, hierarchical world in favor of one in which man (and woman) could shape their destinies and work towards perfecting human society. This helped to challenge the gender hierarchy and political order.[1]

Prior to the 18th century in the Western world gender was not seen as a bio-logical difference but another type of fixed relationship that ordered society. Then it began to be re-conceptualized into binary opposites. Throughout the first half of the 18th century, the city's Quaker and Moravian populations provided for an expansive cultural space for women outside of marriage, but that freedom eroded by mid-century as the population became more diverse.

Women performed most, if not all, of the domestic work in the city, including childcare, food purchasing and preparation (butchering, preserving, cooking), sewing, laundry, cleaning the house, and the chores needed to ensure the home ran as smoothly as possible. This served as the most prevalent source of employment for women. However, women were not limited to a life of domestic work, either unpaid or paid. They held down a host of other occupations: keeping shop, owning and operating a tavern, huckstering, spinning, bookselling, baking, distilling, gloving, mantua making (aka dressmaking), sieve making, soap boiling, tailoring, tinkering, upholstering, boardinghouse keeping, innkeeping, midwifery, teaching school, and laundering. Women accounted for nearly half of all retailers. The world of the 18th century would be one in which women played a significant role in Philadelphia's society.

Women played active roles in the worsening political atmosphere. They were among the Philadelphia merchants who signed the non-importation agreement in their protest against the Stamp Act. Women, as consumers, turned their product choices into political acts, making quiet statements on what to buy and from whom. They participated in spinning bees, working to produce wool fabric in order to lessen the amount imported from England. Though women played essential parts in the earliest days of the unfolding move toward independence, the Stamp Act crisis saw the beginning of the decline in what public political power there was for women. The crisis masculinized political authority, at the same time that Quakers and their more egalitarian views receded from political power. This process began during the Seven Years' War when Quakers began retreating from public life, instead opting to tackle major initiatives like the abolition of slavery through private means and organizations rather than through the political process. The Stamp Act crisis elevated empire-wide policies that overshadowed local concerns. As taxes became the center of the controversy, the ones paying those taxes—the men—took on more political power.[2]

To understand the shift occurring in the years leading up to the Revolution, it helps to understand the lives of women in the first three-quarters of the 18th century. Prior to the Revolution, most women married after the age of 22. Being married immediately granted a husband control over his wife's body, but there were times like in cases of women making very public proclamations of self-divorce from their partner or their decision to run away with another man when that control wavered and fell apart completely.[3]

The economic conditions in Philadelphia meant that marriage was a necessity for many women; however, the women of the city's elite made up the highest percentage of women who never married. Over and over again parallels were being made between liberty and marriage, and added awareness of the boundaries that marriage placed upon women. These ideas were helped along by prominent religions within the city, primarily the Quakers and German Pietist sect, which challenged the notion that marriage should dominate a woman's life.[4]

The household formed the most important social unit in colonial America, where the political, economic, and familial all mixed with one another. At the core of this idea was gender and the belief that the head of the household expected to be deferred to. In most cases, this was a man. But there did exist female-led households, and they came in different shapes and sizes and depended upon the socioeconomic class of the woman. Still, they typically fell in the category of widows with children and women's partnerships with a sister or other female family member. Single women (widowed or not) would join the households of parents, siblings, and other relatives and would often fulfill domestic roles for the family.[5]

Many women of Philadelphia would enter into marriage during their lives. Marriage was not necessarily seen as a romantic situation, but was often viewed through more practical and domestic lenses. Women offered men a solution to a problem rather than some sort of companionship. Henry Muhlenberg complained in his journal, "I could not get along without some female servant ... I would not employ young girls, and old women require servants themselves."[6] His solution was to marry a teenager, who managed the duties of a domestic servant while also bearing 10 children for the German.

Marriage itself was an investment for women because it meant bearing children and raising them. A Philadelphian woman, on average, gave birth to four to seven children, half of whom were expected to survive. Children were often the precursor to taking on a servant or enslaving a woman to help with domestic duties that came along with them. In one Philadelphia district, 62 percent of households with children employed at least one domestic female. It was considered a hardship to raise children without such help. Most of a woman's time as a domestic servant or enslaved individual was spent buying food and preparing it, along with childcare and laundry. Laundry, in particular, was a heavy chore, and washerwomen were often paid as much as servants.[7]

Illustrated view from inside the market stalls on Market Street showing women shopping. The city's women would routinely go to the market to pick up the necessary items for daily living. (Library of Congress)

Most stay-at-home spouses would go out and shop daily—to the baker for bread, or to visit peddlers' stalls along Market Street for fish, eggs, and produce.[8] The wives of tradespeople would often actively participate in the family business. Artisans' wives frequently tended the shop while the husband was away, or ordered and processed materials.[9]

There was not much house cleaning going on, or at least it was not a regular part of the household routine of shopping, cooking meals, doing laundry, childcare, and if a business was run out of the home, helping with the running of the business. A typical family lived in a narrow story and a half building two rooms deep. The sitting room, shop, and kitchen occupied the bottom floor, with bedrooms on the second floor. The sitting room gained more and more prominence over the century as it morphed from the principal bedroom to an area devoted to socializing. For those that could afford it, fine furniture filled the space: tea tables, chairs, settees, etc. It was a place to visit and drink tea, and for women, it was the only actual space available to them to meet together. Socializing in public places was frowned upon for women of a certain stature, which meant coffee houses and taverns were only patronized by middle or upper-class women if they were traveling.[10]

For many women, needlework proved to be the artistic medium that enabled them to exercise their creative energies throughout their lives, with their audience being a private circle of family and friends—and descendants, as pieces would be handed down through the generations.[11]

Needlework was a standard component of women's education and had been for centuries. It began with a girl learning the basic stitches for marking and mending linens and garments. As a demonstration of her skill, she would then progress to creating a sampler. When she was younger, this was a rather plain study in marking stitches but she would produce a more complex ornamental one as she became older and more talented. If the family was more better off and could afford the fabric and materials, then the girl might go on to make purely ornamental needlework creations and receive instruction from a teacher on more elaborate or costly stitchery. This all would often occur between the ages of eight and 15 and would continue until whenever the young woman married, with needlework being replaced by the demands of keeping and maintaining a home.[12]

A sketchbook was commonly used to inspire and practice design ideas for embroidery patterns. These patterns would then be traced out on fabric, with the embroiderer then bringing the design to life through their skill in shading, coloring, and choice of stitches. The designs could be used for silk or canvas work as well as whitework, crewelwork, and quilting.[13] These works were essential pieces and would adorn the walls of their houses and be passed down from generation to generation. In the Graeme home hung needlework depicting a crocodile that the matriarch Ann Diggs Graeme had completed, along with an embroidered picture of a dog that her daughter Elizabeth had finished at the age of 12. She would go on later in life to write a poem, "Lines in Praise of Needlework":

> Oft when the Weary languid hour, I knew,
> And Time with Leaden Foot Slow Crept nor flew
> When Books and writing tasteless seemed around
> No varying Pleasures marked Lifes narrow bound.
> Then has the Needle Stole away the time.[14]

~

While marriage was the norm, not all relationships lasted. At the time, in Pennsylvania, it was not legal to get a divorce, a situation that would not change until 1786. However, there were many ways to circumnavigate the law, such as self-divorce, which was an accepted and even seen as an advantageous and just practice. The practice would often include a spouse printing an announcement in the paper to sever ties.[15]

> WHEREAS Hannah Joyce (whose maiden name was Turner) the wife of Peter Joyce Fitzgerald, hath eloped from her said husband, and lives in a scandalous manner with another man, named Richard Stagtham Thomas, Brass Founder, with whom she has attempted a marriage before the Swedish Minister—These are to warn all persons not to harbour her in such a scandalous manner, nor to credit her on my account, for I will pay no debt of her contracting from the date hereof.
>
> June 2, 1772 PETER JOYCE FITZGERALD[16]

These and other methods, such as utilizing a town crier or slapping up some signs, were used as effective means of dissolving a marriage. As Fitzgerald's announcement demonstrates, the primary function was to sever the financial obligation he entered into with his wife when they married. Even living apart, a husband had the legal obligation to provide financial support, with the Overseers of the Poor working to secure support for deserted wives and children, but he was released from such obligations if his wife eloped. And it stopped the wife from building up debts in her husband's name. Wives participated in the typical exchanges of economic necessity, buying and selling goods, extending credit, accepting payment against debts owed to their husbands, and even assigning bonds. They made these financial decisions and agreements to run their households, and it was accepted that a wife's word could be trusted when the husband was away or preoccupied.[17]

By naming inexcusable spousal behavior, these announcements helped to create new ideas around a woman's autonomy in a marriage focused on her ability to make her own choices. And when women began applying this same doctrine, it became a way for them to seek personal happiness. They did not take this lying down either; many wives responded to the claims that they eloped. Without

A busy street scene in Philadelphia where women and men take in a public speaker. It was expected of a woman of a certain status to be accompanied by a man or other women when in public. (*The Life of Benjamin Franklin*)

denying that they ran away, some still considered themselves married, and they provided reasons for their disappearances, with the most frequent cause being an abusive husband.[18]

Most of these claims of self-divorce came from the working class of Philadelphia, with over a quarter of them being mariners alone. Long voyages away made sailors more vulnerable to a spouse racking up debts in their name, so advertising self-divorce was a means to protect their financial well-being and freedom from debtor's jail.[19]

These self-divorce ads provide the broad strokes hinting at what lies below the surface of each relationship. Husbands would also hit out at a woman's performance as a mother. These were seen as direct attacks against the wife's womanhood. Any mother who would leave her infant could also be considered "loose" and "disorderly," especially since a few advertisements call out the wife for going to live with another man.[20]

Wives became more publicly confrontational in their rebuttals to their husband's proclamations of marital dissolution. They called upon their neighbors and those who knew them to vouch for their character:

> I take this method to give a true state of the case between me and my husband, to convince the public what a brutish, malicious, scandalous fellow he is; for it is well known to all my

neighbours and acquaintance, that I have behaved myself as becomes a good subject of our Sovereign Lord the King, and that I did, by all ways and means, endeavour to get a good honest livelihood, and I can, when called upon, get my neighbours, of sufficient credit, to testify the same, and that I am neither a whore, thief, or a drunkard; but it being my misfortune to marry so disagreeable a person as the said Michael Herbert is.[21]

Wives commonly and publicly stated that they were physically abused, which was the leading cause for them to leave a marriage. It showed there were limits a woman would take when a husband exercised his perceived right to "manage" his wife. In these situations, the wife was expected to seek intervention by going to the community. They could call upon the Justice of the Peace, who, in turn, could issue a bond of a considerable amount against the abusive husband—an early American version of a restraining order. If the husband persisted, the court could collect the bond, and she could receive a court-ordered separation maintenance. Increasingly, wives and women said that this behavior went beyond what a husband could do and what a wife should endure. With these public rebuttals, women were redrawing the line of acceptable behavior in a struggle over power in the relationship.[22]

Though it may be a tricky proposition, Philadelphia at the time made it possible for a woman to leave their husband. Women had the opportunity to live and be self-sufficient thanks to the relative economic stability found in the city, which made being a single woman a viable option thanks to work being found either in a household or through applying their skilled labor to nursing, midwifery, mortuary business, boardinghouse, etc. Economic factors also played a role in wives leaving their husbands as they complained of their husband's failings to provide for their family or squandering away what was rightly theirs.[23]

These are to let the Public know the Reason I live separate from him is this, that in about three Years he spent near Three Hundred Pounds of my Estate, and was never sober one Week in the Whole time; so let this be a Warning, that my Estate shall pay no more for him after this Date.[24]

For husbands, the most common cause for self-divorcing from a wife was "stepping out" on them with another man. Their wives' sexual behavior became the fundamental issue when it came to a marriage falling apart. A significant amount of self-divorced adverts from husbands mention the stepping out of their wives and this only increased over the late colonial era. Some of this increase can be attributed to women exerting more control over their choosing of partners, while the increase also shows that over time more men were willing to come forward and make such declarations.[25]

～

Unmarried women made up a large portion of the female population of Philadelphia. Not all women were wives, as historian Karin Wulf points out. Women spent a significant portion of their lives in an unmarried state, whether that meant yet to marry, never married, widowed, or separated. Single women made up a culturally significant population in colonial Philadelphia, where they headed a fifth of Philadelphia households. There were higher than expected rates of unmarried or never-married women in the city, with widows being more content in that state than widowers.[26]

Single women could make contracts, own property, and be head of a household—essentially possessing the same legal capacities as any man. In Philadelphia, there was an awareness around the idea that marriage, especially remarriage, could be potentially problematic and represented only one possible choice a woman could make. Singleness was a respectable avenue.[27]

Philadelphia's economy necessitated that most unmarried women be part of the workforce in some way, primarily in domestic work or retail. Women were unlikely to get specialized training in a craft or skill, and they had little or no access to capital, which kept them from starting their own businesses. While this was a world of networks and connections, that was only true for men who could flip those family or business connections into tangible financial gains for them, while women had no such access.[28]

Retailing was the common occupation for women who headed their own household. The later colonial period saw 300 women retailers, and at certain periods the

A woman and child walking through Philadelphia's market stalls on a day off showing them all but empty. (Library of Congress)

majority of women who held occupations were shopkeepers. Women also preferred buying from other women, which helped to keep women-run stores open. Shopping became a social activity that women could do together and have fun doing, and that created a consumer culture that benefited women retailers.[29]

Younger unmarried women often spent their time either living at home or in domestic service. For the more upper-middle-class and upper-class families, household labor would be performed by these servants or enslaved women and supplemented by hired servants (usually older women). These domestic laborers would often be unmarried and performed essential services for many urban households.[30] More modest households would use indentured servants. Indentured servants almost always were under 21, with most being either orphans or young girls from the city placed into servitude by their parents. These indentures often included obligations to teach girls to read and write, along with a payment of cash or clothing at the end of their term of service. Young unmarried women almost never lived by themselves or as a boarder. So, they were left to enter some form of domestic service, either married or not. However, marriage did bring with it the possibility of upward mobility in the female world.[31]

Domestic servants were often treated only slightly better than chattels and, after years of service, were sometimes left destitute and in the poor house. As Philadelphia grew, so grew the need for domestic labor, and the number of female indentured servants rose right alongside to fill this need.[32]

Indentured servants' only control over their predicament was to run away and break their contract, though that came with harsh penalties of five extra days for every one day away and reimbursement of any expenses accrued during their recapture. Reimbursement came in the form of adding extra time to their service. Masters sometimes showed little compassion towards their indentured servants; in one announcement one master called his indentured servant a "chunky fat lump" and "stout, fat woman."[33]

Unlike indentured servants, hired female servants needed personal or professional references to present to the lady of the house while being interviewed, and they often worked for shorter periods, days or months at a time rather than years. Hired servants might also work a trial period to ensure their performance would meet expectations. But they did have the power to quit and seek employment elsewhere, which indentured servants and enslaved people did not share. They controlled their labor.

The type of work female servants performed was an endless merry-go-round of chores, disagreeable and sometimes dangerous, and on-call 24/7. Duties shifted with the seasons and the work environment, and could include childcare, wet nursing, laundry and ironing, preparing three meals a day (along with tea), and seeing to the needs of not only the family, but their many visitors and possibly boarders as well. With limited space in a residence, chamber maids sometimes slept at the foot of their mistress's bed. They were called on in the middle of the night for any number of reasons, from sickness to investigating a fire alarm or quieting a barking dog. In winter, the draftier rooms would be closed for the cold months, and everyone crowded into the front rooms, with servants having to wake up early to get the fires going before the family rose.[34]

Women disproportionately made up the residents of the poor house, and many used the house as a maternity hospital when the need arose. All too often, it would be where indentured servants landed after their time was up—sick, destitute, and without any resources.[35] As the 18th century wore on, employers moved away from indentured servants and toward hiring from the bountiful cheap labor available around the city, often in the form of newly arrived immigrants.

Accidental pregnancy could muck up household operations, leaving the family without their servant(s) for considerable stretches. If a woman happened to get pregnant while an indentured servant, she faced stiff penalties, like having her contract extended to make up for any time lost from recovering from the birth as well as repayment for nursing while recuperating. In at least one instance, the Overseers of the Poor bound the children of an indentured servant to the master as well. Extreme annoyance was felt by the household anytime a domestic servant got pregnant. Incidents like these also show the large amount of sex going on outside of marriage in colonial Philadelphia.[36]

This rise in extramarital sexual behavior was openly acknowledged through the grudging acceptance of bastardy, sex work, and an increase in the treatment for sexually transmitted diseases. These trends show that sex outside of marriage and courtship was regular in the 18th century, which led to the formation of a new "pleasure culture." Nonmarital sex allowed women to begin and end relationships at their leisure, and provided a means of avoiding the legal obligations of marriage or submitting to what it meant to be in a patriarchal marriage. As Philadelphia became more cosmopolitan, it began to adhere more to European modes of entertainment, and theaters, dance studios, horse racing, and cockfights began to gain popularity. Along with entertainment grew gambling, drunkenness, sex for pleasure, seduction, and prostitution, leading to the inevitable committee of ministers working together out of their concern over this growing vice. By 1775 even the city's market fair featured plentiful opportunities to get drunk, gamble, and have sex, and it had to be abolished due to the sheer amount of illicit activities taking place.[37]

As the population in Philadelphia tripled, the number of illegitimate children being sired grew tenfold. Women in these situations did not expect to marry the child's father. They reached out to the Overseers of the Poor to establish paternal support, which happened after becoming pregnant but before the child was born. This meant that these sexual encounters were probably casual and short-term. Late in the colonial period, one in three brides was pregnant at the time of marriage. Hundreds and hundreds of Philadelphians freely partook in extramarital sex with no plans of marrying their partner should a pregnancy occur. It was a widespread activity that crossed ethnic and class lines. Philadelphians pursued sex for their own personal enjoyment.[38]

While the legal system had no means to stop bastardy or punish those involved, it was called into play to ensure the father supported his offspring. The system in place, however, was thrown into jeopardy when there were children created from the sexual union of a Black man and a white woman, which happened often enough that the Overseers of the Poor complained to the legislature that enslaved men impregnating white women had become a drain on their resources. However much of an exaggeration that may have been is not precisely known, but the fear of damage to the racial caste system—which justified and protected the idea of slavery—was real. What we do know is that there were many instances where a Black enslaved man ran off with a white woman; in ads seeking the enslaved man's return, the enslaver would say things like, "'Tis supposed he is harboured by some base White Woman, as he has contracted Intimacies with several of that Sort lately."[39]

For a typical illegitimate child's birth, the father was responsible for all of the costs, including paying the birth attendant, doctor, midwife, and pre- and post-delivery nursing care. However, the burdens of single motherhood fell squarely on the mother. This meant not only extra financial burden, but it also compromised her ability to marry, which was a crucial factor in upward economic mobility, and without that path many single mothers were forced to live on the poverty line.[40]

Prostitution played a vital role in the city's sex culture. Many tales printed in the newspapers and almanacs, pamphlets, and plays spoke of men debauching themselves in taverns with the women plying their trade within. Sex work was a fundamental part of the city's fabric and an accepted aspect as long as it didn't cross certain lines. Those lines included protecting the innocence of females who may have been entrapped in the life by either a duplicitous man or a scurrilous Madam.[41]

Houses of prostitution tended to be owned and operated along the waterfront in the alleys by the city's docks, close to the most prevalent source of business— undersexed sailors. All social classes, however, solicited sex workers, and sex work could be found in all parts of the city. Bawdy houses could be found in Southwark, along High Street, and in the Northern Liberties, with the British Barracks in the Northern Liberties serving as a gathering spot for many runaway servant women who anecdotally made up a large portion of sex workers in the city.[42]

Proprietors of these establishments were discreet, which ensured their business … well, stayed in business. A typical encounter with a sex worker entailed traveling down to the city market around 7 p.m. and catching the eye of a lady hanging around there. It was not appropriate for ladies to be out in public unattended by a male chaperone of some kind, and single or working women had no leisure time to be lounging around with so much other work to do, which made it easier to tell the sex workers from the non-sex workers. The lady would ask the john to share his pepper pot, a local soup brought to Philadelphia by enslaved Black people.

From Birch's *Views of Philadelphia* showing Market Street with women together out shopping, which became more and more of a social event. Women preferred doing their shopping from women-owned businesses. (Library of Congress)

After getting full on soup, she suggested they find a place for a night's lodgings and the fees were agreed upon.[43]

Very few sex workers were ever prosecuted for actual prostitution. It was only when sex work butted up against other crimes that the authorities took notice; one such instance was a brawl at a bawdy house that led to the death of a city constable. Bigger concerns were leveled at the growing spread of sexually transmitted diseases, whose spread depended upon having multiple sexual partners. This increase can be seen in the number of cures being advertised in papers, from "Dr. Sanxay's Imperial Golden drops," to "Walker Jesuit Drops," and "Keyer's famous pills."[44]

Over this period sexuality found its way into popular print either through local publications, newspapers, broadsides, almanacks, etc., or through the importation of bawdy literature from (mostly) England and France. It showed there existed a market for such ideas and behaviors. Strong sexual content ran deep throughout the press from 1750 to 1775. Almanacs, in particular, regularly printed items related to sex and gender, and printers around town distributed broadsheets and pamphlets related to prostitution, seduction, and adultery. This popular culture helped to shape and was shaped by Philadelphia's sexual scene.[45]

Starting in the late 1750s and moving throughout the next decade, new tastes for sexualized literature became more prevalent and even became a mainstay for popular almanacs that depicted sexual danger for women and offered a voyeuristic experience for the readers that became part of the urban pleasure culture.[46]

Jaunty poems offered sex up for lively and light humor, reflecting how prevalent nonmarital sex was at the time.[47]

> Scarce had five Months expir'd since Ralph did wed,
> When lo! his fruitful Wife was brought to Bed.
> How now, quo[t]h Ralph—this is too soon, my Kate?
> No, Ralph, quo[t]h she,—you marry'd me too late.[48]

Through poetry and other writings, many women expressed their anxiety over the false flattery they received during the courting process and whether the men were falsely representing themselves. Women, single or in a relationship, still had to deal with the unwanted attention of men. Sarah Eve, daughter of a wealthy sea captain and ship owner, grew up with many of children of the city's elite, recounts Dr. William Shippen, Jr. being a kisser:

> In the morning Dr. Shippen came to see us. What a pity it is that the Doctor is so fond of kissing; he really would be much more agreeable if he were less fond. One hates to be always kissed, especially as it is attended with so many inconveniences; it decomposes the economy of one's *hankerchief*, it disorders one's *high Roll*, and it ruffles the serenity of one's countenance; in short the Doctor's, or a sociable kiss is many times worse than a formal salute with bowing and curtseying.[49]

The newspapers provided nearly the only means for a woman to express their social or political opinions. Hannah Griffitts shared many politically charged verses in the pages of Philadelphia's newspapers. This included her opposition to Ben Franklin's political posturing:

> Oh! Had he been wise to pursue
> The Track for this Talent designed,
> What a tribute of praise had been due
> To the teacher and friend of mankind,
>
> But to covet political fame
> Was in him a degrading ambition,
> For a spark which from Lucifer came
> Had kindled the blaze of sedition.[50]

Women's versifying in print came with plenty of detractors, and by 1772 caused a minor literary controversy as the more conservative elements of Philadelphia had had enough. A "Misericordis" spoke out in the *Pennsylvania Chronicle* against the poems of the likes of "Miss Sappho Hexameter."[51]

For her part, Griffitts would go on to write a highly influential poem for the patriot cause, "The Female Patriots," that first appeared in *The Pennsylvania Chronicle* in 1768.

> Since the Men from a Party, or fear of a Frown,
> Are kept by a Sugar-Plumb, quietly down.
> Supinely asleep, & depriv'd of their Sight
> Are strip'd of their Freedom, & rob'd of their Right.
> If the Sons (so degenerate) the Blessing despise,
> Let the Daughters of Liberty, nobly arise,
> And tho' we've no Voice, but a negative here.
> The use of the Taxables, let us forebear,
> (Then Merchants import till your Stores are all full
> May the Buyers be few & your Traffick be dull.)
> Stand firmly resolved & bid Grenville to see
> That rather than Freedom, we'll part with our Tea
> And well as we love the dear Draught when a dry,
> As American Patriots,—our Taste we deny,
> Sylvania's gay Meadows, can richly afford,
> To pamper our Fancy, or furnish our Board,
> And Paper sufficient (at home) still we have,
> To assure the Wise-acre, we will not sign Slave.
> When this Homespun shall fail, to remonstrate our Grief
> We can speak with the Tongue or scratch on a Leaf.
> Refuse all their Colours, tho richest of Dye,
> The juice of a Berry—our Paint can supply,
> To humour our Fancy—& as for our Houses,
> They'll do without painting as well as our Spouses,
> While to keep out the Cold of a keen winter Morn
> We can screen the Northwest, with a well polish'd Horn,
> And trust me a Woman by honest Invention
> Might give this State Doctor a Dose of Prevention.
> Join mutual in this, & but small as it seems
> We may Jostle a Grenville & puzzle his Schemes
> But a motive more worthy our patriot Pen,
> Thus acting—we point out their Duty to Men,
> And should the bound Pensioners, tell us to hush
> We can throw back the Satire by biding them blush.

Stories and poems were full of rakes and libertines out carousing and womanizing, and their female equivalents, amorous Ladies and Coquets. In these tales, both men and women participated in this sexual behavior.[52]

Not just content with producing their own literature, women also consumed adult literature imported from England. The lending libraries of Philadelphia, which are generally seen as products of the Enlightenment and spreaders of knowledge and reason, stocked their shelves with trashy, highly sexualized novels, making them readily available to the lower and middle classes who couldn't necessarily afford to buy them.[53]

A satiric depiction of patriotic women gathering to pledge their support for the non-importation and non-consumption of British goods in 1774 in response to the Intolerable Acts. (Library of Congress)

Before the 18th century, the long-held belief in gender was complicated. It was situated around the one-body model theory. The body was thought to contain fungible fluids referred to as humors, and the humors could transform themselves from one substance to another. Four humors made up the human body: blood, choler, melancholy, and phlegm, and those were assigned four qualities: cold, wet, hot, and dry. Different combinations of the two sets determined whether you were female or male. The humors also drove a person's sexual behavior. Moist and cold humors were associated with females, while men contained greater portions of dry and hot humors. The humors were not fixed though, creating a fluidity in genders; as humors slid across the scale a male could become more feminine and a woman more mannish. Gender to the people of 18th-century Philadelphia was merely where one's humors rested on any given day. This led to the belief that men and women shared a human anatomy, but men were thought to be more developed and thus superior. Women's genitalia never fully developed because they didn't contain the heat needed to complete the development process, which also played into sexual desire that arose from too much semen building in the body, needing to be released.

In the process this built up the heat in one's body and helped in conception. All of it was essential to a person's health and to aid in reproduction.[54]

In this humoral understanding, there was no biological basis for the differences between genders. Over the course of the 18th century, these views and ideas began to slowly change and evaporate, but not until the 19th century were they overtaken by the more anatomical and biological definitions of gender. Enlightenment ideas began undermining the belief in a fixed hierarchy that had placed male superiority at the apex.[55]

Women's lustiness was presented in the press as part of this one-body model, and it was also dependent on men being the initiator to fulfill those desires. But this lust ultimately corrupted a woman's character and became the driving force to turn her into a sexual temptress.[56]

It also created the opportunity to tell a bunch of cuckold jokes in the popular press in the 1760s and 1770s, poking fun at husbands and offering up examples of the untrustworthiness of female sexuality. The sentiment being projected implied that women could not resist their sexual impulses and would commit adultery. This coincided with an increase in the number of proclamations in the papers announcing self-divorce by husbands stating that their wives had run off with another man. However, like always, there was a rude double-standard playing out with it being alright for men to commit adultery on their nag of a wife. Men had approved means of seeking out extramarital sex, while women were chastised for similar behavior.[57]

~

This era of Philadelphia produced many impressive women. Successful business-women like Rachel Draper and poets like Hannah Griffitts show the independent nature of women in the period. One woman who exemplified the rise of Philadelphia was Elizabeth Graeme Fergusson, a writer and intellectual gadfly, who transcended any limitations placed upon her by Philadelphia's patriarchal society.

She was born to Ann Diggs and Thomas Graeme, a prominent and successful physician in Philadelphia who was also an informal advisor to Thomas Penn. Her mother Ann had come to America with her second husband, Sir William Keith, the deputy governor of Pennsylvania from 1717 to 1726, and Franklin's faux benefactor who had sent Franklin off to London with misplaced dreams of becoming a publisher. After Keith's death, Ann married Thomas, and Elizabeth was their last child, born on February 3, 1737.

At the time in Philadelphia, there were very few trained medical doctors, and Thomas's and Ann's connections with the proprietor and other leaders helped to get him and his family settled and situated as one of the leading citizens of the city with a thriving medical practice. He supplemented this income with official appointments such as naval officer of Philadelphia, member of the Governor's

Council, supreme court justice, physician of the port, and surgeon to the Pennsylvania Hospital.

These lucrative appointments and medical practice helped Thomas keep two homes throughout much of his life in Philadelphia: one which they would rent in the city and live in during the winter months, and a stately country estate in Horsham township to escape the city in the summer. The Horsham home was a true gentleman's estate, known as Graeme Park. Three hundred acres were enclosed by a double row of hedges and dirt sloping up the outer walls to allow deer to enter but not escape, creating a lavish deer park. One visitor called it "gay and blooming ... each field and grove dressed in rich attire."[58]

Portrait of renowned writer and salon host Elizabeth Graeme. (*The Literary History of Philadelphia*)

The mansion overlooking this estate was a three-story manor house. Three rooms occupied each floor. An elegant drawing room was on the first floor, equipped with a harpsichord for entertaining summer guests, with bedrooms occupying the second floor. Adjacent to the house was a stone kitchen and barn, the farmhouse, and other various buildings. These were the luxurious surroundings in which Elizabeth grew up.

Elizabeth was taught by her mother, with her father adding classical language instruction. As she grew older, private tutors supplemented her education. Lessons centered around the Bible and being able to read, memorize, and recite Psalms. She had a great love of languages, learning Greek and Latin, French and Italian, and the family encouraged her to read for leisure, where she developed her passion for literature and writing.[59]

Women of Elizabeth's station were expected to develop a complete set of social skills from their mothers and other older women in their circles who helped them fine-tune their manners and graces. A young lady was often shipped to family friends for extended stays, where they could receive even further instruction as they were more likely to listen to someone who wasn't their mother. There, they developed friendships that would last for the remainder of their lives. Elizabeth experienced just this in her teens when she went and visited her mother's friend in New Jersey. There she learned how to entertain and be entertained.[60]

Her younger years would be some of her happiest days, and it was not until she began to take an interest in the opposite sex that things started to complicate her life and bring on emotional distress. Throughout her teens, she became close or at least acquainted with the other well-to-do children around her age. They would attend dances and hang out with one another; Francis Hopkinson, John Morgan, Phineas Bond, and William Franklin were among her childhood circle of acquaintances.[62]

Thomas Graeme and Benjamin Franklin did not see eye to eye politically. With Graeme's close ties to the proprietors and his livelihood depending on them, he did not appreciate Franklin's near-constant provocations over the Penns' perceived notion that their instructions were law and the struggle over the right to tax the proprietors' lands.[62]

So, in the early 1750s, when his daughter and the illegitimate son of Franklin, William Franklin, began a friendship, Thomas looked upon it with a wary eye. Elizabeth and William flirted back and forth with one another in verse, she 15 and he 21. At the time, he was a desirable bachelor, handsome, amusing, intelligent, and well-educated, and she was much the same. Her family's wealth and position offered a means for Franklin to rise above his bastardly birth.

Elizabeth was an inquisitive teen who wrote and read constantly and who surrounded herself with friends who would intellectually stimulate her. She took to poetry to communicate with her friends and with herself. Poetry played a significant role in 18th-century Philadelphia as many studied the poems of published poets, memorizing the stanzas and quoting to one another while writing up their own imitations of these works to pass among their friends. Elizabeth and her friends exchanged their poems or read them aloud to one another. It acted as a way to exchange ideas and express themselves; it was how they flirted and joked, amusing one another.

The poems between Elizabeth and William often included poetic stand-ins for one another, with William being Damon and Elizabeth, Alexis. Passing flirt tracks between one another, "Damon" would say:

> The truly Wise and happy Man
> Thats he who is not discomposed;
> By others Pleasurs or their woes.
>
> With Alexis call such a happy man a "degenerate,"
> His Life at best a waking Dream
> In short at Most a mere Machine ...
> Cooly they speak they never feel,
> Their Souls are harden'd o'er with Steel![63]

These poems would pass back and forth between the two, stanza after stanza. Their flirtations were going on at the opening stages of the Seven Years' War, with Philadelphia acting as a starting point for many expeditions inland. This tested the bond between Elizabeth and William. The Franklins were very much digging in and fighting the proprietors tooth and nail to provide funds for the protection of Pennsylvania. In addition to their support of the proprietors, the Graemes were friends with William Smith, provost of the Academy of Philadelphia, who had also picked fights with the Franklins over the administration of the academy and ridiculed the Quaker management of the Assembly.

Through these years, the courtship continued, even as William went on a tour of frontier forts with his father in 1756. When the Assembly voted to make Franklin their representative in London, he intended to take William along with him, meaning he would be away from Elizabeth for a considerable amount of time.

For his part, William worked hard to marry Elizabeth prior to his journey, but the Graemes managed to convince the two to wait until his return to see if the spark was still there. They surely hoped that the relationship would fizzle and fade away with an ocean between the two. Which is what ultimately happened; as time stretched out, the letters between them became fewer and none had the expressions of warmth or flirtations that their previous exchanges included. When Elizabeth brought this up, he protested, saying his father's demands left him no time for writing. This led to increasing frustration on Elizabeth's part; she accused him of "Want of Generosity in not having frankly told her that [his] own Levity of Temper, or [his] father's Schemes, or [his] Attachment to a Party, prevented [his] preserving in the tender Passion that [he] had professed." She bared her wounded pride by writing, "Neither the Judgement nor Morals of a Person can be pure when he is that in full Extent of the Word … it would be Folly, nay Madness, to think of running all Risques with [him]."[64]

William interpreted this as her calling off their engagement, and he agreed with it; however, Elizabeth did not see it that way. She continued believing they were formally engaged despite the dwindling correspondence between the two. Word reached her a couple of years later, in 1762, of William's marriage to Elizabeth Downes, a daughter from a wealthy planter family in Barbados.

It had been 10 years, and now Elizabeth was 25, her most eligible years having passed her by in waiting for someone who did not wait for her. In early 1763, the Reverend Richard Peters, a family friend, invited Elizabeth to be his traveling companion to England and Scotland. Peters, at the time, was 60 years old and agreed to take Elizabeth on side trips and introduce her to prominent people around the country.

On the crossing, both experienced intense physical maladies, Peters from chest pains and Elizabeth from her typical headaches and fevers. On landing in Liverpool, they made their way to London to be seen by Quaker physician Dr. John Fothergill for treatment. He shuttled them off to the resort town of Scarborough to drink the mineral waters and bathe in the sea. While there, they took in the races at the track, where she was surprised to meet Laurence Sterne, the author of *Tristram Shandy*.[65]

Now Crys and Oaths are heard around
Applause or Murmurs quick rebound

> The Victor Gay the loser Sad;
> Some Sullen seem; while others Mad
> Fly from the Turf dejected Home
> With empty Pockets pensive roam.[66]

They also danced and played cards. After a couple of months, they were back in London, and slowly Elizabeth began to settle in and started to feel normal once again. She was meeting with old friends and acquaintances in London; however, a sense of melancholy was gathering about her.

> Alone & Pensive & opprest with Pain
> The starting Tear sometimes could scarce refrain.
> Tho' England's Pleasures open to me lay
> Pain barr'd my Entrance & forbad my Way.[67]

Elizabeth took in the sights of London, visiting Westminster Abbey, taking in the art in private collections in homes and castles, traveling to Bristol and Upton, and staying with acquaintances. She then traveled to Scotland to visit Graeme relatives, where she met and became friends with a young divinity student with a flair for poetry, Nathaniel Evans. It was during these side excursions that she received word that her mother passed away on May 29, 1765.

The news devastated her and made her want to return home, which did not happen until the day after Christmas in 1765. Eighteen months in total she had been away, and upon her arrival, her family and friends told her all about her mother's final days, and she read the two letters she had left behind for Elizabeth. These letters instructed her on the selecting a husband:

> We women have it only in our power to deny, I cannot call it a choice, but I hope you will never bestow yourself on any other than one who is generally reputed a good and sensible man, with such a one a woman cannot be unhappy. When you meet with such a one take him with all his faults and frailties (for none are without) and when you have him expect not too much from him, for depend upon it this is like all sublunary things, the higher your ideas are the greater will be your disappointment.[68]

Shortly after her return to Philadelphia, her only remaining sibling, her sister Ann, also passed away. This left Elizabeth as the de facto head of the house. Her father was aging quickly, and she would come to be responsible for her niece and nephew. She was 28 now, unmarried and childless, and decided to dedicate herself to her books and to writing. She turned very introspective, writing an epitaph for her mother's grave and many personal poems.[69]

Over this period, she kept up her friendship with Evans, with whom she traded poems, enjoying the attentions and flirtations but keeping him at arm's length, carrying on much the same way she and William had done. They exchanged poems where she teased him and he would feign outrage; he even offered a sly marriage proposal, which Elizabeth swatted away. While this was going on, she began a literary project of paraphrasing and annotating Psalms, using it as a means to deal with her grief over the deaths of her mother and sister. This project eventually amounted to two quarto-sized volumes of work.[70]

Her version of Psalms 23:

> The Lord supream doth Condescend
> My Path to guard, my Steps to tend:
> The heavenly Shepherd Guides my Ways;
> And Crowns with joy my Prosperous Days.
> He leads me to the Verdant Meads,
> And from the purest Pasturs feeds;
> Or by meandering Waters Sides:
> Where murmuring Fountains smoothly glides.[71]

It had the intended effect of helping her through her grief and the healing process. She renewed her correspondence with Evans, but his health began to decline throughout the summer of 1767, and he passed away on October 29, 1767, presumably of tuberculosis.

To honor her friend, she teamed up with William Smith to assemble a collection of Evans' poems. She headed up a very

Psalm VII from Elizabeth Graeme's ambitious personal project to annotate and paraphrase the Psalms. (*The Literary History of Philadelphia*)

successful subscription campaign to support the cost of publication, totaling nearly 900 copies with orders from the most prominent citizens of Philadelphia to people in Edinburgh, Canada, London, and Barbados. Keeping busy on literary matters, she completed a translation in verse of *Les Aventures de Télémaque* by François Fénelon. She shortened the title to just *Telemachus*. It was a popular work at the time in the colonies and had been a favorite of hers since childhood. It was a massive undertaking, taking up another two volumes, 30,000 lines of poetry, which she completed in the spring of 1769. It was done for her "private amusement" and not intended for publication.[72]

She was still writing poetry, as well as articles, lyrics to songs, prayers, hymns, and essays. She typically corresponded with others through poetry using her alter-ego of "Laura." Early in 1767, she began what could only be considered the first *salon* in the colonies, at which guests discussed art, literature, music, and more. While in Philadelphia, she held regular calling hours on Saturday evenings, allowing friends to drop by their residence for conversation and exchange of ideas. This included the likes of Benjamin Rush, John Morgan, Francis Hopkinson, Mary Hopkinson,

Elizabeth Hopkinson, William Smith, Jacob Duché, the Willing sisters, and many, many others. Elizabeth's salons also served as places for single and married women to meet with men outside of their homes without fear of social disapproval. This salon gained a sterling reputation, leading Elizabeth to become known as a witty, gracious, and brilliant host.[73] Benjamin Rush recalled:

> These evenings were, properly speaking, of the attic kind. The genius of Miss Graeme evolved the heat and light that animated them. One while she instructed by the stores of knowledge contained in the historians, philosophers, and poets of ancient and modern nations, which she called forth at her pleasure; and again she charmed by a profusion of original ideas, collected by her vivid and widely expanded imagination, and combined with exquisite taste and judgement into an endless variety of elegant and delightful forms. Upon these occasions her body seemed to evanish, and she appeared to be all mind.[74]

In response to and inspired by John Dickinson's *Letters from a Farmer in Pennsylvania to the Inhabitants of the British Colonies,* Elizabeth wrote in 1770 a lengthy poem titled "The Dream" or "The Philosophical Farmer." It was also addressed to the colonists and encouraged them to boycott English manufactured goods and told colonial women "to spin and weave their own wool and linen":

> To show proud Albion [England] that you can resign
> Her Manufacturers; and her Trade decline;
> When weighty Taxes do each Good invade
> And strike at Liberty that lovely Maid![75]

She called on Pennsylvanians to give up luxuries and return to simple country life to spurn England: "fear God alone, but never Albion fear."[76]

In December of 1771, Benjamin Rush brought a young Scot, Henry Hugh Fergusson, to the Graeme family home. Fergusson had few prospects of his own but was handsome, affable, and projected a gentlemanly air. Elizabeth had her standard reservations right off about this younger-by-11-years man who came into her life, who seemed to have fixated on Elizabeth. She saw the flawed character behind the handsome mask. Despite that, by March of 1772, she had professed her love for Henry. They kept their courtship secret from her aging, unhealthy, and disapproving father. Henry pushed and pushed for a secret marriage, and though she feared doing so behind her father's back, they wed on April 21, 1772. It quickly became drama, like most secret marriages are, and had all of Philadelphia society talking about it.

It was eating at Elizabeth, not telling her father. She and Henry had lived apart for six months before her father passed away on September 4, 1772, never knowing of the marriage. This began a new period of trouble and frustration for Elizabeth, which would last for the remainder of her life. Following her father's death, control of the estate which had gone to Elizabeth was passed on to Henry, and she could not do anything to Graeme Park without his approval. She dreamt of selling the large estate, investing the money, and living off of that while moving to Philadelphia.

Graeme Park around 1755, years before Elizabeth and her husband, Henry Fergusson, took ownership over her family's estate. (*The Literary History of Philadelphia*)

However, it took over a year for Elizabeth to convince Henry to put Graeme Park on the market, and once up for sale there were no takers, forcing them to continue to live there. The settlement of the will took a heavy toll on Elizabeth, and Henry began spending more time farming than with his wife, causing acute bouts of loneliness and boredom for Elizabeth. She tried to fill her days with needlework and weaving, but these distractions failed to cover the long days alone. Fewer and fewer people stopped by. With the increased financial burdens, she could not host like she once did.

The rest of Elizabeth's story will be discussed a little later in this book. Suffice it to say, her marriage complicated the brilliant life she had built for herself—a peril she recognized just a bit too late. As a single woman of means, she had carefully constructed an independent and fulfilling life; as a married woman, she found herself bound to the whims of her husband.

While extraordinary, Elizabeth's life, accomplishments, and trials were shared with many women in Philadelphia. For most of her life, she managed to navigate Philadelphia society as a single woman; even after marriage, she spent most of those wedded years apart from her deadbeat, loyalist husband. But she was also just one of the legion of women who took to business, took to the arts, took to making their own path in the city.

CHAPTER FIVE

Education is a Battlefield

William Smith had the severe look any good schoolmaster needs to instill fear into the souls of the children under his care and tutelage. He was a man who honed it not only on his students but on nearly every other person in Philadelphia. This made him some allies, but many more enemies.

A sly, arrogant character, his opponents also labeled him as cynical and drunken, ambitious, and slovenly. But not one soul ever questioned his abilities. A vigorous mind buoyed his strong opinions. He fashioned himself as a political cleric who aligned himself closely with the proprietors, conservative Quakers, Old School Presbyterians, and, of course, the Anglicans. Oftentimes, he could be found as the counterweight to Franklin's utilitarianism, veering more and more towards aristocratic and genteel traditionalism in his maneuvering of the College of Philadelphia as a place of pulling Americans up intellectually so that they could be accepted in the European traditions. Like many others during the time, Smith had a wide variety of roles including scientist, writer, historian, publicist, land speculator, clergyman, and politician, but, most importantly, educator. This devotion to education originally led him to Philadelphia, much to the enthusiasm of Franklin—though that would quickly fade. Like Franklin, Smith was a man of his age, and his combative ways shaped and transformed education in Philadelphia, Pennsylvania, and the wider colonies.[1]

Smith applied these talents to education as the Provost of the College of Philadelphia, now the University of Pennsylvania. After wrestling over it with Franklin, he built the school up piece by piece in his own image. In the process, he helped to make Philadelphia an academic and intellectual cauldron in the Americas that paved the way for artistic, scientific, and medical achievements that the colonies had not experienced up to that point.

~

After dropping out of the University of Aberdeen in Scotland, Smith came to America at the age of 23 to tutor the two sons of a British colonel. He arrived in New York City in 1751 and lost no time embedding himself in New York's educational scene by writing pamphlets calling for the founding of a publicly supported college for the colony. Following that, he wrote and published a more philosophical tract, A *General Tract on the College of Mirania*, which laid out his philosophy for education, putting into writing his ideal curriculum, building program, and methods for raising money in a college in the new world.

Mirania was a mythical province, whose educational system created a clear division between the middle-class professions and the more working-class mechanical trades. A mechanical education was taught in English, with students going out into the world by the age of 15. Smith stressed this importance of learning a common language and its impact on creating a common culture:

> They wisely judg'd, therefore, that Nothing cou'd so much contribute to make such a Mixture of People coalesce and unite in one common Interest, as the common Education of all the Youth at the same public Schools under the Eye of the civil Authority. Thus, said they, indissoluble Connexions and Friendships will be form'd; Prejudices worn off; and the Youth will in Time either forget their very Extraction, or from a more liberal Education, and manly Turn of Thought, learn to condemn those little ridiculous Distinctions that arise among the Vulgar, because their Fathers first spoke a different Language, or drew Air in a different Clime.[2]

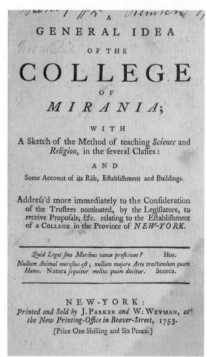

All other students would be taught in Latin with an additional five years of education that stressed the classics, math, natural philosophy, rhetoric, agriculture, history, and politics. There were some electives in foreign languages, the art of fencing, and dancing, with all classes including a heaping portion of morality and religion. To Smith, "the knowledge of what tends neither directly nor indirectly to make better men and better citizens, is but a knowledge of trifles."[3] His vision of Mirania would primarily be responsible for him being sought out to become the first provost of the Academy of Philadelphia.

He first traveled to Philadelphia in the spring of 1753 to enroll his two pupils in the academy. There, he began talking to its leaders, Franklin included, who all but offered him the job of provost for the school, which at the time was a small charitable

Title page of William Smith's *A General Idea of the College of Mirania* that laid out Smith's views on education, which were championed by Franklin and others on the Board of Trustees at the Academy of Philadelphia. (*A General Idea of the College of Mirania*)

institution propped up by Franklin and a few other Philadelphians to meet the educational needs of the city. Franklin, then Board president, recommended Smith to the proprietor, and Smith traveled to become an ordained Anglican minister, which was customary for a president of a school or university.[4]

A benefactor was needed to provide for him financially, which brought him in touch with the Penn family who agreed to underwrite his salary. This would kick off a long relationship between Smith and the proprietors; one that would see him feeling in debt for their largess and often, very often and acrimoniously, at odds with Franklin and his faction in internal Pennsylvania politics. From the beginning, the school depended upon the financial support of the proprietary, and the Board of Trustees encouraged Smith to establish a close relationship with Thomas Penn.[5]

This relationship with the proprietors often set him up as their direct representative and combative force, and he was never one to shy away from controversy. By early 1754, he had settled in Philadelphia, getting to work on educational matters at the academy, and throughout the city and all of Pennsylvania.

Prior to the founding of the Academy of Philadelphia, what education system existed in the city was created and run by the Society of Friends. Quakers, while following, for the most part, the same ideas about education as the English, did not place the same kind of emphasis on classical learning, as it did not generally fall under their egalitarian worldview. Greek and Latin were not required to preach at their meetings; instead, they focused more on humanistic, empirical, and utilitarian endeavors when it came to educating their children.

Early in Pennsylvania's beginnings, there was a gradual shift in responsibility for education from the government to individuals. This would lead in 1698 to the Quakers chartering the Friends' Public School, originally opened in 1689, and the creation within the Philadelphia Monthly Meeting of an Overseers of the Friends' Public School to manage the operations of the school. It combined the teaching of classics with more practical classes in English, mathematics, and surveying. It offered free tuition to poorer students and had a distinct inclusivity policy. William Penn commented that it was a school "where all children and servants, male and female, whose parents, guardians and masters be willing to subject them to the rules and orders of the said schools ... be received and admitted, taught and instructed."[6]

The Public School had a difficult time maintaining stability and went through a constant stream of instructors until 1742, with the hiring of Anthony Benezet. Benezet also emphasized practical education and the need to provide education for women, Blacks, and those in need.

Many younger females were enrolled in dame schools that women privately ran in their homes. They were adaptable and flexible, but along with that, unstable because they were all dependent on the students paying their tuition, making them very short-lived.

Teachers, then as now, were paid very little, and they often sought out additional forms of income. This would lead to a burgeoning evening-school environment in Philadelphia as schoolmasters and teachers taught evening classes to supplement their small salaries. They taught primarily apprentices who had their evenings free and were learning a diverse range of subjects: algebra, geometry, plain and special trigonometry, gauging, and any number of other topics to prepare for work in surveying or navigation. Individual tutors, evening classes, and dame schools provided the bulk of educational opportunities for children in the city. The city's formal education infrastructure developed in fits and starts as there were a limited number of charity and grammar schools that were privately funded, showing the lack of a larger plan, vision, or structural approach.

The Academy of Philadelphia, like many other institutions in the city, was the brainchild of Ben Franklin. In 1749, he penned the tract *On the Need for an Academy*, describing his feeling that organized education created the cornerstones of a civil and engaged society:

> I think with you, that nothing is of more importance for the public weal, than to form and train up youth in wisdom and virtue. Wise and good men are, in my opinion, the strength of a state: much more so than riches or arms, which, under the management of Ignorance and Wickedness, often draw on destruction, instead of providing for the safety of a people. And though the culture bestowed on many should be successful only with a few, yet the influence of those few and the service in their power, may be very great ... I think also, that general virtue is more probably to be expected and obtained from the education of youth, than from the exhortation of adult persons; bad habits and vices of the mind, being, like diseases of the body, more easily prevented than cured.[7]

Growing increasingly exasperated with Quaker handling of Philadelphian matters, Franklin wanted a Quaker-free educational institution that still continued to

From a drawing of Pierre Eugene Du Simitière of the Academy of Philadelphia. (*The Many Sided Franklin*)

provide useful instruction to the working- and middle-class children to gain the skills and education needed in their future work and lives. This led Franklin to emphasize penmanship, drawing, arithmetic, accounts, pronunciation, gardening, planting, grafting, inoculating, and valuable history, like the history of commerce. He explained his objectives:

> Numbers of our inhabitants are both able and willing to give their sons a good education if it might be had at home, free from the extraordinary expense and hazard in sending them abroad for this purpose, and since a proportion of men of learning is useful in every country, and those who of late years come to settle among us, are chiefly foreigners, unacquainted with our language, laws and customs, it is thought, a proposal for establishing an ACADEMY in this province, will not now be deem'd unseasonable.[8]

From its beginnings, Franklin served as president of the Board of Trustees that numbered as many as 24 and was made up of Philadelphia's elite. Because of the largeness of the board, Franklin was not able to shape the Academy in his image.

Once settled into his role as provost, Smith started out reforming and enlarging the academy while also working to establish on the frontier of Pennsylvania charity schools for German children. The German question was one near to many Philadelphians who felt that Germans would never assimilate to their British customs and the English language.

As Germans became more prevalent around the city, fear of them becoming a major political force spread through the Anglo-Philadelphians. Education became a means that could bring about their assimilation and adapting to the English way. Thomas Penn, Smith, and Franklin were all big proponents of this with Franklin writing some xenophobic lines: "Why should Pennsylvania, founded by the English, become a Colony of Aliens, who will shortly be so numerous as to Germanize us instead of our Anglifying them, and will never adopt our Language or Customs, any more than they can acquire our Complexion."[9] He went even further in a letter to his friend Peter Collinson:

> Few of their children in the Country learn English; they import many Books from Germany; and of the six printing houses in the province, two are entirely German, two half German News-paper, and one half German. Advertisements intended to be general are now printed in Dutch and English; the Signs in our Streets have inscriptions in both languages, and in some places only German.

Smith felt much the same when he wrote:

> By a common education of English and German youth at the same schools, acquaintances and connections will be formed and deeply impressed upon them in their cheerful and open moments. The English language and a conformity of manners will be acquired, and they may be taught to feel the meaning and exult in the enjoyment of liberty, a home, and social endearments.[10]

Smith thought that exposing young German students to English would be enough to properly Anglicize all facets of their lives, which started his journey of establishing free schools for German settlers on the frontier of Pennsylvania. It was met with little enthusiasm by the Germans he wanted to "help."[11]

This ordeal allowed Smith to go on the offensive against the Quakers and the Quaker Party, both being the leading factions of the city and Assembly, who he claimed were power-hungry, and whose negligence encouraged the French to make advances in the western part of the colony. Smith went further, advocating for denying Germans the right to vote unless they demonstrated "sufficient knowledge of our Language and Constitution." Further anti-German bias was shown when he called for legal documents to be in English only, and foreign-language publications had to have an English translation.[12]

Smith seemed to want his fingers in an endless well of pies and was deeply involved in the politics of the colony, writing in 1755 the explosive pamphlet *Brief State of the Province of Pennsylvania* which served as a direct attack against the Quaker-led Assembly, taking them to task for continually refusing to adequately defend Pennsylvania, proclaiming a "kind of Independency of their Mother-Country, despising the Orders of the Crown, and refusing to contribute their Quota."[13] By aligning with the Germans, the Quakers were able to take complete control over the Assembly. Smith called on Parliament to take action and impose its will upon Pennsylvanians, wanting it to require "all those who sit in Assembly to take the Oath of Allegiance to his Majesty," knowing full well that Quakers with their aversion to making any sort of oath would never abide by such measure.

While intimately involved with the fight against Quakers and Germans, Smith petitioned and got a new charter for the academy, which now was the "College, Academy, and Charitable School of Philadelphia in the Province of Pennsylvania." This created the first degree-granting institution in Pennsylvania. The academy would still exist and act as a feeder school to the new college. That the new college was not affiliated with any particular denomination made it an anomaly in the colonies as the College of New York was affiliated with the Anglican church, as the New Jersey College was with the Presbyterians. This capped a productive first full year in Philadelphia, where Smith frequently caused a stir with his writings and made significant changes to the school under his charge.

Feeling the cock of the walk, he was ready to keep stirring the pot. The following year he produced a sequel to his previous anonymous pamphlet, titled *A Brief View of the Conduct of Pennsylvania for the Year 1755*. This new pamphlet stated much of the same as before, mostly boiled down to a screed against the Quaker power brokers in the Pennsylvania Assembly, particularly their continued aversion to providing defense legislation. Parliament began threatening to act upon his idea of forcing Assemblymen to take an oath, which led to six Quaker members resigning, though they were replaced by Franklin-approved candidates. The College of Philadelphia served as the only institution conferring degrees in the city and Pennsylvania.

Though the college only handed out 141 degrees between 1757 and 1776, thanks to Smith it established itself as a major cultural center in Philadelphia.[14]

For students, life at the academy and college was often unpleasant as they had to deal with regular violence, either as corporal punishment from the teachers (rapping of knuckles, paddling, etc.) or between the students. New students were put through hazing-like incidents to show their worth. Later in life, Alexander Graydon recalled when he was eight and first entering the academy like all new students, he was forced to fight one of his classmates:

> A combat immediately ensued between Appowen [his opponent] and myself, which for some time, was maintained on each side, with equal vigor and determination, when unluckily, I received his fist directly in my gullet. The blow for a time depriving me of breath and the power of resistance, victory declared for my adversary, though not with the acknowledgement of the party, that I had at last behaved well, and shewn myself not unworthy of the name of academy boy.[15]

Smith's belligerent ways helped to create this combative atmosphere at the Academy.

Outside of the college, he helped to found and became the editor and guiding spirit of the *American Magazine,* which began publication in October 1757 and ran for only a year. The magazine shared Smith's varied interests in theater, politics, religion, natural science, and current events. It had a subscriber base of over 850 that spread from New England to the West Indies. He even managed during that year to take a dig at Franklin by playing down his efforts in the field of electricity and playing up those of Franklin's partner in some experiments, Ebenezer Kinnersley—although Kinnersley quickly jumped up to refute this.[16]

Smith habitually took up a cause, enflamed the drama, and then lost interest in it. He was ambitious and on the lookout for any angle to increase his power or his influence. This had the result of creating an atmosphere where threatening behavior thrived, and Smith played this up as 1756 turned into 1757. The printer of Smith's pamphlets was threatened, causing him to discontinue their sale. And Smith reported that the church was gaining ground in the city and at the college, as it was slowly taking control of the Board of Trustees and he was increasing the time spent in the classroom on religious instruction.[17]

In 1758, Smith became embroiled in more political fiascos, thanks to his involvement with William Moore, a member of the Proprietary Party and a vehement adversary of the Quaker majority. Moore's attacks on the other party led him to be arrested and jailed by the Assembly, to be held until he made a retraction, which he never did. Smith, as a friend and supporter, was brought in and questioned about his knowledge of Moore's attacks on the Assembly. They found Smith guilty too and had him arrested and imprisoned with Moore in January 1758. The Assembly denied both appeals and any sort of habeas corpus.[18]

Smith was called before the Assembly because the assumption was that he wrote Moore's address, and for his part in printing it in *The Pennsylvania Zeitung.*

When presented by the Assembly with the opportunity to retract his libel, he instead doubled down and gave a long oration to the legislative body, denying any illegal activity and promising to appeal all the way to the king. A hundred of his supporters in the audience stood up and applauded him, for which they were arrested, too.[19]

While in jail, life continued much the same for Smith. Students filed into the jail to continue their classes with the provost. He welcomed visitors the rest of the day and even managed to court Moore's daughter, with the two becoming engaged. When the Assembly adjourned in April of that year, Moore and Smith managed to obtain their release. With the specter of re-imprisonment hanging over his head, he headed to England that fall to appeal directly to the Privy Council. The proceedings dragged on into the summer of 1759 when the attorney general and solicitor general made their rulings, freeing both Moore and Smith on the technicality that Moore's invective came while the Assembly was not in session, so his attack was not leveled against an existing assembly. They also ordered the Pennsylvania governor to reprimand the Assembly for their violations against the royal prerogative and a citizen's individual liberties.

Smith made it back to Philadelphia a free man and was around when Governor James Hamilton read before the next Assembly the king's tut-tutting, "therein commanded, in the Kings name, forthwith to signify to you His Majesty's High Displeasure at the unwarrantable Behaviour of the said Assembly in assuming to themselves Powers which did not belong to them, and invading both His Majesty's Royal Prerogative, and Liberties of the People."[20]

Just as this controversy was ending a new one was boiling when Smith began an open campaign against Benjamin Franklin. Franklin managed to make quite a few enemies throughout his long life—that is to be expected from one as opinionated as he was and as plugged into so many political disputes as well. None, however, were as up for mixing it up with him than William Smith. From when he took over as provost of the academy to Franklin's death, Smith enjoyed a 37-year personal squabble with the bespectacled founding father.[21]

Smith was Franklin's equal when it came to ambition. His conservatism came naturally, and he took it upon himself to voice the concerns of Thomas Penn, in large part out of gratitude for his personal endowment of Smith's position at the college. This placed him squarely in opposition to Franklin and the Assembly leadership.[22]

Away from the school, Franklin and Smith would clash over various political issues, the first of which would be the militia bill.[23] Smith and the Proprietary Party preferred that control over any militia rested with the proprietors, while Franklin and his supporters championed the election of officers. As the local militia gained momentum, Smith saw the dwindling hopes of a proprietary-controlled force, so he opened the academy grounds to an anti-Franklin crowd looking to create an alternative militia opposed to the militia law. This stunt landed Smith in another war of words, with some claiming he wanted to become the "Bishop of America" and him labeling Franklin a

"Golden Calf." Tempers flared, and politics seeped into the Academy and College of Philadelphia. The Board of Trustees voted Franklin out as the president of the board, to be replaced by Richard Peters, a Penn loyalist. As a result, the academy became neglected after losing its most prominent champion in Franklin and as Smith focused almost exclusively on the college.[24]

Now with open opposition existing between Smith and the anti-proprietary faction, the Assembly put the screws on Smith and the college, attacking the purse strings in 1759 by outlawing lotteries, which served as a major source of funding for the school. Franklin would add to Smith's and the college's headaches by playing a little 4-D chess. He managed to finagle that a prize due to Smith for a piece of his writing would not be in the form of precious prize money but a decorative prize medal.[25]

Portrait of William Smith, provost of the College of Philadelphia and general antagonist to Franklin and the Assembly. (*The Literary History of Philadelphia*)

This would lead to the most acrimonious and personal set of attacks as Smith began a campaign against William Franklin's appointment as royal governor of New Jersey. In 1759, Smith had written the president of St. John's College at Oxford, maligning Franklin and warning him not to grant Franklin an honorary degree. Though Franklin would receive his honorary degree, when Smith found out, it still perturbed him. Enough so that Smith believed that Franklin was actively working against his fundraising efforts while he was in England in 1762.

This feeling ultimately led Smith to seek out Thomas Penn in London and lay out the story of William Franklin's illegitimacy, and the two tried to thwart his appointment as royal governor by working behind the scenes, scheming amongst peers in Parliament and government officials. It turned out to be too little too late. In a way, both came out winners. William Franklin became royal governor, and William Smith took back with him a tidy sum for the college. From this personal animosity, Benjamin Franklin vowed never to meet the provost again.

Smith returned to Philadelphia in 1764, exhausted with the petty provincial politics that had been his life for the past decade. The next decade, he shied away from provoking direct confrontations with the Assembly and shifted his focus to the college, building up his personal fortune and spreading the Church of England in the colonies.

Just as Smith began to quiet down and recede somewhat from the political realm, a new educational controversy based around the two most prominent doctors in Philadelphia arose as they fought with each other to bring medical education to America at the College of Philadelphia. They fostered connections amongst their brethren within the colonies and provided the colonial cause some sorely needed medical personnel during the war to come.

Up to the early 1760s, medical education in America was all but non-existent. A student would apprentice under a surgeon or physician for several years, learning the practice and business of medicine, supplemented by reading whatever medical texts they could get their hands on.[26]

The life of a medical apprentice involved toiling under their master, at their beck and call, fulfilling any number of duties thrown upon them, from preparing and delivering medicine to taking care of domestic matters—cleaning the office or stoking the fires. A medical apprentice spent, on average, seven years serving their apprenticeship with their free time spent studying.

Because of the lack of formal medical education, many who had the financial means would travel to Europe to seek out further education, apprenticing in teaching hospitals in London before moving on to universities at Edinburgh, Leyden, Paris, or Uppsala. They would then return to Philadelphia and set up a practice. The expense of pursuing a European education was prohibitive, meaning that the doctors of Philadelphia typically came from the expanding merchant class of the city. This first generation of Philadelphia-born doctors would be the fathers of the revolutionary doctors: Thomas Cadawalader, William Shippen, Sr., Thomas Bond, Phineas Bond, Cadawalader Evans, John Redman, John Bard, and John Kearsley, Jr.[27]

By 1752, Philadelphia boasted the foremost set of doctors in the colonies. Having such a roster of able-bodied medical men helped to ensure public confidence, particularly in the middle and working classes, in health and hygiene and undermined quack doctors and the remedies they peddled. The investment in a European education was a good one, as a doctor could make a handsome living, and they represented the most educated group in the city with multiple years of higher education and expansive travels abroad. Their experience and training helped prepare them for civic duties and raised the ethical standards of their colleagues. Throughout this period, the medical profession in Philadelphia grew and grew in terms of numbers, training, professionalism, promotion of the power of medical science, and prestige, with dozens of practicing physicians and surgeons.[28]

One of the first collective movements in the city's medical establishment was organizing a city hospital. Thomas Bond first proposed a general hospital for the city in 1750, circulating a petition for funding from the Assembly, which Franklin wrote up; he didn't sign the petition for political reasons. By 1752, the first hospital came into operation, renting a house from Judge Kinsey on High Street while construction soon started on a new building. The first wing was ready to be occupied by 1756

Scene from Birch's *Views of Philadelphia* that shows the impressive Pennsylvania Hospital, the first of its kind in North America, which provided some of the earliest medical education in the city and the colonies. (Library Company of Philadelphia)

and was located along Eighth, Ninth, Spruce, and Pine Streets. The ground floor included a walking gallery and apartments for people with mental disabilities and provided the most comfortable accommodations for such care in the Western world. And the hospital served as means for delivering clinical observation with 9,000 surgical cases from 1752 to the Revolution, becoming a grand theater of medical knowledge in the colonies.[29]

While the hospital provided a modicum of education, there was still no formal means of acquiring a medical education in Philadelphia or anywhere in America. American students in Europe would commiserate with one another while congregating in London or Edinburgh, but it all amounted to just talk and no action.[30] Medical education wouldn't get started until two friends became enemies upon their return to the city of their birth. The first steps occurred in 1762 when Dr. William Shippen, Jr. delivered a series of anatomical lectures in Philadelphia.

Shippen is just another fascinating character in the Philadelphia story. Benjamin Rush called him indolent but an eloquent, "pleasing and luminous" teacher. Others called him an extrovert and contemplative. Happy and restless. He made his share of lifelong enemies, Rush being one of them, but many more lifelong friends and acquaintances. He worked hard throughout his professional life to break down the taboos surrounding childbirth, obstetrics, midwifery, and providing prenatal care for pregnant women, and he went on to found the first lying-in hospital in America, the equivalent of a maternity ward today. The Shippen House became a center for patriotic activity before the Revolution and was a favorite hangout for George Washington, who lodged regularly there.[31]

The Shippen family was one of the most prominent in the city and the province, and established themselves amongst the city's elite. The first Edward Shippen was an early mayor of Philadelphia, and served as chief justice of the Pennsylvania Supreme Court, and president of the Provincial Council. His children, grandchildren, and great-grandchildren would go on to become political and business leaders in the city and all over Pennsylvania, with William Shippen, Sr., being one of the most prominent early physicians in Philadelphia and one of the original trustees of the College of Philadelphia.

Born in 1736, William the Younger followed in his father's medical footsteps. Though his father was a trustee at the city's university, Shippen himself graduated from the College of New Jersey and held no personal connections to the College of Philadelphia. After his graduation, and with the encouragement of George Whitefield, Shippen sought to put his oratorical skills to use to become a minister. His father had different ideas and funneled him into medicine, sending him to Europe to continue his studies and succinctly expressing his control over his son's education:

> My son has had his education in the best college in this part of the country and has been studying physic with me, besides which he has had the opportunity of seeing the practice of every gentleman of note in our city. But for want of that variety of operations and those frequent dissections common in older countries, I must send him to Europe. His scheme is to gain all the knowledge he can in anatomy, physic, and surgery. He will stay in London for the winter and shall attend Mr. Hunter's anatomical lectures and private dissections, injections, etc., and at the same time go through a course of midwifery with Dr. Smellie; also enter as a pupil in Guy's Hospital.[32]

First arriving in London and working under Dr. William Hunter and Mr. Hawson, Shippen made rounds at St. Thomas's Hospital and attended special midwifery courses with Dr. Colin Mackenzie, who helped normalize male midwives. Next, Shippen enrolled at the University of Edinburgh to get his medical degree, where he developed an early interest in obstetrics. He graduated in 1761 and arrived back in Philadelphia in 1762. He moved in with his father in the Shippen House on Fourth Street with his new wife, Alice Lee, of the Virginia Lees. His cousin Edward Shippen lived just down the street and had a newborn baby, Peggy, who would go on to marry Benedict Arnold.

The Pennsylvania Hospital was struggling financially, which led Shippen to give public lectures, showing its anatomical drawings and casts, to raise funds. Since its opening, the Pennsylvania Hospital had served up a kind of medical education: attending physicians brought their students or apprentices to follow them on rounds or act as dressers of wounds. The students were charged for going on these rounds and those funds went to purchasing medicine or to form the library fund. The hospital itself even entered into indentures with aspiring physicians, and they would serve and live in the hospital for five years and receive instruction in return.[33]

Shippen sold tickets at the London Coffee House at 5 shillings a lecture, and so successful was this first year of lectures that he expanded it to include 60 lectures the following year, including anatomy, surgical operations, bandaging, midwifery, and other topics. Many of the city's intelligentsia attended, with the first lecture given at the State House beginning in November of 1762. The

From a portrait of William Shippen, Jr., whose anatomical lectures in the city laid the foundation for the first medical school in America. (New York Public Library)

lectures then moved to his father's house on Fourth Street. Younger students like Benjamin Rush made up the classes. He also gave biweekly public demonstrations of the drawings and casts from Dr. John Fothergill, a London-based physician and Quaker with many ties to Pennsylvania. Fothergill had encouraged the young Shippen to do the lectures, saying:

> I have recommended it to Dr. Shippen to give a Course of Anatomical Lectures to such as may attend. He is very well qualified for the subject, and will soon be followed by an able assistant, Dr. Morgan, both of whom, I apprehend, will not only be useful to the Province in their employments, but if suitably countenanced by the Legislature, will be able to erect a School of Physic amongst you, that may draw students from various parts of America and the West Indies, and at least furnish them with a better idea of the rudiments of their Profession, than they have at present the means of acquiring on your side of the water.[34]

Some of these lectures were disrupted by mobs since there was a belief Shippen was getting his dissection subjects from graveyards. One such attack on his lecture was known for years as the Sailors' Mob, which interrupted Shippen by breaking windows, assaulting his waiting carriage, and forcing him to make a narrow escape down an alleyway. On multiple occasions, he was forced to leave his house and hide to avoid the mob and placed notices in the papers assuring the people that his corpses came from persons who had committed suicide, public executions, or from the Potter's Field.[35]

The idea of bringing medical education to the colonies was freely canvassed by the young American medical students wandering around London and Edinburgh. Shippen had discussed this with his fellow Philadelphian, John Morgan, as their paths crossed in London to witness the coronation of King George III. The two young physicians spoke in general terms of seeing a medical college founded in their home city, and believed they were the ones to do it. And the two would be at the forefront of the medical profession in America until the Revolution.

John Morgan was impulsive and arrogant, an irritating mixture made all the more so because he was one of the ablest men in the city. And he knew it. He also was the one responsible for establishing the first medical school in America, but thanks to his abrasive behavior he created immense animosity between him and William Shippen, Jr. and many others around the city that would never properly heal.

His was born to a Welsh immigrant merchant who was well known and respected around the city. Morgan was a part of the first graduating class at the academy in 1757, receiving his A.B. (*Artium Baccalaureus*), and afterward entered into an apprenticeship with Dr. John Redman. He also worked at the apothecary of the Pennsylvania Hospital and then entered the Provincial army as a surgeon and served in western Pennsylvania during the Seven Years' War, treating soldiers in the forts that dotted the frontier. He resigned his commission in 1760 and set sail for Europe to continue his medical education.

He spent a year in London after spending time working with prominent physicians there, like the Hunters and Hewson. He then moved on to the University of Edinburgh, where he graduated in 1763, writing a highly respectable thesis on the formation of pus. He also became proficient in injecting organs with wax to show them off in anatomical lectures and presentations, earning a reputation in England and on the continent for this skill which gained him admission to the Academy of Surgery of Paris. Following graduation, he took two years and made a grand tour of Europe, visiting leading physicians in Italy and France. By the end of his journeys, he had been elected a member of the Royal Society of London, admitted as a licentiate of the College of Physicians of London,

Portrait of John Morgan, who created the first medical college in America on his own, which led to a decades-long feud with fellow physician and professor at the College of Philadelphia, William Shippen. (New York Public Library)

made a member of the College of Physicians of Edinburgh, and gained membership of the Society of Belles Lettres of Rome.

While preparing to return to Philadelphia, he began developing his plan for creating a medical school in America. Word of Shippen's lectures in Philadelphia had spread to Edinburgh; Morgan's friend Samuel Bard wrote his father, John, in December 1762:

> You no Doubt have heard that Doctor Shippy has opened an Anatomical Class at Phyladelphia. His character here as an Anatomist is very good & I dare say he shines accordingly at Phyladelphia. You perhaps are not acquainted with the whole of that scheem. It is not to stop with anatomy, but to found, under the Patronage of Doctor Fothergill, a physical Colledge in that Place. Mr. Morgan who is to graduate next Spring, & will be over in the fall, intends to lecture upon the Theory & Practice of Physick, and I dare say is equal to the undertaking. I wish with all my heart they were at New York, that I might have a share amongst them, and assist in founding the first Physical Colledge in America.[36]

In November 1764, Morgan wrote to Dr. William Cullen at the Edinburgh Medical School about his plans: "I am preparing for America, to see whether, after fourteen years' devotion to medicine, I can get my living without turning apothecary or practitioner of surgery. My scheme of instituting lectures you will hereafter know more of. It is not prudent to broach designs prematurely, and mine are not yet fully ripe for execution."[37]

At the time, doctors in America did everything, from seeing patients to fulfilling prescriptions and handing out medicines to performing surgery. Morgan was proposing to focus on one aspect and specialize in that, much like how things were done in Europe where many doctors refused to make their own medicine and left it to the apothecary. When Morgan arrived back in Philadelphia from Europe in 1765, he was seen in Europe as second only to Franklin in terms of scientific prestige and reputation.[38]

What was clear to Dr. Fothergill, in London, and many other medical men around Philadelphia was that Shippen was viewed as the leader of the next generation of physicians. This caused great resentment to Morgan, who had a difficult time showing that he was creating something new, fresh, all his own, and not merely building upon what Shippen had already constructed. Morgan's confidence grew after his tour of Europe and helped to fuel his ideas to go bigger—no one's able assistant any longer but a proven and talented physician in his own right.

On returning to America, Morgan wasted no time in implementing his grand plan for medical education at the College of Philadelphia. He presented it to the trustees of the college just days after his return and formally asked to be made professor of medicine. To support this plan, he handed over recommendations from former Governor Hamilton and Richard Peters (both trustees), and Thomas Penn. William Shippen, Sr., a trustee of the college, missed the board meeting where Morgan's plan was voted on. Sr. and Jr. were seemingly told after the fact.

Illustration showing the buildings of the College of Philadelphia, where many of the city's promising youth from the period received their education. (*An Account of the College of Physicians of Philadelphia*)

They became irritated and then resentful at Morgan's lack of recognition of Shippen, Jr.'s earlier work in providing medical lectures, and his propping himself up as the originator of the plan to create a medical department at the college.[39] The trustees approved the plan and made Morgan the first professor of Theory and Practice of Physic. At the end of the same month, he stood in front of the graduating class of the College of Philadelphia and delivered his "A Discourse Upon The Institution of Medical Schools in America," where he fully laid out his plan for a medical college.

While William Smith was on his contentious fundraising trip to Great Britain in 1762–4, he most likely met up with Morgan, and the young doctor gained his support. This led Morgan to also gain the support of Thomas Penn in 1763, which gave him the confidence to work on his plan for medical education in America, running it by the trio of prominent London physicians, Drs. Fothergill, Hunter, and Watson. So, his idea was known before his return by the proprietor, the provost of the college, some of the leading physicians in London, and the trustees of the college. There was even talk of Shippen's brother-in-law, Arthur Lee, becoming the Materia Medica and Botany professor, so it is not as though the Shippens could have been ignorant of Morgan's plan and idea. The real question is whether they were consulted at all by Morgan.[40]

Most likely, Morgan kept the true purpose of his plan away from Shippen and many others to gain glory for himself. What Shippen did or didn't know remains a mystery, though what is known is that he did not receive any firsthand reports from Morgan himself. The secrecy that Morgan worked with seemed to offend Shippen more than anything else, though he would have preferred having an independent medical school outside of the purview of the College of Philadelphia.[41]

In many ways, that day was the pinnacle of Morgan's career. As Morgan's biographer, Whitfield J. Bell, Jr., puts it: "Never again would he be so famous or his audience so friendly. His whole life had been a preparation for this moment, while from the address, a train of consequences flowed which affected him, the medical school, and the profession in Philadelphia for more than a quarter of a century."[42] Morgan put forth a clear understanding of the dire state of American medicine and the practice of physicians, presenting an alternative vision of what the profession could strive to become and offering up a series of practical solutions that no doubt spoke to the practicality of Quaker Philadelphia. But in the same breath, he created immense hostility towards himself, leading to further professional and personal frustrations.

His "Discourse" presented a bold and revolutionary plan to reform medical education and practice in America. If professional education improved, that would only enhance the quality of the medical profession. His speech at the Commencement, May 30 and 31, 1765, was the talk of the town for the following month.[43]

Morgan spent parts of the "Discourse" discussing Shippen while simultaneously taking full credit for coming up with the plan and being arrogant and patronizing at the same time:

> It is with the highest satisfaction I am informed from Dr. Shippen, junior, that in an address to the public as introductory to his first anatomical course, he proposed some hints of a plan for giving medical lectures amongst us. But I do not learn that he recommended at all a collegiate undertaking of this kind. What led me to it was the obvious utility that would attend it, and the desire I had of presenting, as a tribute of gratitude to my alma mater, a full and enlarged plan for the institution of Medicine, in all its branches, in this seminary where I had part of my education, being amongst the first sons who shared in its public honours. I was further induced to it from a consideration, that private schemes of propagating knowledge are instable in their nature, and that the cultivation of useful learning can only be effectually promoted under those who are patrons of science, and under the authority and direction of men incorporated for the improvement of literature ... Should the trustees of the college think proper to found a professorship in Anatomy, Dr. Shippen having been concerned already in teaching that branch of medical science is a circumstance favourable to our wishes. Few here can be ignorant of the great opportunities he has had abroad of qualifying himself in Anatomy, and that he has already given three courses thereof in this city, and designs to enter upon a fourth course next Winter.[44]

In his application for the professor of Anatomy job directly to the Board of Trustees in September of 1765, Shippen provided his rebuttal to Morgan's jab:

The Institution of Medical Schools in this Country has been a favorite Object of my Attention for seven years past, and it is three years since I proposed the Expediency & Practicability of teaching Medicine in all its Branches, in this City, in a public Oration read at the State House, introductory to my first Course of Anatomy.

I should long since have sought the Patronage of the Trustees of the College, but waited to be joined by Dr. Morgan, to whom I first communicated my Plan in England, & who promised to unite with me in every Scheme we might think necessary for the Execution of so important a Point. I am pleased however to hear that you, Gentlemen, on being applied to by Dr. Morgan, have taken the Plan under your Protection, & have appointed that Gentleman Professor of Medicine.[45]

Shortly after Shippen was made a professor the first announcements of classes began to appear in the *Pennsylvania Gazette*:

As the necessity of cultivating medical knowledge in America is allowed by all, it is with pleasure we inform the public that a Course of Lectures on two of the most important branches of that useful science, viz., Anatomy and Materia Medica, will be delivered this winter in Philadelphia. We have great reason, therefore, to hope that gentlemen of the Faculty will encourage the design by recommending it to their pupils, that pupils themselves will be glad of such an opportunity of improvement, and that the public will think it an object worthy their attention and patronage.

In order to render these courses the more extensively useful, we intend to introduce into them as much of the Theory and Practice of Physic, of Pharmacy, Chemistry, and Surgery as can be conveniently admitted,

From all this, together with an attendance on the practice of the physicians and surgeons of the Pennsylvania Hospital, the students will be able to prosecute their studies with such advantage as will qualify them to practise hereafter with more satisfaction to themselves and benefit to the community.

The particular advertisements inserted below specify the time when these lectures are to commence, and contain the various subjects to be treated of in each course, and the terms on which pupils are to be admitted.

WILLIAM SHIPPEN, Jr., M.D., "Professor of Anatomy and Surgery In the College of Philadelphia."

JOHN MORGAN. M, D. F. R, R., etc., "Professor of Medicine in the College of Philadelphia."[46]

For two years, Shippen and Morgan were the only medical professors at the college. In 1767, the trustees cemented the guidelines for conferring the different types of medical degrees, including a bachelor's degree in Physic and a doctor's degree in Physic. In January 1768, Dr. Kuhn was made professor of Materia Medica and Botany. And in 1769, Benjamin Rush was made professor of Chemistry. Most of the faculty, excluding Thomas Bond (who gave clinical lectures), were young; Rush was 24 when he joined, Kuhn was 28, Shippen was 33, and Morgan 34. In 1768, the college handed out its first medical degrees, 10 in total, to graduates representing a wide range of counties around the Philadelphia area, from Bucks, Chester, and Lancaster counties in Pennsylvania to New Jersey and Delaware, with two coming from Philadelphia.[47]

The medical faculty worked only loosely together where cooperation was not essential for the doing of one's duties. But they hardly liked or trusted one another. Bond wrote to Franklin saying that each was a good professor, but the school was hampered by "one or two Crooked Ribs amongst us."[48]

The faculty were free to teach wherever they wished, either in the college hall or in their own quarters, whatever suited their convenience. All of the classes were small, with a slow trickle of students seeking degrees. Because of the highly specialized nature of their courses, they were left to do as they pleased with no oversight from the administration. And they mainly kept to themselves, meeting together as a faculty only at public examinations and commencements.[49]

The faculty's antagonism was not just limited to Morgan and Shippen. In general, Morgan had petty grievances, like when Rush listed Shippen above him in the dedication of his thesis and taking up the role of seniority at the college. Rush accused Shippen of trying to convince students not to take his courses. Rush and Morgan gleefully watched as Shippen kept getting accused of grave robbing for corpses to use in dissections. And Morgan, Rush, and Shippen all worked on trying to oust Bond as the clinical lecturer for them to deliver clinical lectures themselves.[50]

The drama between Morgan and Shippen did not stop at the medical school, as the two found more opportunities to clash with one another in the drama surrounding

Drawing of William Shippen Jr.'s house where he would routinely hold public dissections, some of which led to riots from the masses who claimed Shippen was grave robbing to get his dissection corpses. (*Annals of Philadelphia*)

the establishment of a medical society in the city while they were busy teaching the first classes at the medical school.

With several young Philadelphia physicians, Morgan organized the Medical Society in February of 1766. It was intended to promote the exchange of medical knowledge and encourage experimentation while enforcing a standard of professional conduct. It was to be akin to the College of Physicians of London and Edinburgh that served as a licensing agency for the physicians of those cities. Morgan hoped the society would issue licenses that would be good throughout all British North America. A great and grand idea in theory, but once again Morgan ran afoul of the Shippens in not letting them in on the idea at all.[51]

Morgan approached Chief Justice William Allen to try to gain official support for his medical society, and Allen complied by writing to Penn, throwing his support behind granting an official proprietor charter to the society, saying that it would make Philadelphia "in some measure the Seat of the Sciences, and, in the physical way, the Edinburgh of America."[52] Once again, Morgan snubbed Shippen in a repeat of the medical school performance, insulting Shippen yet again and creating animosity and clefts among the city's physicians.[53]

The Society invited the older established doctors to join, and some did, but the Shippens declined, and along with them, other prominent Philadelphia physicians declined as well. There was palpable bitterness from the beginning, and it was the "principal factor in limiting its usefulness."[54] The Society met weekly, discussed new publications, and went over complex cases with one another. Morgan approached Penn to charter the Society as a college of physicians with the end result to issue licenses to qualified physicians. William Allen supported the idea; however, Penn thought it was too early to think about such an organization. William Smith opposed it as well, thinking that it would weaken the brand-new medical school: "The Design may be good, but they seem to go too fast; & the Dr. with all his good parts, has given offence to many by being too desirous to put himself at the Head of Things. Such a Charter just now, I fear, would divide instead of unite."[55] Then, when Fothergill came out against the idea, this proved to be the death knell for the charter and society.

The Bonds and Shippens responded by reviving the old American Philosophical Society, and the two societies squabbled with one another in an effort to build their roster of members. Ever prideful, Morgan was the more energetic of the two and added prominent corresponding members from Boston, Newport, New York, and Charleston. By the winter of 1769, the two societies were weaker apart, then ultimately united after Morgan and Shippen both had lost some interest in their endeavors. This new American Medical Society had a long-lasting positive impact in Philadelphia and throughout the colonies and the newly formed country. It called together students and practicing physicians and led to lively participation where they met weekly at the college to read the current literature and discuss medical matters—creating an atmosphere of professionalism that could not have been achieved if Morgan and Shippen continued in leadership roles.[56] After a few months it merged with the American Society for Promoting Useful Knowledge.[57]

All this led to a tense atmosphere when medical classes were to begin in the fall of 1766: an air of personal acrimony and ill will. Shippen had some cause to be grumpy with the continual snubs and slights from Morgan, while it is a little more nebulous why Morgan kept slighting his fellow physician, if not for personal pride and insolence that built upon itself within him and only managed to prolong the quarreling. And while Shippen worked mostly behind the scenes against Morgan in private chats with colleagues, he did not keep wholly quiet. When announcing his lectures in the fall of 1766, Shippen took the opportunity to needle Morgan once again:

> [H]is first course was read in the year 1762 and was premised by an oration, delivered in the State-house, before many of the principal inhabitants of this city, wherein he proposed a plan for the institution of a medical school in Philadelphia, to which he then declared that course of anatomy was introductory.
>
> The use of such an institution, and the practicability and propriety of it at that time, were expressed in these words: 'All these (meaning the disadvantages that attended the study of physic, &c.) may, and I hope will soon be remedied, by a medical school in America; and what place in America so fit for such a school as Philadelphia, that bids so fair, by its rapid growth, to be soon the metropolis of all the Continent? Such a school is properly begun by an anatomical class, and, for our encouragement, let us remember, that the famous school of physic at Edinburgh, which is now the first in Europe, has not had a beginning fifty years and was begun by the anatomical lectures of Doctor Monro, who is still living, &c.;'
>
> Doctor Shippen thinks it necessary, for some reasons, to publish this extract from his oration, to acquaint those who were not present when it was delivered,, that he proposed, and began to execute, a plan for the institution of a medical school in this city four years ago; which, he has the pleasure to inform the public, is now improved, by being connected with the college of Philadelphia, and has succeeded beyond his highest expectations.
>
> As no course of lectures on the theory and practice of physic, is proposed this winter, and as several young gentlemen, who design to settle in the spring, have expressed a desire to be instructed in that useful branch of medicine, the Doctor intends to gratify them, by adding to his course a few general lectures on diseases, in which he will treat of their causes and symptoms, with their indications, and method of cure.[58]

In one announcement, Shippen took credit for the idea of a medical school in Philadelphia and was taking over Morgan's course as well. Morgan wasted no time posting an announcement the following week saying he planned to lecture that winter on theory, practice, and chemistry.[59]

Through adversity, though it was self-inflicted and ego-driven, there developed the impressive educational atmosphere in Philadelphia. The College of Philadelphia began producing the next generation of leaders in the community as the scions of the city and around the Pennsylvania countryside, like Robert Johnston, were sent there to gain an education. The college served as a center of cultural life in Philadelphia. Commencements were open events attended by the public, where they would not only hear enlightening lectures from the professors but would enjoy entertainment in the form of concerts. Some of the first public musical performances took place at the college's commencements, with the college providing the bedrock for the city's flourishing arts and sciences scenes.

CHAPTER SIX

From Deep Within the Soul to the Outer Reaches of Space

Economic growth, expanding educational opportunities, and a myriad of other factors created the atmosphere for America's first collective arts and sciences scene. A burgeoning literati made up of the city's upper and middle classes began to meet and take shape, pushing one another to produce the first genuinely American works in literature, theater, and music. At the same time, they formed a collective of men dedicated to exploring and advancing scientific views and, in the process, making an international impact. Upon the backs of the artists and scientists of Philadelphia, the city began to gain its cultural reputation around the colonies and across the ocean in Britain, France, and elsewhere on the European continent.

Literary in the colonial sense is different from how it is thought about today. Literature came in the form of any sort of written work, such as newspapers, almanacs, magazines, pamphlets, letters, personal poems, and even book publishing. It could take the form of intensely personal and private projects, like Graeme's project of drafting a poetical version of Psalms or the translation of Fénelon's *Télémaque*, which she would share with others who came to her salon. There were also public, published, and political works like popular pamphlets, such as John Dickinson's *Letters from a Farmer in Pennsylvania* or Thomas Paine's *Common Sense*. All of it added up to creating a literate populace and vibrant culture.

And, of course, Benjamin Franklin stood in the center of it all. His literary fame rested upon not one specific writing, though his *Autobiography* would be hailed and still is held in high regard. His vast output and copious interests and activities resulted in letters and pamphlets, parliamentary records, newspaper and magazine articles, and the pages of *Poor Richard's Almanack*.

Franklin also had the advantage of being a printer, and printers often were at the forefront of the literature being produced in Philadelphia. From 1740 to 1775, 42 printers issued 15 newspapers and numerous pamphlets and magazines. This includes Franklin's *Pennsylvania Gazette* but also William Goddard's *Pennsylvania Chronicle*, that was considered the best newspaper of the middle colonies for its skillful and competent prose.[1]

Illustration of the outside of Benjamin Franklin's bookshop, one of the many bookstores in Philadelphia over this time period. (*The Many Sided Franklin*)

Through their connections, printers stood firmly at the heart of cultural and political life in Philadelphia. They tended to think more expansively beyond the confines of the city. New printers of the late colonial period also began expanding the number of current works from Europe available, like *Robinson Crusoe, Paradise Lost, History of Charles V*, and more.[2]

And they printed everything: forms for businesses, the government, and legal practice; handbills and tickets to commencements, plays, and concerts; government records; catalogs for merchants. Almost all of them issued their own almanacs. Sermons and other religious documents constituted a large portion of business, just above the flood of pamphlets that the political and cultural times would soon inspire. As one outrage followed another, these unleashed a series of pamphlets in response, pamphlets responding to those, and the ones responding to those, and on it went. A literate populace eagerly gobbled up these pamphlets. An art form all their own, pamphlets and also broadsheets were often humorous or satirical, slightly offensive; few were fair and even-handed, instead being partisan while they offered immediate responses to the news of the day.[3]

These pamphlets enabled readers of all classes and ethnicities to engage with the controversies, allowing them to feel a part of the ongoing narrative. Newspapers served much the same purpose, informing the public of the comings and goings of ships, letting people know about schoolmasters offering their services, musicians performing, and arts and crafts from around the city. Newspapers offered writers and thinkers a vehicle for them to share their ideas.[4]

Almanacs served as a means to advertise and promote the publisher's business. A year-round advertisement often hung in the house or a tavern that would be thumbed through and consumed all year. They were calendars. They dispensed witticisms. They provided sage advice, passed along astronomical information and offered up probable weather patterns for the coming year.[5]

Fresh newspapers, like the *Pennsylvania Evening Post* and *Pennsylvania Packet*, sprung up during the many different eruptions of discord in the city and would play a significant role in the political controversies. The *Pennsylvania Chronicle* published John Dickinson's "Farmer Letters," whose straightforward prose helped solidify colonial anger against the Stamp Act:

> I am a farmer settled after a variety of fortunes near the banks of the river Delaware in the province of Pennsylvania. I received a liberal Education and have been engaged in the busy scenes of life; but am now convinced that a man may be as happy without bustle as with it. My farm is small; my servants are few, and good; I have a little money at interest; I wish for no more.

The Letters would make Dickinson a celebrity across the American colonies as they were reprinted in all but four colonial newspapers. The pamphlet version of *Letters from a Farmer in Pennsylvania* sold incredibly well and was the most influential American pamphlet until Thomas Paine's *Common Sense*.[6]

Though all were short-lived, magazines like the *Pennsylvania Magazine* and *American Magazine* offered excellent opportunities for budding Philadelphia writers to apply their trade. Paine's first job upon his arrival in the American colonies was as the editor of *Pennsylvania Magazine*, offering him his first platform in America. The magazine's publisher said Paine could not write without a decanter of brandy beside him: "The first glass warmed him, the second illuminated his intellectual system, and when he had taken the third glass it is said he wrote 'with great rapidity, intelligence, and precision, his ideas appearing to flow faster than he could commit them to paper.'"[7] That may be somewhat apocryphal since his publisher and he had a falling-out. William Smith's *American Magazine* was first published in October 1757, and issues were filled with poems, essays, and scientific articles; Smith included the works of students or former students of his.[8] This included the poetry of an academy alum, Nathaniel Evans, whose death at 26 robbed the colonies of one of their finest poets, and whose promise seemed unlimited. He had honed his skills trading flirtatious poems with Elizabeth Graeme. Evans, Graeme, and others utilized scenes and nature around Philadelphia in their poetry, helping to preserve their Philadelphia for future generations.[9] This can be seen in Evans's *Ode*, which he wrote when he was 21 about his youth spent swimming in the Schuylkill and Delaware, fishing, hunting, hiking:

> But hence, ye dear delusions all,
>   'Tis time I tear you from my breast;
>
> Methinks! I hear sweet Reason call,
>   "Be not with empty dreams possest!"
>   Away, ye pleasing shade away,
>   I brook no longer fond delay —
>   Reluctant still ye from me fly,
>
> Your airy forms I see yet flit before my eye!
>
> But come, thou habitant of heav'n!
>   Inspirer of each gallant deed;
>
> Virtue, bright queen, to whom 'tis given
>   The soul for purer joys to breed;
>   High-arch'd, o'er yon cerulean plain,
>   Sublimely shines thy sacred fane,
>   The graces wait its portal nigh,
>
> Which perfect shall endure thro' vast eternity.
>
> Come, and thy gracious aid impart,
>   Each perishing pursuit to tame;
>
> O root out folly from my heart,
>   And thou the full possession claim.
>   Each roving wish, each vain desire,
>   O purge with thy celestial fire;
>   What is the world's, the people's gaze?
>
> Hence with the hubble fame, and idle breath of praise!
>
> Whether, adown the stream of time,
>   I pass with easy prosp'rous sails;
>
> Or o'er its waves I painful climb,
>   Forlorn and toss'd by stormy gales;
>   Still let me check the wanton breeze,
>   Nor be absorb'd in slothful ease;
>   But stedfast steer, when tempests rise
>
> That rend my shatter'd bark, or mount it to the skies.
>
> So come what will, the adverse scene,
>   Or fortune's gay alluring smile,

> Soon shall I keep my soul serene,
>   Superior to all sinful guile;
>   Then, whether Fate's resistless sheers,
>   Shall clip my thread in ripen'd years;
>   Or, *in my Pride*, my doom be spoke,
>
> Undaunted shall I yield, and fearless meet the stroke.[10]

Following Evans' death, William Smith worked to publish a collection of his poems titled *Poems on Several Occasions* (1772). And while alive Evans published a collection of another Philadelphia poet struck down too soon, Thomas Godfrey: *Juvenile Poems on Various Subjects; with the Prince of Parthia, a Tragedy*.[11]

Philadelphia went on to produce one of the more unique literary talents in the colonial era, Francis Hopkinson—a *bon vivant* dilettante who dabbled in satirical prose while also being an accomplished musician. John Adams said of him, "He is one of your pretty, little curious, ingenious men. His head is not bigger than a large apple. I have not met with anything in natural history more amusing and entertaining than his personal appearance, yet he is genteel and well bred, and is very social."[12] Thomas I. Wharton described him thus: "A poet, a wit, a patriot, a chemist, a mathematician, and a Judge of the Admiralty: his character was composed of a happy union of qualities and endowments, commonly supposed to be discordant; and with the humor of Swift and Rabelais, he was always on the side of virtue and social order."[13]

Born on either September 21, 1737, or October 2, 1737, Hopkinson was placed by his mother in the Academy and College of Philadelphia where he graduated in 1757 as part of the first class of the College of Philadelphia and earned his master's degree in 1760. He went on to study law under Benjamin Chew, attorney general of the province, and was admitted to the bar in 1761. Later he would go on to serve in various offices and hold several public positions: secretary to a conference between the governor and Native Americans, which he chronicled in his poem "The Treaty"; secretary of the Library Company, and also its librarian; secretary of the Vestry of Christ Church; and at St. Peters he instructed children in "the art of psalmody." He tried his hand at being a merchant and established his own legal practice out of his house on Race Street above Third Street. After his marriage to Ann Borden in 1768, he gradually moved to her hometown of Bordentown, New Jersey.[14]

In 1772, Hopkinson became collector of the Port of Newcastle and, in 1774, was appointed to a seat on the Provincial Council of New Jersey but resigned his posts in 1776 to become New Jersey's delegate to the Second Continental Congress. While there he managed to get his signature on the Declaration of Independence, afterwards becoming secretary of the Navy.[15] Throughout the Revolution, he published pieces of popular satirical prose and verse like "The Pretty Story" and "Ballad of the Kegs."

These put on full display Hopkinson's satirical chops while maintaining a playfulness that made them popular with the populace. This was never more on point than in his introduction to his book of collected essays and other writings, *The Miscellaneous Essays and Occasional Writings of Francis Hopkinson, Esq.*:

> SIR,
>
> I WAS much pleased when I heard of your intention to publish a Magazine of Monthly Miscellany. For you must know, Mr. Aitken, that I have long had an earnest desire to appear as an author before the respectable public. When I walk out alone, which I frequently do, observations and sentiments arise in my mind, which appear to me as wise and important as many of those which the press is continually obtruding upon the public notice.
>
> TRUE it is, I have never yet been able to collect a sufficient number of these bright ideas to form a regular piece of composition: but I had great hopes, that if a proper occasion should offer, I might be able to furnish a short essay upon some subject or other.
>
> YOU may wonder, perhaps, why I have not tried my hand in some of the public newspapers; but the truth is, that what with your Citizens, your Philadelphians, your Lovers of Liberty, your Moderate Men, and your Immoderate Men, there is no getting a word or two in, edge-ways, amongst them. Now, I look upon your proposed magazine as a pleasant little path, where a man may take an agreeable walk with a few orderly and agreeable friends, without the danger of being jostled to death in a crowd.[16]

Utilizing a Franklin-esque humorous hominess to make accessible his allegories of the British, the king, and Parliament, he fills "The Pretty Story" with neat play on words and a witty narrative to critique British rule. His works from the revolutionary period also showcase his versatility, switching between humorous satires and rousing balladry and blending social commentary with a humorous twang.

As impressive as his literary output was, his contributions to music stand even taller. It was during that first commencement of the College of Philadelphia where one of the earliest musical performances in the city took place with a performance of the "Masque of Alfred," that most likely saw Hopkinson's first public performance on the harpsichord.[17]

Hopkinson was a psalmodist, teacher, organist, harpsichordist, essayist, composer, and improver of the harpsichord. And he stood at the heart of musical life in the city,

Portrait of Francis Hopkinson, *bon vivant* who played a major influence on the cultural landscape of Philadelphia through his writing and his championing of musical performances. (*The Literary History of Philadelphia*)

becoming the first "native poet-composer" of the United States. While no virtuoso on the harpsichord, Hopkinson was better than the average amateur and made up for any perceived lack of technical skills with an unfaltering passion for music. Prior to 1760, the music scene in Philadelphia was nearly non-existent; in the decades following, music progressed rapidly, in large part due to Francis Hopkinson's efforts. American music during the colonial period imitated the music scene of England and was buttressed by the influx of musicians from England, Germany, France, and Italy who supported and participated in the burgeoning culture.[18]

Hopkinson began learning the harpsichord at 17 in 1754 and received instruction from James Bremner, who was the organist at Christ Church and for whom Hopkinson would fill in for as organist for several years.[19] Hopkinson had some personal volumes of collected music, which included his first compositions and also pastoral songs from operas, cantatas, hymns, duets, and anthems. From about 1763 to 1766, Hopkinson held a series of "Subscription Concerts" that featured chamber music where a dozen or so amateur musicians got together to play concertos and other pieces for the enjoyment of the crowd. This was a formal version of the gatherings many families would hold at their houses so people could come together to play music.[20]

Hopkinson wrote a collection of songs and anthems from 1759 and 1760, which include many originals, including "My Days Have Been So Wondrous Free," which music historian Oscar Sonneck calls "unquestionably the earliest American song on record." Other original compositions showcase his branching out into writing cantatas and miniature grand operas, one of the first Americans to do so. Though they were charming they were old-fashioned for the period.[21] Around 1764, a keyboard composition manuscript was pieced together, which included 115 pieces arranged for the keyboard. He titled it "Lessons" intended for personal use and for other keyboardists around the city to use.[22]

The first public concert in Philadelphia took place on January 25, 1757, arranged by John Palma. A series of other early concerts were well regarded and had wide-ranging appeal: one brought George Washington to the city.[23] Other musical endeavors in the city involved James Bremner arranging and conducting benefit concerts in the city in 1764 and 1765. Giovanni Gualdo, a wine merchant/musician and teacher, held several subscription concerts showcasing many of his own pieces in the late 1770s.[24]

> At the Assembly Room, on next Thursday, (being the sixteenth of November) will be performed a Grand Concert of Vocal and Instrumental Musick; with Solos played on different instruments: the concert to be directed by Mr. Gualdo, after the Italian method.
>
> Tickets at a Dollar a piece to be had of the Waiter at the London Coffee House, and at Mr. Gualdo's in Front-street, near the Bank-meeting. To begin exactly at half an hour after Six o'clock.
>
> N.B. Hand Bills will be printed mentioning what pieces shall be performed in the two acts. The evening to be ended with a ball (if agreeable to the Company) without further Expense.[25]

Philadelphia's music scene couldn't have happened without a supply of instruments and scores that were aided by music stores. Michael Hillegas owned and operated the first music store in the colonies in Philadelphia from about 1759 to 1774. With the booksellers in the city not meeting the demand for music compositions, Hillegas saw an opportunity and established his store. Philadelphia thirsted for instruments and music-related supplies, and Hillegas supplied the city's amateur players who otherwise wouldn't have access to music. Adams described him: "Hillegas is one of our continental treasurers; is a great musician; talks perpetually of the forte and piano, of Handel, etc., and songs and tunes. He plays upon the fiddle."[26]

He advertised instruments for sale and music, much of which was secular in nature, which is curious since most documented musical performances were sacred. This opens the possibility that a whole other level of music was being performed throughout the city. There were plenty of people interested in teaching themselves to play an instrument, the violin and German flute being the most popular. Over the years, Hillegas enlarged his inventory and the type of instruments he provided, including the kind of music to play on those instruments and a good selection of supplies such as rosin and reeds.[27] His store would end up taking a backseat to the rising political controversies engulfing the colonies, and Hillegas would go on to become the first treasurer of the United States. What the colonial period lacked in actual music, it made up for in enthusiasm for the art, laying the foundations for the golden age of Philadelphia's music scene, 1790–1850.[28]

The earliest known concerts or performed music came courtesy of plays, which would be operas of a fashion, featuring an accompaniment on harpsichord and intermissions often filled with instrumental music.[29] Thomas Kean and Walter Murray headed the first professional theater company in the colonies and got their start in Philadelphia. They formed in January of 1749 and first came to Philadelphia in the spring of 1750, performing at former mayor William Plumstead's warehouse on Water Street. And right from the beginning the performances received protests from the city recorder and the Quakers, Baptists, and Methodists.[30]

The next professional company did not come through until 1754: the Hallam Company from Great Britain, later known as the American Company. In 1750, William Hallam was bankrupt, so he sent his brother, Lewis Hallam, along with his wife, children, and a troop of actors to America to raise some money. They practiced all the way over the seas to the New World. Landing in Yorktown they quickly got to work in Williamsburg: "The first large company of professional Thespians and certainly the best that the British colonies of North America had yet seen."[31] They continued on their tour to Maryland and completed a successful season in New York. Some Philadelphians who attended those New York City shows persuaded the company to visit their city for a season.[32]

To prepare for this, Hallam sent one of his actors to apply to the governor of Pennsylvania to test the waters and see how they would be received. This kicked off an extensive debate within the city with a virulent diatribe against theater appearing in the *Pennsylvania Gazette*, written by "A.B.":

> Should I pretend to give a View of the Wickedness of the Theatre, I should not know where to begin, or to what Length the Subject would carry me. For whether I insisted on the Lewdness of Impiety of most of the Plays themselves; on the infamous Characters of the Actors and Actresses; on the scandalous Farces they commonly tag the gravest Plays with, or, above all, on the inhumanly impudent Dances and Songs, with which they lard them between the Acts; I say, which so ever of these Particulars I insisted on, each of them would furnish Matter for a great many Pages … [T]he ingenious Contrivance of the Managers entirely prevents the good Effects of any worthy Sentiment expressed in the Play, by introducing a painted Strumpet at the End of every Act, to cut Capers on the Stage in such an impudent and unwomanly Manner, as must make the most shocking Impressions on every Mind.[33]

The following week, a "Y.Z." provided a rebuttal, saying it was a free country where people could enjoy whatever wasn't injurious to others. A group of petitioners, "Inhabitants of this City of several Christian Denominations," went to the mayor to prevent the building of the theater and the presentation of plays. All of this was for naught and the Hallam Company came and had a profitable season, although Governor Hamilton limited it to 30 performances.[34] Their repertoire included Rowe's *Fair Penitent*, Garrick's *Miss in Her Teens*, *King Lear*, *The Merchant of Venice*, *Richard III*, *Romeo and Juliet*, *Hamlet*, *Othello*, Marlowe's *Tamerlane*, Lillo's *George Barnwell*, and comedies by Farquhar, Addison, Cibber, Steele, Garrick and Fielding. They provided at least one benefit show for the "Charity School," most likely put on to endear themselves to the community and show off their good intentions. William Smith attended the benefit show, a performance of Colley Cibber's *The Careless Husband*, lending the event a semblance of official approval.[35]

The Hallam Company would not come back around until April 1759, this time under the new direction of David Douglass, an actor who lived in Jamaica. He had married Hallam's

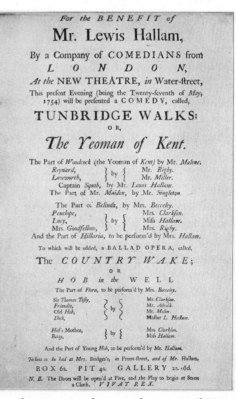

An advertisement for a performance of Lewis Hallam's American Company from their 1754 season. (*Philadelphia: A History of the City and its People*)

widow and reformed his old troop from London under the name of the Company of Comedians in 1758. Douglass constructed a new theater in Southwark called the Theater on Society Hill. This was done to circumvent Philadelphia prohibitions but was only used for that season.[36]

They performed in many genres: comedies, tragedies, farces, and pantomimes. This kicked off a new round of protests in the newspapers, and a group of members of both the Presbyterian and Quaker communities went back to the governor to protest. Douglass countered these actions by having his contractors build the theater and petition the governor, saying that if it weren't built, they would be out of pocket in money and time. After consulting the Provincial Council, Governor Denny found "that the Prohibition of plays was a most unreasonable restraint of the King's Subjects from taking innocent Diversions." The players played more benefits shows, this time for the Pennsylvania Hospital.[37] Several Philadelphians chastised the hospital for taking funds from the theater company, and the hospital had to defend itself, saying it was "not authorized to direct the Treasurer to refuse the money lately raised by exhibiting a stage play near this city." Douglass, to assuage the outrage of local cultural leaders around the 1759 season, agreed to put on the verse play *The Prince of Parthia*, which would be the first play written by an American to be performed. However, the playwright, Thomas Godfrey, close friends to Nathaniel Evans and Francis Hopkinson, and another protégé of Smith, could not finish it in time to be performed for that season.[38]

Seven years would go by before Douglass' company would return in 1766–7, and with the fervor of the Stamp Act still fresh, the company renamed itself the American Company to downplay any ties it had to England.[39] Douglass built the first permanent theater in 1766 on South Street above Fourth Street, which was named the Southwark Theater. It survived until being demolished in 1912 but had ceased being a theater in the early 19th century when it was repurposed as a distillery.[40]

Like previous seasons, the 1766–7 season saw its fair share of protestations. Merchants complained the theater was siphoning off money from the city while also arguing, contradictorily, that it was causing men and women to spend too freely. This all had the effect, they said, of depriving Philadelphia's impoverished of assistance. Once again, the governor had to step in to limit the season to two months, though Douglass managed to have it extended. In February of 1767, the Assembly petitioned Governor John Penn to halt the operation of the new theater. Penn refused, which kicked off another round of religious protests through the newspaper that called theater a place for degenerates, and was clear that "if you live in the use of this diversion, you have no grounds to hope, that you have the spirit and heart of a Christian." The theater was the "devil's abode, where he holds his filthy court of evil spirits" full of debauchery and effeminacy. And it was being blamed for corrupting the political system:

At a time, when pleasure seems to be the grand idol of our cares, and dissipation the object of our wishes, it is really a matter of serious concern, to behold the great encouragement that is given to follies and diversions, of every kind, in this city ... When we examine the rise and fall of states, and trace the causes by which whole nations have sunk at once from the height of glory into more than Gothic barbarity, we shall find them to be principally owning to the luxury and effeminacy of the times.[41]

Companies were small, so an actor occasionally had to take multiple parts in the same play. It also led to some unfortunate casting, like Juliet being played by Mrs. Hallam and Romeo being played by her son. The barrier between the actors and the audience was a thin one. The two would often interact freely with one another throughout the show. Every class of folks from Philadelphia was in attendance. And since actors were seen as on par with vagrants, with low moral standing, the audience didn't think twice about tossing eggs at them if the performances were not up to their satisfaction. It could get rowdy. The stage itself was more just a platform from where characters could speak. The costumes were elegant though not historically accurate, and you could buy tickets for that night's show at local taverns.[42]

A report from a 1764 New York play sums up the experience: "How great then is my disappointment and vexation, when instead of a modest and becoming silence, nothing is heard during the whole performance but laughing and talking, very loud squalling, overturning the benchs, etc. Behaviour more suited to a broglio than a musical entertainment."[43]

Supporters of theater life in Philadelphia praised its ability to bridge the emotional gaps between the classes and calm nerves, and even Anglican clergyman praised its ability to spread Christian virtue: "Every fool, coxcomb, and villain, may see himself represented upon the stage as clearly as in a mirror ... For vice and folly have never received severer lashes than those that had been liberally inflicted on them by dramatic writers."[44]

This debate continued throughout the 1766–7 season and only had the effect of increasing the popularity of the theater. The company put on around 100 performances between November 1766 and July 1767, showing 42 plays, 27 of which were new. There were complaints about the number of young people in attendance, meaning apprentices and servants got out and took in the theater alongside the gentry.[45] The last colonial season ran from October 1772 to March 1773 at the Southwark Theater. The following year, the First Continental Congress passed a resolution that encouraged frugality and discouraged "every species of extravagance and dissipation, especially of horse racing ... gaming, exhibitions of shews, plays and other expensive diversions and entertainments."[46]

The first American playwright, Thomas Godfrey, was born in Philadelphia in 1736. His father apprenticed Thomas off to a watchmaker, but his heart was in writing poetry. He spent his free time composing verse, with his poem "Invitation" published by Smith in *American Magazine*. Smith was impressed with the young

Godfrey's talent, and he became close friends with Hopkinson and the painter Benjamin West, who was soon destined to go to London and embark on a highly successful career there. While at the College of Philadelphia, Godfrey likely participated in a school production of *Alfred*, a pageant-like opera that had a little bit of everything, that was put on during the holidays of 1756–7 and served as part inspiration for his later play, *The Prince of Parthia*.[47]

Smith also helped Godfrey get a commission in the Fort

> By Authority.
> NEVER PERFORMED BEFORE.
> By the AMERICAN COMPANY,
> At the NEW THEATRE, in *Southwark*,
> On *FRIDAY*, the *Twenty-Fourth* of *April*, will be
> presented, A TRAGEDY written by the late ingenious
> Mr. *Thomas Godfrey*, of this city, called the
> ## PRINCE of PARTHIA.
> The PRINCIPAL CHARACTERS by Mr. HALLAM,
> Mr. DOUGLASS, Mr. WALL, Mr. MORRIS,
> Mr. ALLYN, Mr. TOMLINSON, Mr. BROAD-
> BELT, Mr. GREVILLE, Mrs. DOUGLASS,
> Mrs. MORRIS, Miss WAINWRIGHT, and
> Miss CHEER.
> To which will be added, A *Ballad Opera* called
> ## The CONTRIVANCES,
> To begin exactly at *Seven* o'Clock.--*Vivant Rex & Regina*.

An advertisement announcing the performance of Thomas Godfrey's *Prince of Parthia* by the American Company, the first play written and performed by an American. (*The Prince of Parthia, A Tragedy*)

Duquesne campaign. After that, he settled in North Carolina, where he finished *The Prince of Parthia*, in 1758. It would become the first play by an American writer to be presented on an American stage, being first performed by the American Company in his hometown on April 24, 1767. After three years in North Carolina, Godfrey came back to Philadelphia. He would die there in August of 1763 after a short illness at the age of 27. Some critics have said if he had been given more time to hone his craft, he could have become the "American Keats."[48]

The year 1767 would almost bear witness to another first, that of a new wholly original comic opera composed and presented in the colonies. Andrew Barton, possibly the pseudonym for Colonel Thomas Forest of Germantown, wrote and published the libretto for *The Disappointment; or the Force of Credulity.*

> THO' distant far, from fam'd Britania's isle,
> Where comic-scenes, call cynics forth to smile;
> Our artless muse, hath made her first essay
> T' instrust and please you with a modern play.
> Theatric-bus'ness was, and still shou'd be,
> To point out vice in its deformity;
> Make virtue fair! shine eminently bright,
> Rapture the breast and captivate the fight.
> No matter which, the pulpit or the stage,
> Condemn the vice and folly of the age;
> These are our boast, and on sure ground we stand,
> Plead virtues cause throughout this infant land;
> We mount the stage, and lend an helping hand.
> Wits, fools, a knave and conjurer to night,
> The objects make both of your ears and sight.

A band of dupes are humm'd with idle schemes,
Quit solid sense for airy golden dreams.
Our flatt'ring muse thinks she's some merit gain'd,
Pursuing truth, and things (like truth) well feign'd.
The subject's suited to our present times,
No person's touch'd, altho' she lash their crimes;
Nor gall or copp'ras tincture her design,
But gay good humour breathe in ev'ry line.
If you condemn her—she for censure stands;
But if applaud— then thund'ring clap your hands.[49]

Forest knew plenty about credulity; he had been dabbling for years in pranking the many believers in the popular pirate stories at the time, going as far as creating fake confessions of pirates, leading to even more phony treasure locations.[50]

The Disappointment was obscene and coarse but comical in its skewering of many well-known locals who were thinly veiled in the libretto. The plot centers around the hunt for Blackbeard's hidden treasure and the ridiculous lengths to which many would go to recover it. The American Company agreed to perform the opera and began rehearsals. An ad was placed for the first production, but since the play included so many apparent references to locals—enough to lead to potential legal actions—warned off by many, Douglass took heed. He pulled the production, announcing its cancellation: "*The Disappointment* (that was advertised for Monday), as it contains personal reflections, is unfit for the stage."[51]

⁓

Just as Franklin helped define the literary output throughout this quarter century, he also helped create an atmosphere where scientific discoveries were made regularly, mostly through his electricity experiments and the fame that came from that. He also spearheaded the creation of the American Philosophical Society with local botanist John Bartram, which in Europe came to be known as "Franklin's Society."[52]

Science often worked as a unifying force, a collegial one. For his electricity experiments, Franklin worked with a circle of fellow experimenters, utilizing the Library Company resources and fostering a scientific community aided by the coming of the medical school and the medical societies.[53] His book, *Experiments, and Observations on Electricity*, was as successful as a work of science could be at the time, going through five editions in English, an additional three in French, and German and Italian editions. It benefited from the electricity fad going on at the time that was receiving worldwide attention. But Franklin would not be the first American to be recognized by the leading scientists of Europe; that honor would go to John Bartram.[54]

Both were helped along by Peter Collinson, a prominent merchant based in London. Collinson acted as a scientific promoter of sorts who was also largely responsible for lifting the scientific discoveries of John Bartram and making them known across all of Europe. He was a great connector who played an essential role in promoting the works of Franklin and connecting the landed gentry in England with botanists around the Empire to furnish trees and other delights for their palatial estates. A Quaker, he had many ties to Pennsylvania; though a draper by trade, his true passion lay in gardening. He taught himself the science of botany and used his personal and business ties in America to collect seeds and plants found across the Atlantic. This is how he began his 30-plus-year correspondence with Philadelphia-based botanist John Bartram. Their relationship started in 1733 and continued till Collinson's death in 1768, and Collinson couldn't have asked for a better partner and collector. Bartram not only provided Collinson with thousands of unique seeds and specimens but also the inquisitive mind, discerning eye, and relentless pursuit of knowledge, of one of the most talented field botanists and naturalists.[55]

As the earliest native botanist in America, having been born in Darby, Chester County, Delaware, in 1699, Bartram did not receive much by way of formal education: a basic country school education supplemented with studies in Greek and Latin. Early in his adulthood, he acquired some physic and surgery skills, enough for the local community to promote him to neighborhood doctor, and he showed a knack for producing medicines. He built his own house, cleared the land, and created the botanical garden himself. A mysterious visitor and admirer of Bartram—who purported to be a Russian named Iwan Alexiowitz, but could have also been a literary invention by J. Hector St. John, aka St. John de Crevecoeur[56]—provides a tidy description of Bartram's house:

> His house is small but decent; there was something peculiar in its first appearance which seemed to distinguish it from those of his neighbors: a small tower in the middle of it not only helped to strengthen it but afforded convenient room for a staircase. Every disposition of the fields, fences, and trees, seemed to bear the marks of perfect order and regularity,—which, in rural affairs, always indicate a prosperous industry... After a little time I perceived the Schuylkill, winding through delightful meadows, and soon cast my eyes on a new-made bank, which seemed greatly to confine its stream.[57]

Bartram was a gentle soul, cheerful but in a no-nonsense way.[58] He talked about how he educated himself in botany after witnessing a daisy in the field he was tilling:

> I cast my eyes on a daisy; I plucked it mechanically, and viewed it with more curiosity than common country farmers are wont to do, and observed therein very many distinct parts, some perpendicular—some horizontal. What a shame, said my mind, or something that inspired my mind, that thee shouldst have employed so many years in tilling the earth, and destroying so many flowers and plants, without being acquainted with their structures and their uses! This seeming inspiration suddenly awakened my curiosity, for these were not thoughts to which I had been accustomed. I returned to my team, but this new desire did not quit my mind.[59]

He would travel all over North America, from the Great Lakes to Florida, to collect specimens. His travels fueled his correspondence with European scientists, relaying his discoveries and collections to benefit science and commerce.[60] He first proposed the idea of a society promoting natural history in 1739, and then teamed up with Franklin in 1743 to form the first iteration of the American Philosophical Society. The early members were middle-aged men of high standing in the city, but few of them held much enthusiasm for the society and soon it was just Bartram and Franklin doing most of the work. Bartram called them "very idle Gentlemen [who] will take no Pains" and by 1746 the society evaporated away. He had an independent streak, as demonstrated by his disownment by the Quakers over his denial of the divinity of Christ. Bartram's son, William, who would often tag along on his botany journeys, became a respected botanist in

Profile of the great botanist, John Bartram, whose seed collection trips helped him amass a wealth of knowledge on the plants of North America. (*The Romance of Forgotten Men*)

his own right. William's book, *Travels through North and South Carolina, Georgia, East and West Florida, the Cherokee Country, etc.* (1791) would go on to influence the likes of Coleridge and Wordsworth.[61]

By 1750, Bartram was already an established and esteemed botanist, highly respected throughout the kingdom. These plant explorations Bartram undertook were underwritten by Collinson, providing the Londoner with new, exotic American seeds for his clients. The more clients Collinson acquired, the more time Bartram could spend traveling and collecting. In 1761, he brought back the first pecans from a trip to the Ohio river and Pittsburgh. He would travel extensively throughout the South, the Carolinas, Virginia, Georgia, and Florida, making acquaintances and corresponding with the botanists there, such as Dr. Alexander Garden (for whom Gardenia is named). In 1765, thanks to Collinson's efforts, Bartram was named botanist to the king, which came with a 50-pound-a-year stipend and instructions to botanize East Florida, which he embarked on with his son in 1766.[62]

Not content with being a botanist and plant explorer, Bartram wrote an appendix to Thomas Short's *Medicina Britannica* on American medicinal plants. He was also interested in other topics, such as bird migration and geology. During the revolutionary period, Washington, Franklin, Hamilton, and Jefferson all spent time at Bartram's garden and "found peaceful repose from their arduous tasks in the capital of the new republic."[63] Bartram was one of the first to theorize that streams eroded their valleys instead of finding them already made, and was also an early proponent of the theory that "the greatest part of this country ... had formerly been under water." He corresponded with some of the greatest naturalists of the day: Linnaeus, Gronovius, Clayton, and Kalm.[64]

~

Some 20 miles outside of Philadelphia, in Norriton, there lived the other great scientific mind of the age: David Rittenhouse, the renowned mathematician, astronomer, and clockmaker.

Born April 8, 1732, in the stone home his grandfather had built at Norriton, Rittenhouse grew up a sickly child and it became apparent to his farmer father that young David was not suited to the rigors of farming. His carpenter uncle provided him with some education and left Rittenhouse his tools on his death, which he would use for his instrument-making and, eventually, clockmaking. This served as the right kind of stimulation for David's precise mind and suited his manual dexterity. Rittenhouse's father, Mathias, provided his reluctant support by buying his son the clockmaker tools he needed and allowing him to build a workshop on the farm along the road heading into town. David did not look back, becoming a clockmaker in 1750, producing some of the finest clocks in Pennsylvania, and working at it until the Revolution diverted his attention elsewhere.[65]

During one of his many sick spells, while at Yellow Springs, Chester County for his health, Rittenhouse consumed Newton's *Philosophiæ Naturalis Principia Mathematica,* leading to his fascination with astronomy. Putting together the two loves of astronomy and instrument-making he built the first telescope ever fashioned in America, writing to his friend and mentor, Reverend Thomas Barton: "I am spending my time in the old trifling manner, and am so taken with optics, that I do not know whether, if the enemy should invade this part of the country, as Archimedes was slaid while making geometrical figures in the sand, so I should die making a telescope."[66]

Rittenhouse had met Barton when the latter had come to Norriton

Portrait of David Rittenhouse, clockmaker, instrument maker, astronomer, scientist, and revolutionary. (National Portrait Gallery)

in 1751, with the two striking up a quick friendship, and the older man acting as a personal tutor to Rittenhouse, exposing him to Greek and more modern scientific tracts and letting him access his impressive library. Their relationship was further cemented when Barton married Rittenhouse's sister.[67]

His public coming-out occurred in 1763 when the governor's secretary, Richard Peters, called on Rittenhouse to help in the dispute over the border between Pennsylvania and Maryland. This brought him to the attention of the intellectual and political base in Philadelphia and got him additional work as a surveyor for the proprietor in the disputed boundary line between Pennsylvania, Delaware, and Maryland, and the boundary between Pennsylvania and New York. His surveying career extended to working with William Smith, making surveys to connect the Delaware with Lake Erie by canal.

By the mid-1760s, Rittenhouse had grown bored with making clocks and began experimenting with other types of devices like a metallic thermometer, culminating in the building of his orrery, a mechanical device that tracks the movement of the objects in the solar system: Sun, planets, moons. The project took up a large part of his time and mental effort; the intense calculations, planning, and precise construction tested his skills. When complete, Rittenhouse's orrery showed that his grasp of mathematics, physics, and astronomy was second to none in Pennsylvania or all of North America.

> I did not design a Machine, which should give the ignorant in astronomy a just view of the Solar System; but rather astonish the skilful and curious examiner, by a most accurate correspondence between the situations and motions of our little representatives of the heavenly bodies, and the situations and motions of these bodies, themselves. I would have my Orrery really useful, by making it capable of informing us, truly, of the astronomical phenomena for any particular point of time; which, I do not find that any Orrery yet made, can do.[68]

Rittenhouse built his orrery to simulate the motion of Mercury, Venus, Earth, Mars, Jupiter, Saturn, and their known moons. Using the tables of the day while making his calculations, he set up an orrery so accurate that you could select any day 5,000 years before or after 1770 and make accurate observations of the planets and moon.[69]

> This machine is intended to have three faces, standing perpendicular to the horizon: That in the front to be four feet square, made of sheet brass, curiously polished, silvered and painted in proper places, and otherwise ornamented … The two lesser Faces are four feet in height, and 2 feet 3 inches in breadth … The whole may be adjusted to, and kept in motion by a strong Pendulum Clock, nevertheless, at liberty to be turned by the winch and adjusted to any time past or future.[70]

Over the course of three years, 1767–70, Rittenhouse worked on the orrery and when complete Princeton University purchased it. This brought condemnation from Smith and most of Philadelphia for selling it out of state, enough that his loyalty to Pennsylvania was called into question. He assuaged the anger by making a second, better one for the College and Academy of Philadelphia, which he completed in 12 months. It became a prized possession of the college and graced the seal of the University of Pennsylvania for several years.[71]

For these achievements, the College of Philadelphia bestowed on him a Master of Arts for "being well assured of the extraordinary progress you have made by a felicity of natural genius in mechanics, mathematics, astronomy, and other liberal arts and sciences, all of which you have adorned by a singular modesty and irreproachable morals."[72] The poet Joel Barlow paid tribute to Rittenhouse in his poem "The Vision of Columbus":

> See the sage Rittenhouse, with ardent eye,
> Lift the long tube and pierce the starry sky;
> Clear in his view the circling systems roll,
> And broader splendors gild the central pole.
> He marks what laws the eccentric wanderers bind,
> Copies creation in his forming mind,
> And bids, beneath his hand, in semblance rise,
> With mimic orbs, the labors of the skies.
> There wondering crowds with raptured eye behold
> The spangled heavens their mystic maze unfold;
> While each glad sage his splendid hall shall grace,
> With all the spheres that cleave the ethereal space.[73]

But still, Rittenhouse did not publish his observations and had no concrete accomplishments, as his superior clocks were being enjoyed privately by those who purchased them. For as grand as all this work is, it pales in comparison to Rittenhouse's efforts with the grand scientific event of the age, the Transit of Venus, in 1769.

The act of Venus passing in front of the Sun presents a tiny speck, one arc-minute across, for astronomers to observe and track. A little beauty mark sliding across the vastness of the Sun. As it did so in 1769, astronomers could use the measurements from recording precisely four contact points to determine the distance from the Earth to the Sun: what is called an astronomical unit. And then, from that, the distances could be figured out between all known celestial bodies. The idea was first theorized by famed comet finder Edmond Halley who, after journeying to St. Helena in 1677 to observe the Transit of Mercury, realized that "if two observers were widely separated in latitude, they would see a transiting planet move along different chords as it traversed the Sun. If each observer timed the transit from beginning to end, the shift in the planet's position—its parallax—could be calculated and used to determine the Earth-Sun distance, a separation called one astronomical unit (a.u.)."[74] He further theorized that the most accurate measurement would occur during the Transit of Venus. The Transit of Venus occurs in pairs that are separated by eight years, and the pairs happen more than a century apart. This rarity of occurrence has helped the transit loom large in the history of astronomy, and it excited astronomers for nearly a century as they waited for the next Transits of Venus in 1761 and 1769.[75]

Though they had more than enough time, the British planning in 1761 was rushed; the Royal Society of London was headed by future Astronomer Royal Nevil Maskelyne, who led an expedition to St. Helena while he sent another one to Sumatra that included Mason and Dixon. But the Seven Years' War put the travel plans in jeopardy. Mason and Dixon cut short their trip to Cape Town, South Africa, while Maskelyne's observations were plagued by cloudy weather.

What observations were made were tainted by significant variations in the times of contact amongst observers at the same site. This hampered efforts to better calculate the distance between the Earth and Sun. It also increased the pressure on making the most out of the 1769 transit.

Because much of this transit could not be observed across Europe, expeditions were dispatched across the globe, including Captain Cook's to Tahiti, where a third of his crew, including the Royal Society astronomer sent with them, would die of fever, and where the observatory set up on Tahiti was named Point Venus in its honor. Another astronomy team was sent to Hudson Bay.[76] However, since there was no guarantee these expeditions would make it on time (or at all) or they would not encounter poor weather conditions at the time of the transit, it was important to have as many observers as possible. The 1769 observation would yield the first reliable estimated distance between the Earth and the Sun. More practically, these observations also enabled more accurate calculation of longitudes, improving the accuracy of maps and sea charts.[77]

The American Philosophical Society was in correspondence with the Royal Society of London and joined in on the international effort to observe the Transit of Venus in 1769. Franklin had actually promoted Massachusetts as the only province capable of producing a team to go and observe the transit in America to Maskelyne. But Philadelphia was chosen as an observation site because more of the transit could be observed.

PHILOSOPHICAL

TRANSACTIONS.

PART II.

XLI. *Account of the Transit of* Venus *over the* Sun's *Disk, as observed at* Norriton, *in the County of* Philadelphia, *and Province of* Pennsylvania, June 3, 1769. *By* William Smith, D. D. *Provost of the College of* Philadelphia; John Lukens, *Esquire, Surveyor-General of* Pennsylvania; David Rittenhouse, A. M. *of* Norriton; *and* John Sellers, *Esquire, one of the Representatives in Assembly for* Chester *County; the Committee appointed for that Observation, by the* American Philosophical Society, *held at* Philadelphia, *for promoting useful Knowledge. Communicated to the said* Society, *in Behalf, and by Direction, of the Committee, by Doctor* Smith; *and to the* Royal Society *of* London, *by* Nevil Maskeline, B. D. *Astronomer Royal.*

GENTLEMEN,

Read Nov. 23, 1769.   AMONG the various public-spirited designs, that have engaged the attention of this Society since its first institution, none

VOL. LIX.   P p   does

Title page of the William Smith, David Rittenhouse, and John Lukens account of their observation of the Transit of Venus in the very first printing of the *Transactions of the American Philosophical Society*. (*Account of the Transit of Venus Over the Sun's Disk, as Observed at Norriton*)

Three different teams at three different locations around and near Philadelphia were agreed upon. One would be stationed in the State House garden, another at Cape Henlopen, and the third at the Rittenhouse farm in Norriton.[78]

Rittenhouse calculated the anticipated times and explained the importance of the transit to the Philosophical Society. The proprietors, the Assembly, and other public institutions chipped in to provide the funds and supplies to make observations successful. They supplied the Cape Henlopen observation with a telescope, timekeepers, and other instruments; they also erected a platform observatory behind the State House and furnished it with a powerful reflecting telescope, micrometer and other instruments. This observatory would go on to serve as the stage for the first reading of the Declaration of Independence.

For the most part, Rittenhouse had to build his observatory himself, which he started in November 1768 and finished in April 1769. He personally constructed much of the equipment used at Norriton, although Smith secured him a telescope from Thomas Penn and an astronomical quadrant from the surveyor general of New Jersey.[79] Rittenhouse was left to handle much of the preparation at his observatory; Smith wrote: "Our other engagements did not permit Mr. Lukens, or myself, to pay much attention to the necessary preparations; but we knew that we had entrusted them to a gentleman on the spot, who had, joined to a complete skill in mechanics, so extensive an astronomical and mathematical knowledge, that the construction, use, and management of all the necessary apparatus are perfectly familiar to him."[80] Rittenhouse fabricated an equal altitude instrument, a transit telescope, and a timepiece, and spent months determining the latitude and longitude of the observatory, rating the clocks, and making preliminary computations.[81]

The observation at Norriton was filled with tension. The days leading up to the transit were rainy and cloudy, leading to apprehension on the part of those doing the observing: Rittenhouse, William Smith, and John Lukens, surveyor general of Pennsylvania. The night before the rain abated and the skies cleared, making for perfect conditions on June 3, the day of the transit, as Smith recalled: "The weather became perfectly clear in less than the space of one hour, and continued the day following, as well as the day of the transit, in such a state of serenity, splendor of sunshine, and purity of atmosphere, that not the slightest appearance of cloud was to be seen in the whole heavens."[82]

Smith was stationed at the reflector telescope inside the observatory while Rittenhouse and Lukens took control of the refractors outside. Rittenhouse and Lukens had three assistants: one to prop up their heads as the telescopes would be at extreme angles and the other two to relay signals from the observatory. At 2:10:30 p.m., when Rittenhouse had predicted first contact, Smith called out to everyone to be attentive. It was at this moment that Rittenhouse fainted. He had been battling an illness in the weeks leading up to this, and that weakened state, combined with the excitement and anticipation, proved too much. After being the first one to announce the presence he made no comment for six to seven minutes, which most likely means he was out during that period. Lukens missed first contact because he was ostensibly scanning around.[83]

> The Sun was so intensely bright on the day of the transit, that it was found best, early in the forenoon, to lay aside the coloured glasses, brought with the reflecting telescope from England; and to put on deeply-smoked glasses, which Mr. Lukens prepared in their room; and which gave a much more beautiful and well-defined appearance of the Sun.[84]

Smith described the tenseness felt among the group as they waited for that first contact:

> And to do the company justice, during the 12 minutes that ensued before the first contact, there could not have been a more solemn pause of expectation and silence, if each individual had stood ready to receive the sentence that was to give him life or death. So regular and quiet was the whole, that, far from hearing a word spoken, I did not even hear the feet of the four counters, who had passed behind me from the windows to the clock; and I was surprized, when I rose up and turned to the clock, to find them all there before me, counting up their seconds to an even number.[85]

Then Venus finally slipped into view, as Rittenhouse attested:

> As Venus advanced, the point of the pyramid still grew lower, and its circular base wider, until it met the light which crept round from the points of intersection of the two limbs: so that when half was entirely surrounded by a semicircular light, best defined on the side next to the body of Venus, which continually grew brighter, till the time of the internal contact. Imagination cannot form any thing more beautifully serene and quiet than was the air during the whole time; nor did I ever see the Sun's limb more perfectly defined, or more free from any tremulous motion; to which his great altitude undoubtedly contributed much.[86]

Smith observed:

> All at once, I saw something strike into it like a watry pointed shadow, appearing to give a tremulous motion to that part of the Sun's limb … This appearance was so different, the disturbance on the Sun's limb so undulatory, pointed, ill-defined, waterish, and occupying a

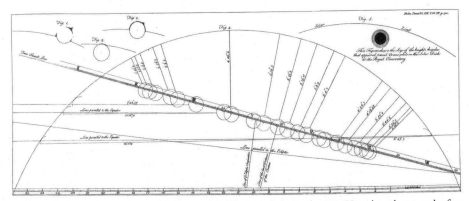

David Rittenhouse's observational drawing of the Transit of Venus, showing Venus's path across the face of the sun. (*Account of the Transit of Venus Over the Sun's Disk, as Observed at Norriton*)

larger portion of the limb than I expected, that I was held in a suspence of five or six seconds, to examine whether it might not be some small skirt of a watery flying cloud.[87]

And for the next four and a half hours, the three observed Venus as it floated across the face of the Sun. Rittenhouse immediately started on the calculations and calculated the Sun's distance at 92,940,000 miles. Today, it is estimated at around 92,955,807 miles.[88] The 1769 Transit of Venus observations were the centerpiece of the first volume of the *Transactions of the American Philosophical Society* and helped to establish the American Philosophical Society's reputation on an international level.[89] The Americans provided their observations and findings to the British, who used them as part of their own calculations. The Philadelphia transit mission was more of a statement of intent from the city and American scientific community showing that they were on the same level as their counterparts anywhere else in the world.

The Transit of Venus did more than any other event of the period to bring together the leading men of the city in a common cause. They worked together in the name of science. While science brought them together, it was politics—vicious partisanship—that drove wedges between all of them and would set the stage for the coming Revolution.

CHAPTER SEVEN

Pamphlets, Paxtons, and Politics

Political landmines lay strewn throughout Philadelphia over this period, testing relationships as old partnerships crumbled and new ones formed around local politics and colony-wide controversies leading to confrontations with the Crown. For Philadelphia's part, the last quarter century of its colonial existence saw a maturing of political rancor swirling around, clashing, raising tensions with little resolution until that final break happened, setting America on the path to Revolution.

Franklin was at the center of things as usual. But as he was away in London attending to the political business of the Pennsylvania Assembly, new political leaders emerged in Philadelphia and steered the city in a tug of war between the proprietors and the Quaker Party. An absent father to his colony, Thomas Penn played a significant role in creating the political situation in the city and across Pennsylvania. His bravado and inability to compromise with the Assembly helped to create the political conditions that ensured support for the revolutionary cause when the time arrived.

~

Conflict existed between the Assembly and proprietors as early as the 1740s. The coming of the Seven Years' War placed increased strain on the relationship, and as this animosity grew it came to define Pennsylvanian politics for the next decade. Thomas Penn inherited majority control of the proprietorship in 1746, which he shared with his brother Richard, upon the death of their father, John Penn. Since he was the eldest, he owned three-quarters of the estate and handled colony affairs on his own. He immediately started issuing orders to his governors in Pennsylvania to oppose any attempts at taxing his land by the Pennsylvania Assembly.

That the Assembly assumed the right to tax the Proprietor's land dates to the 1701 charter, that created the system of government in Pennsylvania. A unicameral legislature of 34 members, popularly elected, made up the Pennsylvania Assembly. This was supplemented by a Provincial Council whose members acted as advisors to the governor. The Penns had not lived in Pennsylvania for a long time and appointed governors to act as their executives. In the years before Thomas Penn took over, the Assembly operated with a great deal of autonomy and took advantage of the Penns' hands-off approach, wresting away much power at the proprietor's expense, which Thomas Penn sought to reverse. Penn harbored great unease about the Assembly and saw that it would not waste any opportunities to take advantage of him. So, he spent his time and effort ensuring his personal lands were not taxed rather than seeing to appropriately governing Pennsylvania. He issued strict instructions to his governors but being an ocean away hindered any effective attempt at governing.

Portrait of Thomas Penn, proprietor of Pennsylvania during this period and major antagonist of the Pennsylvania Assembly. (*The Many Sided Franklin*)

The Pennsylvania Assembly was different from the other colonial assemblies. It was more heterogeneous with a diverse mixture of nationalities and religions. It met and adjourned at its pleasure, not subject to dissolution from the governor. The speaker of the Assembly wielded unusual power for the time, such as nominating members to committees and the ability to check any stalling tactics from the opposition party.[1]

This growing tension and animosity between Penn, his supporters in Pennsylvania, and their opponents in the Assembly was exacerbated by the coming of the Seven Years' War, and the constant need to raise funds to support the war cause. Before the war, pacifist Quakers still dominated the Assembly but quickly lost control of their namesake party to the likes of Franklin. The first fight over defense spending occurred late in 1754 when Governor Robert Hunter Morris and the Assembly faced off over how to raise the money. The Assembly passed legislation that allocated £50,000 for defense spending, funded by a tax on estates, including the proprietor's lands. The governor vetoed the bill, saying the proprietor's land was exempted. This led to no bill being passed and no supplies being raised for the defense of Pennsylvania's vulnerable frontier, but matters were pressed after General Braddock's defeat in July 1755.

This kicked off an acrimonious back and forth between Penn and the Assembly that would be played out year after year throughout the Seven Years' War. Penn replied to the Assembly that since his family had granted the people of Pennsylvania the right to popularly elect the Assembly and then granted that body the ability to assess land and tax it, his lands should be exempted from taxation thanks to the historical generosity of the Penns. The Assembly did not see it that way, thinking that the Penns should make some sacrifices themselves while the amount they were being taxed was small compared to the whole, about 1 percent or £500. The governor argued that since the proprietors did not vote in the Assembly, they could not be taxed by them. This was an example of taxation without representation.[2]

Ultimately, for Penn and the governor, it was more the principle of the thing and not moving an inch to set a precedent for the Assembly to use. The Assembly was not budging either, in order to prevent an increase of the proprietor's power and to protect the colony's rights. The summer of 1755 and much of the fall were spent with this political sniping, as violence spread out on the frontier that required the Assembly's full attention. Pressure to make a deal was increasing, which finally came at the end of November after Thomas Penn offered up a £5,000 gift for the colony to use for defense in exchange for his property to be exempt from taxes. The Assembly agreed to count the gift as a tax. This deal was helped along by a gaggle of disgruntled western Pennsylvanians, a couple hundred strong, showing up in Philadelphia and demanding assistance. In a precursor to the Paxton Boys affair a few years later, Franklin spoke to this delegation, and the next day, a contingent of Quakers capitulated in the Assembly, and the bill was finally passed.[3]

When a new governor showed up in Philadelphia the following year, the Assembly butted heads with him over the same issues, which led to Franklin being appointed their agent to negotiate directly with Penn in London regarding their list of grievances. These included the governor's lack of power, the circumvention of the Assembly's right to raise internal taxes by not allowing any taxes on the Penns' lands, and the Penns near complete control over the judiciary. Penn gave Franklin the runaround in London, taking his time after receiving from Franklin the list of grievances. When he did finally respond to them, he brushed them all off, saying he had a "Right, and are so advised, to prevent any Injury being done" to his estate.[4]

As violence on the frontier required more and more money, the back-and-forth taxation battles between the Penns and the Assembly always ended with the latter capitulating and not taxing the proprietor's lands. This carried on until 1759, when the Assembly bribed the then-governor, William Denny, to pass a defense bill that finally allowed for the taxation of the proprietor's lands.[5]

With little legal recourse due to Denny's betrayal, Penn retaliated with an obfuscation campaign that included not providing the assessors with any information about his lands, which prolonged the assessment period, hoping that the law would be repealed by the time the information was finally collected. He lodged a formal complaint with the Boards of Council and Trade. The Assembly feared a repeal would tank the colony's economy as money had already been printed and was being distributed. The opponents of Penn saw royal government as the cure to their Pennsylvania political woes and would start a decades-long campaign to offer it up as a solution, only losing steam when the colonies lost faith in the ability of Parliament to govern anything. This campaign was spearheaded by the speaker of the Assembly, Joseph Galloway.

An exceptionally gifted and independent thinker who was the political boss of Pennsylvania for 20 years, as well as a key figure at the First Continental Congress and the leading Tory figure in the middle colonies during the war, Galloway's later defection to the British during the Revolution has retroactively clouded his importance in colonial political affairs. He was born in Maryland in 1731, with the family moving to just outside Philadelphia in 1740. Galloway did not attend college but "read law" and was admitted to the bar in the fall of 1749.[6] He started his own practice focusing on land disputes, and it grew rapidly. His clients came from the tri-state area, Pennsylvania, Delaware, New Jersey, where he reaped the benefits of the haphazard surveys being done and conflicts that came up as a result. He frequently tried cases against opponents like John Dickinson on his way to becoming Pennsylvania's most prominent lawyer.[7] Galloway's father and Dickinson's father were engaged in a lengthy legal land dispute when both boys were young, foreshadowing the clashes between the sons decades later.

At precisely the same time he was entering politics, the Quaker Party began shifting, following the death in 1750 of long-time religious and political leader John Kinsey that weakened the party and strengthened the proprietary faction. This led the new speaker of the Assembly, Isaac Norris, to court non-Quakers like Franklin and Galloway to bolster support. However, that support only went so far, as Franklin frequently clashed with Quakers over additional funding for frontier protection.[8]

In 1755, Galloway began his anti-proprietary political journey by teaming with William Franklin and George Bryan to write up a piece that claimed Thomas Penn's friends were working with the French to overthrow the Assembly, while also bashing William Smith's position at the college as a *quid pro quo* for his political writings.[9] This would lead to a

Portrait of Joseph Galloway, speaker of the Pennsylvania Assembly and leader of the influential Assembly Party, the strongest provincial party in all of the colonies. (New York Public Library)

partnership with Benjamin Franklin in 1756 that would dominate Assembly politics in Pennsylvania for the next 20 years, while in the process turning the Quaker Party into America's most potent assembly faction.[10]

Galloway led the Assembly charge, battling Penn and his governors throughout the upheaval brought about by the Seven Years' War, as each new spending bill brought about new rounds of acrimony between the Assembly and the proprietors. The continued exemption of Penn's estates from taxes from 1755 to 1758 led members of the Quaker Party (also referred to as the Assembly Party) to consider Thomas Penn to be little more than a tax dodger. It would result in Franklin's first mission to England to enter into head-to-head negotiations with Penn to reform the Pennsylvania government but not to replace it, "to solicit the Removal of our Grievances, occasioned by Proprietary Instructions."[11] The 15-month negotiations failed, and the two became mortal enemies; after December 1758, Penn refused to see Franklin. The military threat on the frontier ceased from 1760, so the Assembly no longer had to bow down to every proprietary demand. This led to several years of stalemate between the Assembly and the proprietors.

All this set the scene for 1763, when a new governor, John Penn, arrived, a nepotism hire as he was Thomas's nephew who had racked up lots of debt in England and obtained black-sheep status in the Penn family. He arrived in Pennsylvania at the end of October, only to find himself thrust knee-deep into the Paxton Boys saga.

~

The Paxton Boys revolt has its foundations in the policies of Galloway and the Philadelphia establishment. As more and more European settlers populated the western counties of Pennsylvania, the Assembly did not grow in number of seats or redistrict to account for the rise in population in the west, as a result there was disproportionate representation that benefited Galloway and his power base in and around Philadelphia.[12] The counties on the Schuylkill dominated the Assembly and the Quaker Party, which meant legislation was also disproportionately centered around eastern concerns. Hugh Williamson put it succinctly: "For God's sake, are we always to be slaves, must we groan forever beneath the yoke of three Quaker Counties." Westerners placed the blame on the Quaker leaders and the Assembly and not on the governor or the proprietor. The feeling was that eastern politicians did not understand or want to understand their unique issues.[13] Because of this animosity, Philadelphia politicians had little impetus to make any changes.

Further tensions existed in the west since that area was on the frontlines of the Seven Years' War, bearing the brunt of violence and hostilities, while eastern assemblymen squabbled with the governor and proprietor over taxation of Penn's land. Delaying passage of the funding bills meant increased hardships for the Westerners.

When Pontiac's War, a Native American uprising in the Great Lakes region, flared up in the summer of 1763 with a series of violent incursions along the frontier, settlers and inhabitants from the backcountry fled east, crowding in towns while the governor and the Assembly could not pass any legislation to fund a defense bill to provide additional soldiers and relief for the west. The backcountry settlers were greatly suspicious of Native Americans who lived amongst white European settlers. This intense fear and hatred ultimately led to the massacres by a riotous group from the town of Paxton that marched to a Native American village in Lancaster County on December 14 and killed six Conestogas while burning and destroying their houses and property. The mob, consisting of primarily Scots-Irish Presbyterians, returned on December 27 and murdered the 14 Conestogas that escaped the earlier attack, including the women and children.[14]

Late in December 1763, rumors began spreading of the possibility that the Paxton mob might march toward Philadelphia and kill the peaceful Moravian Lenape and Mohicans who had been brought there for their protection. This led to a scramble in Philadelphia to find them a safe new home. They passed through New Jersey on their way to New York, where they were denied entry. While they were on their journey out of the city and the province, tensions abated for the time being.

Carton depicting events surrounding the Paxton Boys' march on Philadelphia that shows Franklin going to meet with the marchers in Germantown. (*The Many Sided Franklin*)

However, members of the Paxton Boys were preparing for their return with Captain Robinson, who was responsible for transporting the Native Americans, saying, "If they return to Philada & our People should Get mad again on our Frontiers & come down, We shall certainly have many lives lost as this seems to be a Determination to try who is Strongest."[15]

By the end of January 1764, the Native Americans were on their way back to Philadelphia, and discontent was quickly brewing on the frontier as a result. The men of Paxton began forming companies and collecting arms and funds for a new march on the city.[16] They passed by David Rittenhouse's place, where he remarked on their state:

> About fifty of the scoundrels marched by my work-shop—I have seen hundreds of Indians traveling the country and can with truth affirm, that the behaviour of these fellows was ten times more savage and brutal than theirs. Frightening women, by running the muzzles of their guns through windows, swearing and hallooing; attacking men without the slightest provocation; dragging them by the hair to the ground, and pretending to scalp them; shooting a number of dogs and fowls—these are some of their exploits.[17]

At the beginning of February, things came to a head when the march reached nearby Germantown. There were rumors that thousands were moving toward Philadelphia, but in reality, there were no more than 250. Benjamin Franklin rose to the occasion, acting as chief adviser to Governor John Penn, and the Franklin home became the unofficial headquarters for Philadelphia's preparations for the Paxton Boys. Spies stationed along the road of the marchers provided valuable intelligence:

> Sunday, February 5, they appeared in Germantown. Monday, Philadelphia residents made the trip to Germantown to give the "Hickory Boys" (what they called themselves) a look.[18]

And a tense night gripped the entire city.[19]

Woodworks were erected around strategic points in the city, and 12 cannons were loaded with grapeshot. Philadelphians themselves had mixed feelings about it all. Many favored the Paxton Boys and their complaints with the Assembly, saying they would face no resistance from large swaths of the population. Many others were passive supporters, primarily Presbyterians. The German population of the city, too, refused to bear arms to repel any Paxton invasion.[20]

> Tuesday, Franklin, accompanied by Benjamin Chew [the governor's attorney general and advisor], Willing, and Joseph Galloway, went out to Germantown to meet with the Paxton crew meeting with them in a large room at a tavern. They met for several hours and eventually agreed to disperse the group and have them go home, and the assembly and Governor will hear the grievances of the Westerners. Two leaders were selected, Matthew Smith [who was directly responsible for the murders of Native Americans that started off the whole ordeal] and James Gibson, to draw up an official declaration of grievances.[21]

This served to relieve the threat to Philadelphia. Still, the west stewed, particularly after Galloway and the Assembly Party summarily ignored their list of grievances as they moved on to reignite the royal government scheme. And there erupted shortly after a prolonged pamphlet war on the streets of Philadelphia.[22] This war saw an unprecedented amount of literature being put forth by Philadelphia's many printers; over the summer of 1764, 63 pamphlets and some of the earliest political cartoons in the colonies were printed, distributed, consumed, and debated in the city.[23]

More pamphlets were generated over the Paxton Boys than any previous issue in Pennsylvania history and they ran the gamut of formats from songs and plays to essays, parodies, and caricatures, many of which acted as a precursor to the revolutionary era a few years later.[24] Both supporters of the Paxtons and their opponents contextualized the march within the larger issues of the times and marketed their works to a broader audience. In the cartoons produced, Franklin was often depicted as an onlooker cheering on the Quakers to win elections while also betraying them or anyone else to get an office.[25]

The Paxton supporters were more successful in portraying Quakers as frauds and hypocrites, all too happy to proclaim their pacifist ideals when it was frontier families facing violence. When it was their own safety on the line, however, they would do anything to protect themselves.[26] The Paxton affair managed to bring together Germans and Scots-Irish and made the Quakers and the Assembly appear unrepresentative, inconsistent, and insincere.

The biggest issue was Governor Penn's refusal to sign a new spending bill unless it included verbatim language already agreed to concerning the taxation of the proprietor's lands at no higher than the lowest rate of any uncultivated lands. This kicked off a massive PR blitz as the Assembly wanted to shape public opinion and saturate Philadelphia and Pennsylvania with royal government propaganda.[27]

Franklin led the media storm through the *Pennsylvania Gazette*, printing thousands of copies of the Assembly's resolves and messages between the Assembly and John Penn. The leaders in the Assembly sent messengers to every house in town to announce a mass meeting to discuss a petition for royal government at the State House in April 1764. They distributed free liquor to get signatures to protest the proprietary government, in the end managing to gather 3,500 signatures.[28]

This started a flurry of pamphlets and letters to newspapers, including ones from David James Dove, whose anti-Quaker pamphlets defended the Paxtons and blamed the Quakers and the Assembly for the predicament that led to the march. Hugh Williamson, a professor at the college, wrote another anti-Quaker screed where he claimed the Quakers were in a conspiratorial cabal with the Native Americans and actively worked to stall bills because they did not care about the frontier folk. Isaac Hunt defended the Quakers and Assembly Party, studying each religion and its suitability to govern, and concluding that the Quakers were the most virtuous and wise. Franklin and Galloway each contributed their own pamphlets, which led to more anti-Quaker pamphlets. At the end of the Assembly's May session, they approved a committee to draw up a petition to the king for a change in government. The next day, John Dickinson showed up to the party.[29]

Dickinson delivered a powerful speech in the Assembly arguing against the royal government. He argued that the timing was wrong, and Pennsylvania already held many privileges that other colonies did not, foremost among them being freedom of religion. The fear was real that the Church of England could be established as the official religion under royal control. He made a logical and legalistic argument against the change in government, which formed the biggest obstacle to Franklin and Galloway. The speech was turned into a pamphlet, with Smith writing the preface. It would prove very influential in swaying voters in October.

Galloway responded with his own speech/ pamphlet and provided counters to Dickinson's arguments. He could not resist taking personal jabs at Dickinson and Smith, calling Smith a "common enemy to the Liberties of America." Smith did not take it too personally, but Dickinson did and challenged him to a duel, kicking off a feud between the two that lasted throughout the war. Dickinson called Galloway a "magnanimous bug" who was "addicted to the occult sciences."

THE

SPEECH

OF

JOSEPH GALLOWAY, Esq;

ONE OF THE

MEMBERS for PHILADELPHIA COUNTY;

In ANSWER to the

SPEECH of JOHN DICKINSON, Esq;

Delivered in the HOUSE of ASSEMBLY of the PROVINCE of PENNSYLVANIA, May 24, 1764.

On Occasion of a PETITION drawn up by Order, and then under the Consideration of the HOUSE, praying His MAJESTY for a ROYAL, in Lieu of a PROPRIETARY GOVERNMENT.

WITH A

PREFACE by a MEMBER of the ASSEMBLY.

Audi et alteram Partem.

PHILADELPHIA Printed;

LONDON Reprinted, and Sold by W. NICOLL, in St. Paul's Church-Yard. M DCC LXV.

[Price Two Shillings.]

1764.

Title page of the pamphlet version of Joseph Galloway's speech calling for a royal government for Pennsylvania, a cause that Galloway never really gave up on. (*The Speech of Joseph Galloway, Esq.*)

This culminated with the two coming to blows when Galloway struck Dickinson with a cane outside of the State House when Dickinson copped to writing an anonymous pamphlet attacking Galloway. They tussled and were separated.[30]

The problem Galloway had was that he did not put forth any explanation as to why a change in government was needed, beyond disdain for the proprietors.[31] With Smith's arrival back from England fresh off securing his freedom from the Privy Council, he used clergymen from around Philadelphia and Pennsylvania to support the opposition to changing to a royal government, and these clergy managed to gather 15,000 signatures on a petition against the effort.[32] All of this activity set the stage for the election that October, with the issues surrounding the Paxton Boys and royal government prompting citizens to debate and to choose sides.[33]

The election would be the closest in the colony's history. The polls opened for two days, and the summer of pamphleteering brought voters out in record numbers. Both sides rounded up as many as they could, bringing lame and aged citizens into the polls on chairs. All told, 4,000 votes were cast, and Franklin and Galloway were defeated. Galloway lost the Speakership and a seat altogether in the Assembly. The Proprietary Party successfully sounded the alarm of the loss of control that would have stemmed from changing the government, with Dickinson proclaiming, "Have we not SUFFICIENTLY FELT the effects of royal resentment? Is not the authority of the Crown FULLY ENOUGH EXERTED OVER US?"[34]

The tumultuous year of 1764 provided a coming-out party for John Dickinson, who would soon become one of the greatest political minds of the colonial era. Dickinson was born in 1732 and raised in Kent County, Delaware. His father was a successful grain grower who served in the local Assembly and as a County Court Judge. Dickinson studied law in London in the 1750s, and when he came back, he quickly built a highly successful legal practice by putting in long hours to the point of exhaustion. His practice and investments in land and commercial endeavors made him a wealthy man.[35]

A

R E P L Y

TO

A P I E C E

CALLED THE

S P E E C H

OF

JOSEPH GALLOWAY, Esq;

By JOHN DICKINSON.

" Yes, the laſt pen for freedom let me draw,
When truth ſtands trembling on the edge of law.
Here, laſt of Britons! let your names be read ;
Are none, none living? Let me praiſe the dead,
And for THAT CAUSE which made your fathers ſhine,
Fall by the votes of their unhappy line."
POPE.

PHILADELPHIA Printed :
L O N D O N,
Re-Printed for J. WHISTON and B. WHITE, in Fleet-ſtreet,
MDCCLXV.

Title page of John Dickinson's pamphlet, *A Reply to a Piece called The Speech of Joseph Galloway*, from the tumultuous summer of 1764. (*A Reply to a Piece Called The Speech of Joseph Galloway*)

While not a member of the Society of Friends, he shared many of their sentiments and held Quaker beliefs thanks to being so intimately involved with them and their culture.[36] He frequently suffered from debilitating illnesses, headaches, and chest pains, and was quick to temper, leading to some prominent quarrels with Galloway in 1764, John Adams in 1775, and James Madison in 1787.[37]

Though 1764 proved raucous, 1765 would be even more monumental to the colonies as a whole. The first order of business for the new Assembly was to respond to a letter from the Rhode Island Assembly calling for a collaboration between colonies to present a united front against stamp duties.

Parliament inserted itself into the political discourse of every one of the colonies when it began deliberating the passage of the Stamp Act in the spring of 1764. Just the hint of this external taxation was enough to throw the colonies into a collective fury that helped cement them together like no other event had before. The Act would end up overshadowing local political affairs, placing many of them on the

One of the first American political cartoons showing a crowd outside the city's courthouse on Market Street in the excited build-up to the contentious election of 1764. (*The Many Sided Franklin*)

back burner until the repeal of the Act came in March of 1766. Even after that, tempers still ran hot.

Multiple factors ratcheted up Great Britain's national debt, not the least of which was a seven-year-long war that simultaneously enlarged the empire while also stirring up hostilities with the Indigenous population. The leaders in Parliament were put off by the colonials' aversions toward being taxed and believed that colonials needed to share the burden of supporting the empire like any other colony. They believed that the North American colonies were inferior to Great Britain and subject to being controlled just like everyone else. Revenue was needed to keep the empire afloat, and support the British troops stationed along North America's frontier.[38]

The Proprietary Party was ready to strike when news of the Stamp Act reached Pennsylvania in May 1765. They argued that this was positive proof that Parliament and the British government wanted to deny Pennsylvania its liberties. Dickinson quickly released a pamphlet attacking a speech Galloway gave in 1764 and warning of encroachments to their liberties if placed under royal control, timely on the heels of the Stamp Act. Dickinson led the vocal opposition while Galloway and the Assembly Party remained quiet.[39]

The Assembly Party was stunned by the outcry against the Stamp Act and the support the Proprietary Party received. It became dangerous to be even remotely pro-Parliament in public. Even though the Assembly Party did not favor the Stamp Act or care much for Parliament, it managed to look like it supported the Act and compounded its mistakes when one of its leaders, John Hughes, became a ministerial agent.[40]

Hughes's appointment provided the Proprietary Party the proof that the Assembly Party was conspiring to hand Pennsylvania over to the Crown. Galloway was trying to position his party as one of moderation, showing dislike but also wanting reconciliation while trying to paint the Proprietary Party supporters and leaders as violent revolutionaries. He made his plea under the guise of "Americanus," arguing Americans should oppose the Stamp Act, but not with loud talk or violent action; new alternative means of taxation should be sought.[41] His efforts focused on preventing violence and rallying moderates against the Proprietary Party in an effort to get reelected and gain control of the Assembly.[42]

Fueled by hostility sparked by the Stamp Act, Proprietary Party leaders helped raise a mob on the evening of September 16 to attack the houses of Hughes, Galloway, Franklin, and Samuel Wharton. Galloway gathered his loyalists, the White Oaks, an 800-strong association of ship carpenters and mechanics, and placed them all over town to quiet down any semblance of violence, and the mob retired.[43] Bells rang throughout the city. Bonfires blazed on Philadelphia's streets.[44]

On October 5, the ship carrying the stamped paper and Hughes's commission arrived, and thousands gathered at the State House. There were many calls for Hughes to resign his post and for his house to be torn down, and the White Oaks were again mobilized to protect Hughes and his home. Galloway and others struck a deal with Hughes that he wouldn't enforce the Stamp Act in Pennsylvania until other colonies did.[45]

Galloway and the rest of the Assembly Party managed to prevent the violence and significant property destruction seen in other major cities in America, like in Boston where protestors hung in effigy the stamp collector there, beheading the effigy, and then ransacking his house.[46] Despite Parliament's actions, he remained suspiciously loyal during the Stamp Act crisis, so much so that people charged him with wanting the Act. While he opposed Parliamentary taxation and was happy to have the Act repealed, he was more alarmed by the response than the Stamp Act itself. There was a great outcry, leading him to be called a Tory.[47]

All of this was happening on the eve of the next Assembly election, which would be hotly contested again and full of vitriolic claims (one public slander was that Chief Justice William Allen had sex with one of his enslaved women, and another that Ben Franklin had actually authored the Stamp Act). Rumors flew that Galloway had tried to keep Pennsylvania from sending representatives to the Stamp Act Congress. These public tirades showcased the Proprietary Party's specialization in libel, and demonstrated to the public that the Assembly Party had no good comebacks other than blanket denials.[48]

What it lacked in mastery of the political dark arts, the Assembly Party made up for with its machine politics. Galloway had systematically built up a highly organized political infrastructure that his opposition could not match. He realized that the failure of 1764 rested upon ability to recruit votes, so his party adapted by rounding up German immigrants to naturalize them, making them eligible to vote. They bribed men in taverns with drinks to secure their votes, and the White Oaks ferried voters into to the State House to cast their ballots. All of these maneuvers led John Penn to describe the Assembly Party political machine as a "Macedonian Phalanx not to be broken by any force that can be brought against them in this Country."[49]

Polls were open for three days from October 1 to 3 to ensure voters had enough time to cast ballots, resulting in massive turnout: nearly 80 percent of eligible voters participated. It was an Assembly Party landslide, with it claiming all eight seats from Philadelphia County, the one city seat, eight seats in Chester, and four seats in Lancaster County.[50]

Victory for the Assembly Party meant a return to the movement to shift government control to royal authority. Franklin, who had been in England since November 1764, was instructed to continue working in England towards a royal government.[51]

~

The Stamp Act served as the springboard for another central Philadelphia political figure, Charles Thomson, who would be a lynchpin in galvanizing Philadelphia to the revolutionar cause to action and following along with the rest of the colonies.

He was born in Gorteade, Ireland, on November 29, 1729. His mother died while Thomson was still very young, and his father sailed for America with Charles's siblings in 1739. On the voyage over, though, his father died, orphaning him in the middle of the Atlantic. Upon arriving in New Castle, Delaware, Charles was placed in the care of a blacksmith, and when he overheard talk of being apprenticed to him, he promptly ran away. While on the road, a lady took an interest in the lad and placed him in the school of Francis Alison at Thunder Hill, in southern Chester County, Pennsylvania.[52]

Thomson was intellectually curious, easily picked up new languages, and was politically ambitious. He was of the prime movers behind restarting the Junto in 1750 with other young bright Philadelphians, which led to Franklin helping to get him appointed as a tutor in Greek and Latin at the Academy of Philadelphia, the predecessor of the

Profile of Charles Thomson, the Sam Adams of Philadelphia, who helped steer the city toward radical action against the British. (*Philadelphia: A History of the City and its People*)

University of Pennsylvania. He taught there and at the William Penn Charter School throughout the 1750s.[53]

During the 1750s, he acted multiple times as the secretary to conferences with Native Americans, working tirelessly on their behalf and securing their confidence. Secretaries at treaty conferences served a vital function as they were responsible for accurately recording the proceedings, but many would not do so in order to manipulate the treaties after the fact for European colonists' advantage. Thomson took this to heart and went out of his way to make sure the various tribes received justice, striving to make sure nothing dishonest happened on his watch:

> I need not mention the importance of the business we are come about. The welfare of the province and the lives of thousands depend upon it. That an affair of so much weight should be managed with soberness all will allow. How then must it shock you to hear that pains seem to have been taken to make the King drunk every night since the business began. The first two or three days were spent in deliberating whether the King should be allowed the privilege of a clerk. When he was resolute in asserting his right and would enter on no business without having a secretary of his own, they at last gave it up, and seem to have fallen on another scheme, which is to unfit him to say anything worthy of being minuted by his own secretary. On Saturday, under pretense of rejoicing for the victory gained by the King of Prussia, and the arrival of the fleet, a bonfire was ordered to be made and liquor given to the Indians to induce them to dance. For fear they should get sober on Sunday and be fit next day to enter on business, under pretense that the Mohawks had requested it, another bonfire was ordered to be made and more liquor given them.[54]

The Native Americans so respected him that he was adopted into the Delaware tribe and given the name "Wegh-wu-law-mo-end" meaning "The Man Who Tells The Truth." He became a leading authority on Native Americans and even wrote a book on Native American affairs, *An Enquiry into the Causes of the Alienation of the Delaware and Shawenese Indians from the British Interest* (1759).[55]

In the 1760s, Thomson took up being a merchant, opening a general store on Market Street that sold various goods, and he spent five years almost wholly dedicated to this store. Through it, Thomson gained an intimate knowledge of the trans-Atlantic trade which put him at the forefront of the Stamp Act debate. The economic downturn following the end of the Seven Years' War prompted him to take more notice of politics.[56] The Stamp Act crisis was his first foray into politics, and he embraced the colonial cause wholeheartedly, eventually becoming known as the "Sam Adams of Philadelphia."[57]

Following the passage of the Stamp Act, no one was as active as Thomson in opposing the measure in Philadelphia. In a letter to Franklin, he expressed the frustrations in the city:

> Arbitrary courts are set over us, and trials by juries taken away: The Press is so restricted that we cannot complain: An army of mercenaries threatened to be billeted on us: The sources of our trade stopped; and, to compleat our ruin, the little property we had acquired, taken from us, without even allowing us the merit of giving it; I really dread the consequence. The parliament

insist on a power over all the liberties and privileges claimed by the colonies, and hence require a blind obedience and acquiescence in whatever they do: Should the behaviour of the colonies happen not to square with these sovereign notions, (as I much fear it will not), what remains but by violence to compel them to obedience. Violence will beget resentment, and provoke to acts never dreamt of: But I will not anticipate evil; I pray God avert it.[58]

Thomson's actions during the crisis won him support from the mechanics, artisans, and small shopkeepers whose political awareness and voice were growing and becoming keener due to the Stamp Act and the falling prestige of the Assembly.[59]

When Bostonians sent a letter to Philadelphia seeking support for resolutions they were adopting as a result of the Townshend Acts in 1768, which imposed taxes on imports into the American colonies, there was a meeting at the London Coffee House, where Philadelphia merchants opposed general boycotts, saying it was a ruse on the part of Boston to get them to destroy their trade, and they refused to act. During that meeting, Thomson implored action, saying, "If we do not exert ourselves now when TAXED by Parliament … when shall we exert ourselves?"[60]

He began working with Dickinson to try to get prominent Philadelphia merchants to protest against the Townshend Acts, and to unite with Boston and New York merchants.[61] Thomson had some success in guiding the mechanics and artisans to join forces with the more radical merchants to put pressure on the conservative merchants, who eventually came into line with the non-importation agreement in place in Boston at the time. A letter from Franklin to Thomson was published concerning the Townshend Acts: "In short, it appears to me that if we do not now persist in this measure till it has had its full effect, it can never again be used on any future occasion with the least prospect of success, and that, if we do persist another year, we shall never afterwards have occasion to use it."[62] This partnership with Franklin aided Thomson's organizing efforts with radicalized merchants, traders, and mechanics. Ultimately, it was this faction that moved Pennsylvania towards revolution and independence.[63]

The quest for royal government remained a central political point for the Assembly Party until 1768. Then, as yet another incursion by Parliament against the rights of Pennsylvanians, the Townshend Acts spelt the death knell for royal government and further fractured the political balance in the commonwealth. Former opponents became new allies and vice versa. Franklin and Galloway's once strong friendship and partnership floated away as Franklin embraced the patriot cause, and Galloway increasingly became more loyal to the Crown. Thomson and Dickinson were at odds with one another but became the closest of associates and collaborators.[64] After the Stamp and Townshend Acts, it became clear that Parliament threatened Pennsylvania's liberties just as much as the proprietors did, which meant the end of the quest for royal government and the beginning of the next chapter in Pennsylvania politics.

The Stamp Act and the Townshend Acts generated a powerful boycott of British-made goods in the form of the non-importation movement. The leading advocate of this was John Dickinson, who initially proposed it in his *Letters from a Farmer in Pennsylvania* to get merchants to see the value of commercial coercion. Meanwhile, Galloway and other Assembly party members actively worked to sabotage intercolonial efforts against the Townshend Acts.[65]

Dickinson was 35 at the time of the *Letters* and was one of the most successful lawyers in the American colonies. He wrote *Letters from a Farmer in Pennsylvania* anonymously, posing as a farmer living the ideal American life, one distinctly Pennsylvanian in its simplicity and rationality.

Through a series of 12 letters published from New Year's Eve in 1767 into 1768, in Galloway's new newspaper, the *Pennsylvania Chronicle and Universal Advertiser,* Dickinson pulled from his legal creativity to show the difference between regulating trade and the power to tax—only one of which he argued that Parliament possessed.[66]

Frontispiece of John Dickinson's *Letters from a Farmer in Pennsylvania* showing a portrait of the author. *Letters from a Farmer* was one of the most influential works in the colonies prior to open conflict erupting between Great Britain and the American colonies. (*Philadelphia: A History of the City and its People*)

Let these truths be indelibly impressed on our minds—that we cannot be happy without being free—that we cannot be free without being secure in our property—that we cannot be secure in our property, if, without our consent, others may, as by right, take it away—that taxes imposed on us by parliament, do thus take it away—that duties laid for the sole purposes of raising money, are taxes—that attempts to lay such duties should be instantly and firmly opposed—that this opposition can never be effectual, unless it is the united effort of these provinces—that, therefore, benevolence of temper toward each other, and unanimity of counsels are essential to the welfare of the whole—and lastly, that, for this reason, every man amongst us, who, in any manner, would encourage either dissention, diffidence, or indifference between these colonies, is an enemy to himself and to his country.[67]

The letters proved influential in coalescing the colonial ideas around British policies. Throughout his writings, Dickinson opposed the idea of taxation without representation, which became central to the colonial rally-cry. He argued that as British subjects, American colonists should enjoy the same rights and protections as those living in the homeland. Never before had a work united the ideas swirling up and down and all around the colonies. It instantly made Dickinson a national figure.

Aiding Dickinson's arguments and angering the colonies even more was Lord Hillsborough, Secretary of State for the Colonies for was instrumental in implementing the Stamp Act and Townsend Acts, issuing a circular letter on April 21, 1768, which called on the governor to dissolve any colonial assemblies that supported non-importation. This riled up those who were previously apathetic or opposed to non-importation and threatened Pennsylvania's most precious right to Assembly. It proved a disaster to Galloway and the Assembly Party, for it showed that a royal government would be as arbitrary as the proprietor's. And it showed that sucking up was to no avail.[68]

This led to Franklin telling Galloway in a letter from August of 1768 that Hillsborough had told him that the dream of a royal government was dead. Franklin said it was a dead matter to him as well, and he wouldn't be advocating for it anymore. This caused a rift between Franklin and Galloway that never was repaired. The quest for royal government became caught up in the larger colonial-wide politics of the passage of the Stamp Act and, along with the subsequent passage of the other hated acts by Parliament, led to a shift in Pennsylvania's political fascinations at the time.

The atmosphere in Philadelphia was such in 1770 that Galloway sought election again not from the city, but from Bucks County. He won, but the Quaker Party would never wield quite the power that it once had. The urban working-class support it enjoyed defected to become an entity all its own, with Dickinson and Thomson pulling the strings with help from Franklin.

This new entity began calling itself Whig and had Presbyterian leanings. After the repeal of all but one of the Townshend Acts (the tax on tea remained), Philadelphia merchants did away with the non-importation agreement, and from 1770 to 1773, they continued as if nothing had happened—business as usual with Britain. However, there was a dramatic rise in smuggling. In Philadelphia, wealth was becoming more concentrated at the top while the rest of society stagnated.[69]

In those brief early years of the 1770s, an anxious calm settled over Philadelphia. Thomson worked tirelessly, but ultimately unsuccessfully, to keep the fervor of the protests against British rule alive. He organized a "Committee of Tarring and Feathering" to prevent ships carrying tea from docking in Philadelphia in defiance of the boycott. However, the Assembly pursued its own agenda of not stirring the pot with the home country.[70]

Tensions increased across the colonies throughout the early years of the 1770s. Additional taxes were still being levied, such as the Tea Act and the subsequent protest in Boston in the form of the Boston Tea Party. This kicked off retaliatory measures by Parliament and the Crown, the Intolerable Acts, which saw the closure of Boston Harbor in a measure passed on March 31, 1774, to take effect on June 1, 1774. Riders spread out, carrying the news across the colonies, calling for the other colonies to unite with them to stop importations from Great Britain and the West Indies, to preserve their liberties so that "justice, social happiness, and freedom" could triumph over oppression.[71]

Philadelphia learned of the Boston Port Act on May 14, and Paul Revere arrived on the 18th with an appeal from Boston's Committee of Correspondence. Thomas Mifflin, Joseph Reed, and Charles Thomson started planning how to gain support for intercolonial action. This rested upon the help of John Dickinson. At the same time, the city's moderate and conservative factions were already moving to quell any radical behavior in the city's response to Boston's appeal. Knowing this was the case, Thomson and his compatriots called a meeting for May 20 at the City Tavern and planned to outflank these conservative voices and commit Philadelphia and Pennsylvania to aiding Boston, engaging in intercolonial cooperation, and defending America's liberties.[72]

Working with Reed and Mifflin, Thomson knew they needed John Dickinson in order to garner support for the non-importation agreement. Thomson laid out his strategy:

> As the Quakers, who are principled against war, saw the storm gathering, and therefore wished to keep aloof from danger, were industriously employed to prevent anything being done which might involve Pennsylvania farther in the dispute, and as it was apparent that for this purpose their whole force would be collected at the ensuing meeting, it was necessary to devise means so to counteract their designs as to carry the measures proposed and yet prevent a disunion, and thus, if possible bring Pennsylvania's whole force undivided to make common cause with Boston. The line of conduct Mr. D. had lately pursued opened a prospect for this. His sentiments were not generally known. The Quakers courted and seemed to depend upon him. The other party from his past conduct hoped for his assistance, but were not sure how far he would go if matters came to extremity, his sentiments on the present controversy not being generally known. It was therefore agreed that he should attend the meeting, and as it would be in vain for Philadelphia or even Pennsylvania to enter into the dispute unless seconded and supported by the other colonies, the only point to be carried at the ensuing meeting was to return a friendly and affectionate answer to the people of Boston, to forward the news of their distress to the southern colonies, and to consult them and the eastern colonies on the propriety of calling a congress to consult on measures necessary to be taken. If divisions ran high at the meeting, it was agreed to propose the calling together the Assembly in order to gain time.[73]

Their plan was to start the meeting out strong with an aggressive push to demand that the city enforce a unilateral boycott of British goods that would last until the

Intolerable Acts were repealed. They would hammer this idea to alarm moderates, when Dickinson would stand up and put forward a more cautious response that would carry the meeting. The plan wholly depended on Dickinson, who had slid away from public service in the early 1770s. Mifflin, Reed, and Thomson rode out to meet Dickinson at his Fairhill residence mid-day on the 20th and spent the next couple of hours convincing Dickinson of the plan, which he agreed to. They rode off for the meeting separately to avoid appearing to be the conspiratorial cabal they were.[74]

Two hundred of Philadelphia's leading merchants, lawyers, and citizens packed the City Tavern. Reed stood up first, read the letters from Boston, and laid out the crisis to the crowd. This was followed by Mifflin and Thomson demanding that Philadelphia put into place the non-importation boycott that the Boston committee requested. Thomson's passions and lack of sleep overwhelmed him, and he fainted.[75]

It was now the merchants' part, and they played the role just as Thomson's trio had predicted, shouting down the demand and expressing their disapproval of the proposal. The meeting was spiraling out of control. Dickinson rose, quieted the crowd, and spoke about petitioning Governor Penn to call the Assembly into session to consider this crisis. When he said his piece, Dickinson walked out. Thomson revived and called the meeting to order and put forward a motion to petition the governor while replying in support of Boston's letter, which the group quickly approved and called for the creation of a committee to draft the reply to Boston, send correspondence to the Southern colonies, and create and circulate a petition to the governor.[76]

It was a victory for Thomson and Philadelphia's radical element to get support for Boston while joining in the growing intercolonial resistance to British policy—a far cry from trying to suck up to the Crown to try and obtain special considerations, which was the policy that Galloway had endorsed to no avail.

This led to the first of a series of special committees that would meet adjacent to the Assembly and in lieu of it when it was out of session—filling in the gap in the legislative branch, though the committees were outside the bounds of any type of legality. The only real opponents to the radical elements were wealthy Quaker merchants with no actual political adherents, just their financial might and decades of solidifying their political roots. When Governor Penn received the petition, he immediately rejected the idea, which only benefited the radical movement. Penn's rejection of the petition kicked off additional public assemblies and sparked rapid political action. The summer of 1774 was spent building another committee, which would become known as the Forty-Three, to address the changes and challenges facing the colony. The most important outcome of the Forty-Three was that it prompted the creation of a solidified resistance movement. In less than a month, Thomson had convinced Philadelphians of the need to be united amongst the colonies and to pursue a policy of resistance through committees and mass meetings.[77]

On June 17, the Massachusetts House called on committees from the other colonies to meet in Philadelphia on September 1. Other colonies followed suit and began electing delegates. The Assembly, still led by Galloway, convened in June 1774 and tried to get ahead of the message by approving the Continental Congress, but said that only they, as the legally elected representatives of all of Pennsylvania, had the authority to select delegates for the Congress. The Forty-Three on July 21 marched two by two to the State House and formally presented their *Resolves and Instructions to the Assembly* and demanded that three of their members be included as delegates to the Congress.

> The Trust reposed in you is of such a nature … that it is scarcely possible to give you particular Instructions respecting it. We shall therefore only in general direct, that you are to … exert your utmost Endeavors to form and adopt a Plan, which shall afford the best Prospect of obtaining a Redress of American Grievances, ascertaining American Rights, and establishing that Union and Harmony which is most essential to the Welfare and Happiness of both Countries. And in doing this, you are strictly charged to avoid every Thing indecent or disrespectful to the Mother State.[78]

The Assembly criticized the Committee's work and its very existence, took its deliberations behind closed doors, and ignored the instructions and nominees.

On the eve of the First Continental Congress, the radicals won two bureaucratic victories in getting the Congress to meet in Carpenter's Hall rather than the State House and selecting Charles Thomson as the secretary, a position he would hold until 1789. It was a local triumph for Philadelphia's mechanics and artisans to get away from the conservative hotbed of the State House.[79]

Guiding Galloway throughout 1774 and 1775 was his desire to exclude Dickinson from gaining any sort of prominence, as they had been battling one another for the previous decade over royal government. Galloway believed resisting British policy would upset the ever-shifting balance of power within Pennsylvania politics, jeopardizing his power in the process.[80]

In the build-up to the First Continental Congress, Dickinson led the charge in Philadelphia that called for a Provincial Congress, for Pennsylvanians to gather and discuss their positions going into the upcoming Continental Congress. However, Galloway ignored these recommendations and proposals, excluded Dickinson and his supporters from being delegates to the Continental Congress and told the delegates to work on a reconciliation plan with Great Britain. Galloway then appointed himself the chairperson of local arrangements for the arriving colonial delegates, which garnered him much hatred in and around Philadelphia. This culminated in the October election, while the Continental Congress was going on, when Dickinson won his Assembly seat back. The Assembly removed Galloway as speaker, and elected Dickinson as a delegate to the Congress.[81]

Delegates of the First Continental Congress arrived in Philadelphia in the fall of 1774 to discuss the Boston Port Bill and the so-called Coercive Acts jointly. For most of these leading individuals in the colonies, it was their first time in Philadelphia, and they marveled at the city. The Philadelphia of 1774 was flourishing. It was the largest city in British North America, home to a bustling port and over 30,000 residents. More houses were built in Philadelphia in 1774 alone than in Boston in the preceding decade. The city and suburbs extended for two miles along the Delaware river, which served as a thriving waterfront, "the great mart of America." The market on High Street was the most impressive in America and rivaled those in Europe. The hospital, the college, the Bettering House, the State House, and the growing walls of the new jail served as ornaments for the city's grand appearance. One new visitor called Philadelphia "the most regular and best laid out city in the world."[82]

Members of the Congress visited the Library Company, whose collection was available to the delegates for free. They toured the Pennsylvania Hospital and the Poor House. They gazed upon the Schuylkill Falls and visited the Welsh fishing club, Fort St. David's. They dined with the members of the American Philosophical Society. Even John Adams admitted, Philadelphians "have more Wit, than We. They have Societies; the philosophical Society particularly, which excites a scientific Emulation, and propagates their Fame."[83]

Galloway was grumpy throughout, condemning the Congress even as it assembled in his city. He called into question its motives, consistency, and sincerity as any delegates were trying to find a way to couple empire with liberty, which Galloway did not think possible. Galloway was fearful of any movement towards independence hampering his ability to work with other delegates.

On September 6, Congress agreed to appoint a committee to "state the rights of the Colonies in general, the several instances in which these rights are violated or infringed, and the means most proper to be pursued for obtaining a restoration of them." Committee members decided to figure out what constituted American rights before working on any sort of declaration of rights. This led to the debate surrounding natural rights and rights from the English constitution.[84]

This was followed on September 8 by Galloway taking part in the debate on the sources of colonial liberty, with some wanting to base that liberty on natural law and English common law precedents that protected the rights of subjects. Others thought it was a dangerous precedent to place it in natural law and thought the English constitution was sufficient enough. Galloway stepped in to support only the English constitution.[85]

Throughout the proceedings, Galloway time and time again asserted himself in the arguments and debates. He was trying hard to make it all about himself. He believed that the colonies needed representation, but at the same time, as British and colonial subjects, they were subordinate to the Crown and Parliament. And he felt that he alone could bridge these two truths. Others couldn't understand the inherent set-up or try to rectify it.[86]

Galloway became withdrawn and secretive and pushed to petition the king to induce the ministry to accept negotiations in an effort at reconciliation, which showed his high belief in the power of words and wording. He managed to raise awareness of independence through his constant accusations that it was what the leaders of the colonial cause wanted, even though it was a sentiment that was seldom raised. All he managed to do was to get himself ignored, increasingly ostracized by other delegates, and isolated from the proceedings. He proposed a Plan of Union that would create an American branch of Parliament to hold jurisdiction over all colonial legislation; it was debated and thrown out, even expunged from the record, with Galloway repudiated for being too cautious while the delegates endorsed the Suffolk Resolves, a set of resolutions passed as a result of the situation in Boston that asserted colonial rights and condemned British actions, and adopted non-importation.[87]

This was a different game from internal Pennsylvania politics, and Galloway seemed not to wrap his head around the fact that he could not control everyone involved in the proceedings. He thought highly of himself and his powers of persuasion but was not prepared to have his ideas ignored, or even openly derided, by the body.[88]

Many of the Congress delegates who arrived in Philadelphia wanted to meet the author of the *Letters from a Farmer in Pennsylvania*, and Dickinson did not disappoint. He wined and dined the delegates at his estate and impressed them with his support for their cause. Once he became a delegate, Dickinson wrote and revised several significant documents, emerging as an important political figure in Congress and Pennsylvania.[89]

The Congress adjourned at the end of October of 1774. The most important achievements were a pact amongst the colonies to boycott British goods starting in December of that year and a pledge to reconvene the following year, setting up 1775 to be a pivotal moment in American history and the history of Philadelphia.

CHAPTER EIGHT

1775: A Change is Going to Come

As 1774 concluded and the dawn of 1775 crept over the horizon, the American colonies teetered on the precipice. The coming year would see the battles of Lexington and Concord, the fighting at Bunker Hill and the siege of Boston, American forces seizing Fort Ticonderoga, and the formation of a new colonial army headed by George Washington. It was a transitional year, when all that came before it crescendoed only to either blossom or crash in 1776.

Philadelphia acted as the nerve center conducting the cause, where the struggles from the previous quarter-century all played out throughout the year. The political actors remained front and center. The abolitionist movement took its first organized steps. Benjamin Franklin would make his return. And the Second Continental Congress would convene in the city and lead the united colonies in revolution against Great Britain and on the path towards independence.

January

At the start of 1775, Pennsylvania was on a political knife edge. Moderate and conservative factions became emboldened in their opposition to the increasingly radical shift in rhetoric going on around them in the city. They were gathering to prevent these elements from pushing for further reforms and policies beyond what Congress already proposed.

The Pennsylvania Assembly had met on December 5, 1774 to consider the proceedings from the First Continental Congress, and by the 10th, they had approved the acts unanimously. The Assembly then elected Edward Biddle, John Dickinson, Thomas Mifflin, Joseph Galloway, Charles Humphreys, John Morton, and George Ross, the same delegation who attended the first congress, as delegates to the Second Continental Congress. As the non-importation agreement loomed, Philadelphia merchants ramped up their purchase of British goods for the coming freeze in trade.

In response to the First Continental Congress's call for the Association, a collective agreement among the colonies to boycott British goods owing to their oppressive measures, a committee, the Sixty-Six, convened to ensure Pennsylvanians adhered to this, urging policies to support non-consumption and economic independence. The Sixty-Six sought a self-sufficient economy to withstand the loss of imports by having Pennsylvanians craft their own textiles, produce their own paper, distill their own liquor, and manufacture their own salt. The new committee also sought production of saltpeter and gunpowder, and it established local societies around the province to encourage local production. As a result, throughout the year, the industrial output of Pennsylvania began to increase slowly but steadily, providing increased political power to those in charge of these efforts.[1]

Under this pressure, the Pennsylvania Assembly acquiesced. On January 25, it agreed to execute the provisions of the Association and took steps to prepare for the defense of Pennsylvania.

February

Parliament informed the king on February 7 that Massachusetts was in a state of rebellion, and stood ready to support him. The king responded 10 days later, asking Parliament to increase the land and naval forces in America.[2]

Later in the month, David Rittenhouse delivered an "Oration on Astronomy" to the American Philosophical Society. A packed audience, including the governor, the Assembly, and many of the leading citizens, came to hear Rittenhouse deliver a lecture on his astronomical exploits and receive a first-class education on the cosmos.[3]

Rittenhouse finally moved to Philadelphia in 1770, renting a house on the southeast corner of Seventh and Mulberry Street. The following year, the Assembly awarded him funds to create a third orrery, saying it and its creator served as "a testimony of the high sense which this House entertains of his mathematical genius and mathematical abilities." Just after moving to Philadelphia, his wife, Eleanor, passed away, a shock that stayed with him for the rest of his life.[4]

In 1773, he started to provide Philadelphia and Pennsylvania specific astronomical projections for local almanacs, whereas before they were copying those from other places like Boston. This gave him additional publicity, and his name started to take on a stamp of authority. As someone who had all but stayed out of the political realm, it was to great interest that he delivered his oration on February 24, 1775.[5] And he interjected his scientific thoughts on tyranny and his wish for those in Europe to embrace those in the New World:

> But when I consider, that *luxury* and her constant follower *tyranny*, who have long since laid in the dust, never to rise again, the glories of Asia, are now advancing like a torrent irresistible, whose weight no human force can stem, and have nearly compleated their conquest of Europe; luxury and tyranny, who by a vile affectation of virtues they know not, pretend at first to be the patrons of science and philosophy, but at length fail not effectually to destroy them agitated I say by these reflections, I am ready to wish—vain wish! That nature would raise her everlasting bars between the new and old world; and make a voyage to Europe as

impracticable as one to the moon. I confess indeed, that by our connections with Europe we have made most surprizing, I had almost said unnatural advances towards the meridian of glory; But by those connections too, in all probability, our fall will be premature. May the God of knowledge inspire us with wisdom to prevent it; Let our harbours, our doors, be shut against luxury.[6]

March

Franklin, still in London, wrote to the Assembly with the letter arriving on March 8, informing them that the king received Congress's petition graciously and said he would pass it along to Parliament:

> This is just to inform you, that having received the Petition of the General Congress to the King, we immediately communicated the same to Lord Dartmouth Secretary of State for the American Department, as the regular Official Method, and that by which only we could have Expectation of obtaining an Answer. His Lordship this Day inform'd us, that he had laid the same before the King, that his Majesty had been pleased to receive it very graciously, and to say, it was of so great Importance, that he should, as soon as they met, lay it before his two Houses of Parliament.[7]

When it was printed in newspapers around the colonies, the news excited the public, who thought Congress had saved America.

However, old political hands like Galloway knew otherwise, and he made one last push to save the union with the publication of his pamphlet *A candid examination of the mutual claims of Great-Britain, and the Colonies, with a plan of accommodation on constitutional principles*, in March of 1775. In it, Galloway argues for Parliament's authority over the colonies and severely criticizes the decisions of the First Continental Congress:

> When we see the country we live in, where agriculture, elegant and beneficial improvements, philosophy, and all the liberal arts and sciences have been nourished and ripened to a degree of perfection, astonishing to mankind; where wisdom and sound policy have even sustained their due authority, kept the licentious in awe, and rendered them subservient to their own, and the public welfare; and where freedom, peace and order, have always triumphed over those enemies to human happiness, oppression and licentiousness; now governed by the barbarian rule of frantic folly, and lawless ambition: When we see freedom of speech suppressed, the liberty and secrecy of the press destroyed, the voice of truth silenced: A lawless power established throughout the colonies, forming laws for the government of their conduct, depriving men of their natural rights, and inflicting penalties more severe than death itself, upon a disobedience to their edicts, to which the constitutional magistracy, in some places by force, and in others willingly submit:—The property of the subject arbitrarily, and without law, taken from him, in pursuance of those edicts:—When, under their influence, America is arming in the east and west, against the parent state:—I say, when we see the colonies, needlessly, and while the path to their safety and happiness is plain, and open before them; thus pushing on with precipitation and madness, in the high road of sedition and rebellion, which must ultimately terminate in the misery and ruin: It is the duty of every man of least abilities, to try to reclaim them from their folly, and save them from destruction, before it be too late.[8]

His calling out the entire Continental Congress and the people of the city led to bitter criticism. Franklin, when hearing of Galloway's plan, wrote to him: "I have not heard what objections were made to the plan ... nor would I make more than this one, that when I consider the extreme corruption prevalent among all orders of men in this old rotten state, and the glorious public virtue so predominant in our rising country I cannot but apprehend more mischief than benefit from a closer union." Its publication started off another mini pamphlet war that spring with Dickinson and others publishing a rebuttal, *An Address to the Author of the "Candid Examination"*, and of course, that could not stand and led to a rebuttal from Galloway.[9]

Thomas Paine, in the *Pennsylvania Journal*, would write a passionate plea against slavery in the same vein as Anthony Benezet, attacking the institution on moral grounds and the hypocrisy of white Americans saying they were enslaved to the British when they were, in turn, enslaving so many others:

> A
> CANDID EXAMINATION
> OF THE
> MUTUAL CLAIMS
> OF
> GREAT-BRITAIN,
> AND THE
> COLONIES:
> WITH
> A PLAN of ACCOMMODATION,
> on Conftitutional Principles.
>
> By the AUTHOR of LETTERS to a NOBLEMAN on the Conduct of the AMERICAN War.
>
> NEW-YORK:
> Printed by JAMES RIVINGTON, early in MDCCLXXV.
> AND NOW
> Republifhed by G. WILKIE, in St. Paul's Church-Yard;
> and R. FAULDER, in Bond-Street.
> MDCCLXXX.

Title page of Joseph Galloway's pamphlet, *A Candid Examination of the Mutual Claims of Great-Britain, and the Colonies.*

> That some desperate wretches should be willing to steal and enslave men by violence and murder for gain is rather lamentable than strange. But that many civilized, nay, Christianized people should approve and be concerned in the savage practice is surprising and still persist, though it has been so often proved contrary to the light of nature, to every principle of justice and humanity, and even good policy, by a succession of eminent men, and several late publications.[10]

Benjamin Franklin would leave London to make his way back to Philadelphia on March 21, and on the same day Thomas Penn passed away. With him died the last vestiges of old Pennsylvania. The great adversary of the Assembly, of Galloway, and of Franklin was gone. His son, John Penn, became the chief proprietor, but following the Declaration of Independence, the Pennsylvania Assembly would dissolve the proprietorship once and for all.

April

On April 14, at the Tun Tavern on Second Street, 10 men gathered. Mostly the group was made up of Quaker artisans and small retailers influenced by the humanitarian message of Benezet and others. They were brought there by the increase in the number of cases where freed Blacks and other people of color were being kidnapped and sold back into slavery. Various reports were arising where this happened, but one case in particular troubled the assembled men. An Indigenous woman, Dinah Nevil (Neville), and her three children were brought to Philadelphia with the intention of selling them to a Virginian. While in the city, Dinah declared herself freeborn, and that she and her children were being illegally enslaved. Two Quaker men, Israel Pemberton and Thomas Harrison, took the opportunity to sue on her and her children's behalf for their freedom. The mayor wanted to examine the case further and kept the family at the city workhouse while he investigated the matter. Thanks to the Revolution, it took years of delays and appeals for a decision to be made, and it was ultimately determined that Nevil and her children were not illegally enslaved. At that decision, Thomas Harrison purchased the family in 1781 and granted them freedom.[11]

As a result of their deliberations that day, the 10 men formed "The Society for the Relief of Free Negroes Unlawfully Kept in Bondage," which in turn became the first antislavery society in North America. A committee was formed to handle the reports of kidnapped free Blacks, investigate each case, and report back to the society. The society would meet again in May, August, and November, with its lawyers intervening in other cases that year similar to Nevil's. The Revolutionary War brought a long

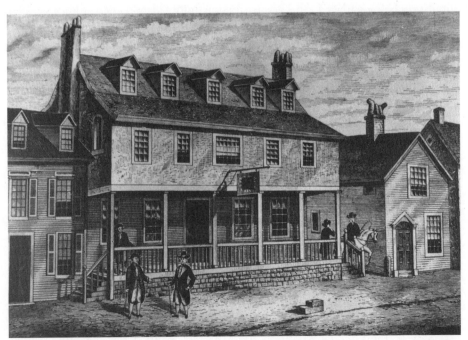

Here at the Tun Tavern the first American organization was created to combat the horrors of enslavement, "The Society for the Relief of Free Negroes Unlawfully Kept in Bondage," which after the Revolution would morph into the Pennsylvania Abolition Society. (National Archives)

pause in their actions, and they would not resume activity until 1784, with their minutes stating, "The National commotions that have prevailed for these last several years are the only reason why the company has not met together according to the rules established for its government." By then, the society had adopted a broader goal of freeing all enslaved people and turned into the Pennsylvania Abolition Society.[12]

Throughout the Revolution, Anthony Benezet kept calling out the hypocrisy of the cause for liberty while at the same time depriving Black enslaved peoples of their liberty: "How many of those who distinguish themselves as the Advocates of Liberty, remain insensible and inattentive to the treatment of thousands and tens of thousands of our fellow man." Benezet was a determined pacifist who also argued that if it was alright to violently resist British rule than it was equally alright for enslaved people to violently resist their enslavement. In the summer of 1783, two free Black people committed suicide in the city when they were charged as being runaway slaves. They had reached out across Philadelphia for help, but it all fell upon deaf ears, so instead of being re-enslaved, they chose death. This greatly affected Benezet, who spent the remaining months of his life trying to address the situation which led to their suicides.[13]

By 1775, only one in five of Philadelphia's Black population was free. By the end of the century, that number would dwindle to only 1 percent of the city's Black population being enslaved. This was partly due to Philadelphia becoming a popular destination for free Black people either from the South or the Caribbean in the waning years of the Revolution and the remainder of the 18th century. There was also an increase in the rate of manumissions as Quakers began a concerted effort to free all enslaved people. They formed committees at their meetings to apply pressure on members to free their slaves. This helped Philadelphia become the first large free Black community in North America, establishing itself as the center of free Black life in the United States.[14]

These advances, however, did not change many of the white residents' views that their Black neighbors were inferior and also unfit for freedom. But the strength of the Abolition Society and its prominent members, like Franklin and Benjamin Rush, led to growing feelings on the eve of the Revolution that ultimate freedom was near, aided by the increase in manumissions, the prevalence of anti-slavery pamphlets, and rumors that the British were going to free enslaved people if a break with the mother country did occur. So, in 1775, a somewhat hopeful atmosphere existed for the Black population of Philadelphia. However, as historian Gary Nash notes, "not a single document remains to inform us how Philadelphia's slaves and free Blacks might have viewed their world as the colonial era drew to a close."[15] The promise of those hopes would not be felt until 1780 and the passage in the Pennsylvania Assembly of the Gradual Abolition Act. The Act, while being the first piece of legislation to codify abolition in the New World and America, failed to free a single enslaved person and kept slaves who were born before its passage as enslaved people for life, and only freed enslaved people born after March 1, 1780, after 28 years of slavery, which also held true for any child born to them. Total abolition would not arrive in Pennsylvania until 1847.

~

April 24 was a day of celebration in Philadelphia. It was St. George's Day: a time to celebrate the patron saint of England and to toast the current king, George III. That day, Robert Morris was toastmaster at the lively festivities going on at the City Tavern when in burst a rider to disrupt the party. They brought news of the battles of Lexington and Concord, which took place on April 19 when British troops attempted to seize colonial military supplies at Lexington and clashed with colonial militia. The skirmishing continued on to Concord igniting the already simmering tensions between the American colonies and Britain. A riot briefly erupted inside the tavern and an electric shock coursed through the city.

The following day, 8,000 people crowded around the State House. They all pledged to defend the colony, the city, their rights, and their property. Pennsylvania's Committee of Correspondence took charge of military affairs in the city, preparing to train and supply the rapidly forming militias. This was all being done outside of the legal authority of the Assembly, which would not meet again until May 1. As the Assembly met, the new army of Pennsylvania was training outside on the grounds of the State House, leading to the martial atmosphere in the city.

Philadelphia was priming itself for war. The radical committee, the Sixty-Six, saw that it was inevitable and led the planning, putting pressure on the Assembly to raise the funds necessary for the defense of Pennsylvania. The moderate Assembly, still controlled by the likes of Galloway, did not want to be directly involved with any sort of armed resistance and only allocated a fraction of what was being called for. While the Sixty-Six wanted £50,000, the Assembly provided £7,000: £2,000 for defensive purposes and £5,000 for building stores. It would then adjourn and leave the Sixty-Six and the Committee of Safety in charge of Pennsylvania affairs until the next time it convened in June, hoping the military situation would be better understood at that time. The Committee of Safety was a 25-person organization that essentially became the executive branch for all of Pennsylvania for the remainder of the year. Half-moderate and half-radical, the Committee found common ground in furthering the armed resistance against the British.[16]

Robert Morris had sworn his allegiance to America and the colonial cause by being appointed vice president of the Committee of Safety, with Franklin serving as the president. With what funds and influence it possessed in the power vacuum, the committee was responsible for inter-province supervisory military powers, and Morris set about procuring gunpowder, organizing the militia, fortifying the river, and supplying military outposts, batteries, and battalions with ammunition and weapons.[17]

The building to the left with the awning is the City Tavern where on St. George's Day revelers first heard word of the battles of Lexington and Concord that brought the city to immediate action. (Library Company of Philadelphia)

May

Benjamin Franklin arrived back in Philadelphia on May 5 and was promptly elected by the Assembly to be a delegate to the Second Continental Congress, which was converging on the city.

As the Pennsylvania Assembly was wrapping up its lackluster session, the members of the Second Continental Congress convened in Philadelphia, on May 10, with the first session lasting until August 1, 1775, a total of 84 days. After this adjourned, delegates reported back to their colonial assemblies and committees and waited to hear about the response of the king to their petition and to make plans for the Second Continental Congress.[18]

Congress held no real authority to pass laws or levy taxes. It couldn't enact a draft or issue bills of credit, merely make recommendations. Each colony imbued their delegates with different instructions, mostly related to consulting, advising, and providing agreement that they should focus on restoring peace with Great Britain. Most of those there wanted to be a part of the empire, though as a more equal partner. Those attitudes shifted though, over the course of the Second Continental

Congress, as they became more and more hostile towards Britain, leading towards declaring their independence the following year. John Dickinson led the conservative faction as they held out hope for some sort of reconciliation with Britain and pushed for a second petition to the king.[19]

The State House acted as the regular meeting place for the Continental Congresses in Philadelphia, housing the 68 delegates. Committees did most of the work of Congress, and there would be 38 different committees throughout the Congress focusing on any number of topics. Day one of the Second Continental Congress saw the first committee being appointed. Work started off slowly, though, in the first two weeks of Congress when officers were elected, delegate credentials were read and approved, rules of parliamentary procedures were approved, and other bureaucratic measures were taken. This had John Adams complaining about the pace: "Our unweildy Body moves very slow. We shall do something in Time, but we must have our Way ... Such a vast multitude of Objects, civil, political, commercial and military, press and crowd upon us so fast, that We know not what to do first ..."[20]

At the beginning of the session, the day began for delegates at around 10 a.m., but as more and more business poured in, that crept up to 9 a.m. and then 8 a.m., with the day lasting to 3:30 p.m. at the beginning but stretching as late as 6 p.m. towards the end of the first session as the long sunny summer days allowed. They would meet six days a week and take Sundays off. The president called the daily session to order. The first order of business usually related to presenting any critical communications that he had received, where they were discussed by the whole, sent to the relevant committee, or sent to the "we'll get to it later" pile. Committees would report on the various issues that had arisen under the responsibilities, such as securing necessary supplies or finding the finances for those supplies, and, once presented, those reports would be debated and any recommendations coming from the reports or from the debate would be put up for a vote.

The out-of-town delegates were entertained daily by the people of Philadelphia, so much so that it started to affect the health of some. Thinking it a reflection not only of themselves but of the city, people of all stripes went to great lengths to put their best foot forward and offered elaborate hospitality. They saw it as an opportunity to show off, but by the end of the first session the mood was changing, and it became a more restrained atmosphere that stressed frugality and moderation. The delegates enjoyed the same festivities as the locals, as all delegates attended the commencement of College of Philadelphia on May 17.

John Adams was taken aback by the luxurious greeting he received from some of the inhabitants. Saying of one Quaker he dined with, "this plain Friend, and his plain, tho pretty Wife, with her Thee's and Thou's had provided us the most Costly Entertainment—Ducks, Hams, Chickens, Beef, Pigg, Tarts, Cream, Custards, Gellies, fools, Trifles, floating Islands, Beer, Porter, Punch, Wine ..." The following day he reported a similar spread, "Dine at Mr. Powells ... a most sinfull Feast again!

Everything which could delight the Eye, or allure the Taste, Curds and Creams, Jellies, Sweet meaths of various sorts, 20 sorts of Tarts, fools, Triffles, floating islands, whipped Sillabubs ... Parmesan Cheese, Punch Wine, Porter ..."[21]

One Philadelphian whose life became consumed by the proceedings of Congress was Charles Thomson. As secretary of Congress, he became the living embodiment of it. He was taking minutes, revising them, recording, publishing, and maintaining multiple sets of journals, while performing increasingly odd jobs for Congress that popped up, like issuing letters of marque and drafting correspondence from the Congress. Thomson kept not only the journals of the Continental Congress but a total of eight different sets of records.

June

On June 15, Congress elected George Washington as commander-in-chief of the new Continental Army. He would leave shortly afterward to be replaced as a Virginia delegate by Thomas Jefferson. Many issues were constantly popping up that required the Congress's attention, from political, military, Native American, and financial affairs, to securing the basics needed for the newly organized army, like gunpowder.

Painting showing John Adams nominating George Washington to be made commander of Continental Forces in the main Assembly room in the Pennsylvania State House where the Second Continental Congress met. (Library of Congress)

The summer months provided non-stop activity for the Congress. They spent their days in committee answering communications pouring in from various locales, drafting responses to those, creating a postal system in order to get those letters delivered, debating and passing more resolutions concerning trade, and considering Franklin's "Plan of Union". They were making plans for the defense of the colonies, and besides creating a Continental Army and choosing a commander-in-chief for it, they were busy debating and electing other generals and officers to fill out its ranks, creating a hospital department to oversee treatment for the wounded, and founding the first American Navy. In order to do all of this, they authorized a continental currency, issued bills of credit, and elected two treasurers to keep an eye on financial matters.[22] As John Adams complained, "Our debates and deliberations are tedious."[23] Simultaneously, Congress was developing the minutiae of governing and conducting a war while considering the bigger picture of the war and the campaigns, creating a long-term plan for fighting.[24]

This atmosphere created long working days for the delegates as they labored and debated and played politics in the sweltering heat of the summer of 1775. And many delegates, when the day's session was over, would retire to their quarters, which varied drastically, with some delegates boarded together while the more well-off ones like John Hancock rented houses all for themselves, to draft correspondence to their home assemblies and deal with any number of local and personal matters that arrived in the latest packet. Many delegates were worn out physically and exhausted with the grinding routine.

To blow off steam, delegates created private clubs where they could meet outside the pressures of Congress. They would visit the local taverns. The Treasury Committee regularly met at the City Tavern to conduct meetings. This allowed Philadelphians to hear firsthand the news going on in Congress. The city became a waypoint for soldiers heading to Northern battle zones or Southern troops returning home. It also became a place where troublesome prisoners were sent and housed in the new jail.

William Smith gave the first of three public orations on June 23. He spoke at Christ Church to members of the Pennsylvania militia and the Continental Congress. He extolled the actions being taken by the colonists due to Great Britain's "unconstitutional exactions, violated rights, and mutilated charters."[25] He justified the steps being taken to resist the colonial rule of Britain while still not looking back in anger "to the times of ancient virtue and renown" and looking ahead "to distant posterity." His next sermon, as part of the first Continental Fast Day to honor the battles of Lexington and Concord, and the occupation of Boston, offered prayers for forgiveness and invoked divine guidance for King George III, asking for both sides to stop and think about their previous fruitful and meaningful relationship and to restore that.

Then, in February 1776, he delivered a funeral oration in honor of General Richard Montgomery and the Continental soldiers and officers who died during the Canada Campaign. Speaking to a crowd of 4,000 that included all of the dignitaries in the city, after praising the sacrifice for liberty, he pivoted to provide the most direct call for restoration of the relationship between the colonies and England: "I am happy in knowing that ... the delegated voice of this continent, as well as of this particular province, supports me in praying for a restoration of the former harmony between Great-Britain and these colonies upon so firm a basis as to perpetuate its blessings, uninterrupted by any future dissension, to succeeding generations in both countries."[26]

At a funeral honoring those who gave their lives for the cause, his call for reconciliation did not go over well. And many who were in attendance did not wait long to push back. If anything, it showed that Smith had stayed consistent, but the times had changed around him. He followed that up with another strange chapter where he, through a series of letters printed in the papers of Philadelphia, provided rebuttals to Thomas Paine's *Common Sense*, which was first printed in January of 1776. Going under the name of Cato, Smith supplied the most vehement attacks against Paine's arguments, going point by point through *Common Sense* with a counter-narrative. It was a weird performance. Then, as now, *Common Sense* was and is hailed as a masterpiece of effective political rhetoric, and to try to bring it down brick by brick was a fool's errand. Even Paine said in his rebuttal to Cato's rebuttal, "Art thou mad, Cato, or art thou foolish? or art thou both? or art thou worse than both?" Smith's former pupil, Francis Hopkinson, got in on the fun, penning a "playful tract" that took aim at Cato and his foolishness, saying all he was doing was trying "to persuade the people to put their trust in the rotten tree [British colonial government] ... the people shall root up the rotten tree ... and Cato and his works shall be no more remembered among them. For Cato shall die, and his works shall follow him."[27]

This ultimately led Smith to be thought of as a loyalist, and matters became too hot for him in Philadelphia, particularly after the end of British occupation, when he was forced to flee to Maryland. His handful of years there were quite productive as he worked on founding two new colleges, Washington College and St. John's College. After the war, he made his way back to Philadelphia and continued at the college there, also continuing his land speculating ways in Central Pennsylvania, founding the town of Huntingdon. He passed away in 1803—one of the great and original antagonists.

As part of raising a new Continental Army, Congress voted on forming eight rifle battalions from Pennsylvania. The Committee of Safety was created to oversee the creation of these battalions: The Committee of Safety was just one of several institutions and groups exerting political and economic influence on the province. The assembly, local committees of observation, committees of militia officers, and others were representing and competing with one another. Conservative elements, the elder statesmen, warred with younger, radical zealots over who had political authority in the colony. Old political alliances faded in the winds of revolutionary change. New alliances forged by a new political elite of a different character grew out from the ranks of the militia, targeting those not loyal to the continental cause.[28]

Throughout June 1775, voluntary companies were forming, and the City Committee began pressuring the Assembly to recognize these voluntary associations as a regular organization. They wanted the Committees of Safety and Defense to act independently in case of an invasion and have discretionary power to raise funds through credit to meet the defensive needs of the colony. The Assembly agreed and handed over power to the Committee of Safety, then promptly adjourned until September. The Committee would fill in the gap while the Assembly was adjourned. Things were moving too fast for the Assembly to be effective leaders in times of war.

The Pennsylvania Committee of Safety began electing officers and making assignments for Pennsylvania's militia, with one of those being now-Dr. Robert Johnston. Following his education at the Academy and College of Philadelphia, Johnston had continued his medical education, taking a path laid down by Shippen and Morgan by attending the University of Edinburgh. Upon arriving back in Pennsylvania, Johnston moved to his family's home in Antrim Township in then Cumberland County, now Franklin County, and opened up a practice near Greencastle. He stayed there for a couple of years, seemingly content; however, with the outbreak of the Revolutionary War, he and his brothers headed the call and joined up to serve Pennsylvania and the American cause.[29]

Shortly after Johnston joined the Sixth PA Battalion, Washington ordered them to support the campaign in Canada. The Canada Campaign had begun in June 1775 as a way to cut off one entry point for British forces coming into America and to put to rest any British recruitment efforts to get the Six Nations involved in the war. After taking Montreal, Colonial forces were repelled at Quebec City, where they began a retreat down the St. Lawrence River. The Sixth Battalion arrived just in time to be thrust in as reinforcements during that retreat, seeing its first action at the Battle of Trois-Rivieres.

Johnston himself would have a long and storied service in the Continental Army, rising to be the director general of the Northern Department and later serving in the Southern Campaign, seeing to colonial prisoners of war in South Carolina. He was one of the last remaining surgeons serving the American cause when the Treaty of Paris formally ended the war.

July

During those long, hot summer days of July, John Dickinson reached the zenith of his political power when his Olive Branch Petition was sent to the king. Up to that point, he had been a shining example of the champion of American rights. Then afterward, he would systematically destroy that reputation.

He could not abandon his belief that reason would prevail, and the empire be saved. As a result, he urged sending another petition to the king in hopes of reconciliation. The petition called for a restoration of peace, appealing directly to King George III for him to address grievances and restore harmony between the colonies and the Crown, while still proclaiming loyalty to him. As part of it, Dickinson said the colonies would pay for the tea dumped in Boston Harbor. Outside of the petition, Dickinson started to argue that the timing for true independence was not right. No federal government existed in America. There was no foreign support. And speaking as a Pennsylvanian, an internal revolution was brewing, and no steady government existed. Like all other appeals to the King, the Olive Branch Petition was rejected. And a year later Dickinson would find himself the primary opponent in Congress to the Declaration of Independence, setting himself up to become one of the first American traitors.[30]

Portrait of the influential politician and lawyer John Dickinson, whose continual objections to independence meant he soon became scorned by the British and Americans alike. (National Portrait Gallery)

Meanwhile, his long-time political opponent suffered a quicker but similar fall from patriotic grace. The revolutionary fervor and the radical shift in Pennsylvania politics soured politics and public life for Joseph Galloway. This led him to leave Pennsylvania politics in the summer of 1775 to live on his country estate, rebuffing Franklin's attempts to get him to join the patriot cause. While at his country house in Trevose, he was like a prisoner as mobs visited his property regularly, threatening to tar and feather him, only to be deterred by what friends he had left. One gang even planned to hang him.[31]

Galloway considered himself retired from politics, but would have an infamous return during the British occupation holding various administrative roles, and afterward, he fled to England, where he continued to advocate for reconciliation with Britain.[32]

At the end of the month, two Philadelphians, Michael Hillegas, the owner of the music store, and George Clymer, were named joint treasurers of the Continental cause and began working towards organizing the financial morass the Continental Congress found itself in.

August

The First Session of the Second Continental Congress adjourned on August 1. For most, that meant returning home to report directly back to Congress. However, in Philadelphia, the radical local committees that had sprung up kept up their activities.

Throughout the year, these committees had begun usurping the power of the Assembly. They took it upon themselves to dictate policy for all of Pennsylvania and left the Assembly to play catch-up, and as a result, Pennsylvania was becoming more and more radical. The committees began aligning the province towards the goals of Congress and, within that, the radical, free-thinking elements. The still-sitting governor, John Penn, was all but ignored and did nothing but sign measures passed by the Assembly and appoint a few civil officials.

The committees represented a silent revolution in internal Pennsylvania politics from May 1774 up till July 1776. Over the course of this time, nearly 300 Pennsylvanians would end up serving on civilian or militia committees, many of which were new to the political arena. They were the artisans and mechanics who had been so vital to supporting Galloway during the Paxton Boys affair and helped back Thomson. In normal times, many of them would have never entered public service or politics, but this injection of new blood ushered out the old regime. Their passion changed the face of Pennsylvania politics.

The institutions that had been in place since Pennsylvania's founding, built into the province's charter and fought for and debated by the people of Pennsylvania for much of the 18th century, were quickly crumbling apart. While an elected oligarchy ruled Pennsylvania, the democratically elected leaders tended to come from the same class of landed, wealthy merchants, farmers, and lawyers. This new influx of political participation from more diverse fields and classes rapidly reshaped Pennsylvania. The old elites were being pushed aside, and they did not put up much of a fight.[33]

As a result, a series of radical committees was formed. They were short-lived and transformed into other committees, which spawned more committees as the situation necessitated. In August, the Sixty-Six would be getting a successor of 100 members (76 from the city and 12 each from the Northern Liberties and Southwark). This committee became known as the First One Hundred and was made up of artisans, retailers, and mechanics, all from the middle and working class of Philadelphia. It was nominally there to enforce the Continental Association focus on efforts to not consume unsold British imports and to control the prices of goods. But it had also morphed into suppressing dissent and making preparations for war. The members were all men. Women were not allowed to enter the political realm.

September

When the night of the second turned to the third, a hurricane, aptly named the Independence Hurricane, swept through Philadelphia. Amateur Philadelphia meteorologist Phineas Pemberton described the night: "Stormy and showery. A violent gale from NE to SE the preceding night with heavy rain, lightning, and thunder."[34] Luckily, the structures of the city were protected from the lightning by Franklin's lightning rods.

The Delaware and Schuylkill both rose high and flooded into the streets, entering into several businesses along Front Street. Damage was done to the docks and warehouses; as one observer put it: "Much damage in the stores on the wharves, among sugar, salt, and other perishable articles; wood, staves, plank, &c. was washed off the wharves."[35] Ships and other small craft at dock were battered with many being destroyed, meaning merchants took heavy losses. Ships riding out the storm on the river were violently grounded on the banks of the Delaware. While Philadelphia got off lightly, the storm caused severe damage up and down the coast from North Carolina to Newfoundland, leading to a total of 4,000 deaths.

At the beginning of the hostilities between the colonists and British forces, Elizabeth Graeme was away from the action going on in Philadelphia and having to make do with descriptions from friends who stopped out at Graeme Park. It also began to be increasingly tricky for Tories or those still loyal to Great Britain to live, work, and operate in the area. Her husband, Henry Fergusson, was very much for reconciliation with Great Britain, saying to Benjamin Rush at one point:

> Are then our resentments so high, is revenge so sweet a thing, that to distress Britain in a few particulars, we will expose ourselves to every horror the imagination can paint?—Our cities destroyed, our fields uncultivated, our plains strew'd with death and ruin and to what end all this? Why to be enslavd at last: for depend upon it when things are reduced to the utmost extremity, not only England and the other powers in europe will squeeze and harness us, but demagogues among ourselves will spring up to tear the vitals and suck the blood of this once happy happy country.[36]

His arguments grew louder, and many worried for his safety as expressing Tory sentiments in Philadelphia as 1774 turned to 1775 became a dangerous proposition. Finally, in September 1775, he left for Great Britain ostensibly on a business trip, and it would be the last time he would ever be at Graeme Park. And the last time Elizabeth would ever see her husband. Despite his letters exhorting her to be with him in London, she refused and remained in Pennsylvania. Following the war, Graeme Park was briefly confiscated by the Pennsylvania government for being the property of a loyalist. Elizabeth regained ownership after years of appeals and remained there, writing and publishing more of her poetry. Due to financial constraints, she was forced to start selling Graeme Park towards the end of the 18th century, and she would pass away there in 1801 at the age of 64.

It became policy in Philadelphia to identify and then ostracize loyalists. Groups, committees, and, in the city, a militia formed to seek out loyalists and harass them. This led to one dry goods retailer being reprimanded by a committeeman for trying to sell the remaining British linen in his possession. He hired Isaac Hunt to defend and represent him, who immediately challenged the Committee's right to regulate commerce. The case bounced around subcommittees and plenary sessions of the First One Hundred. After two weeks of deliberations and intense public pressure, Hunt agreed to publicly apologize for questioning the authority of the committee.

On the day of the public apology, September 6, 1775, 30 militiamen gathered Hunt from his home and escorted him around town in a cart for a couple of hours to make his apology to the townsfolk: "At every halt that was made, he rose and expressed his acknowledgments to the crowd for their forbearance and civility."[37] When the procession passed by the house of Dr. Kearsley, a known "extremely zealous" Tory, he threw open a window and fired a shot into the crowd. The militiamen stormed into his home and seized him. They chucked Hunt off the cart and replaced him with Kearsley, who they then started parading through the streets, and the people began throwing abuse upon him. As one who witnessed these proceedings later wrote:

> He was seized at his door by a party of the militia, and, in the attempt to resist them, received a wound in his hand from a bayonet. Being overpowered, he was placed in a cart provided for the purpose, and, amidst a multitude of boys and idlers, paraded through the streets to the tune of the rogues' march. I happened to be at the coffeehouse when the concourse arrived there. They made a halt, while the Doctor, foaming with rage and indignation, without his hat, his wig dishevelled and bloody from his wounded hand, stood up in the cart and called for a bowl of punch It was quickly handed to him; when, so vehement was his thirst, that he drained it of its contents before he took it from his lips.[38]

Later, Kearsley wrote to Parliament complaining about the patriots. These letters soon leaked out, and he was in hot water once again. A subcommittee of the First One Hundred formed to hear charges against Kearsley, whom they had arrested, and they searched his home for any other papers containing "base and cruel invectives against the liberties of America" but before the investigation could continue the Committee of Safety stepped in to take over jurisdiction of the case. The committee sentenced Kearsley to indefinite sentences in the jail at Carlisle, where he passed away during the war. Hunt left town and lived the remainder of his days in the Caribbean.[39]

A British Major Skene rode into the city and was quickly detained, and a guard stood watch at his lodgings at one of the taverns. As Alexander Gray recounted:

> I well recollect the day that the guard was paraded to escort him out of the city on his way to some other station. An immense crowd of spectators stood before the door of his quarters, and lined the street through which he was to pass. The weather being warm, the window sashes of his apartment were raised, and Skene, with his bottle of wine upon the table, having just finished his dinner, roared out, in the voice of a Stentor, God save great George our King. Had the spirit of seventy-five, in any degree, resembled the spirit of Jacobinism, to which it has been unjustly compared, this bravado would unquestionably have brought the major to the lamp post, and

set his head upon a pike; but as, fortunately for him, it did not, he was suffered to proceed with his song, and the auditory seemed more generally amused than offended.[40]

The second session of the Second Continental Congress reconvened on September 3, 1775, and continued undisturbed until December 12, 1776. During this period, there were a lot of comings and goings in and out of the city due to Congress's actions: orders, reports, messengers carrying news of the ever-increasing operations, and delegates leaving to investigate activities for themselves. Daily attendance was never high. Even on momentous occasions like the signing of the Declaration of Independence, there were 50 in attendance, though 90 or more delegates were, in theory, attending or supposed to be attending Congress.

October

The beginning of October marked another election in Pennsylvania, and it quickly became the most hotly contested one in Philadelphia since 1764. More so than any other election, a large number of candidates put their names forward for sheriff and coroner and for the city and county's Assembly seats. When the results came in, the Assembly had shifted firmly behind the call for armed resistance.

It quickly took up a bill for mandatory militia service for freemen, leveling a fine on those who would not serve. Petitions poured into the Assembly from the Committee of Safety, the First One Hundred, militia officers, Philadelphia's Committee of Privates, and the Quaker Yearly Meeting, some calling for conscription while others, the Quakers, said this would violate their religious freedoms and the charter of 1701.

This led to the passage in November of the new militia law that called for compulsory service. Every able-bodied freeman was to attend 20 drills in the spring and summer of 1776. Poor relief funds would be allocated to support families impacted by the loss of their families during this time. Miss a muster day, and a fine was levied against you. All troops in active service were placed under the direction of the Assembly or the Committee of Safety, following the same guidelines as the Continental Army. Included in the same bill was a hope for reconciliation with Great Britain and a repudiation of independence, something that would hinder the province's government as independence became more and more likely and accepted.[41]

~

John Morgan was a cautious patriot and was slow to come around to the continental cause. He held no strong political beliefs, generally respected British laws and customs, and had no great desire to shake the political foundations in place since it had been so prosperous for himself. Over the fall of 1774 and spring of 1775, he met socially with the leaders of the Continental Congress, getting to know them personally, and mostly sat on the sidelines observing and saying little, until he was appointed to succeed Benjamin Church as the second director general of the hospital department of the Continental Army in October.[42]

Meanwhile, William Shippen, Jr. was even slower to join the patriot cause, becoming the chief physician to General Hugh Mercer's flying camp in the summer of 1776. Even though he had an entire department to oversee, Morgan still saw Shippen's commission as another attack on his command and became convinced that Shippen was out to take his job, which is eventually what happened after, of course, more bickering and recriminations between the two, this time on a national level. In January 1777 Morgan was replaced by Shippen.

Morgan would then spend the next three years trying to repair his reputation and sully Shippen's. He enlisted the help of Benjamin Rush, and in 1780, court martial proceedings were levied against Shippen. He beat the charge and was reinstated as director general of the medical department, which he would resign in early 1781. Shippen would go on and lead pretty much the same life he had before the war, while Morgan began a steady decline in health and prestige, leading to his death in 1789 at the age of 54.

November

For Robert Morris, 1775 would bear witness to his entrance into politics, where he was elected to the Pennsylvania Assembly that fall and served on the Committee of Safety. Quickly elected to serve in the Continental Congress, in November he was assigned to two important committees, the Secret Committee of Commerce and the Committee of Secret Correspondence.

His firm, Willing and Morris, started in September to acquire arms and ammunition for the Continental Congress, using its contacts throughout the Atlantic world to secure these and create a network to supply the Continental Army throughout the war.[43] When it came time to begin his duties on the Secret Committee of Commerce, Morris tapped into those previously established networks he had built up over his decades as a successful merchant. He helped set up privateering routes in the West Indies and opened commerce with the French. He put into motion efforts to procure arms, powder, cannon, clothing, etc., and ways to pay for all of this, and he headed up distribution efforts once the goods arrived in America. And since Willing and Morris were the leading merchants in the city, they received a large portion of contracts. This somewhat dubious arrangement would lead to many claiming that Morris was a war profiteer, which wasn't totally true or false. But Congress kept on supplying them with contracts and even went so far as to place regular soldiers to guard the firm's warehouses.[44]

News arrived in November that the king would not consider Dickinson's Olive Branch petition. In this uncertain time, the Pennsylvania Assembly adjourned once again and left control of Pennsylvania in the hands of the Committee of Safety and other committees. One person who was becoming more and more active in these committees was David Rittenhouse. He was a member of the Mechanics Association and served on the Committee of Correspondence. He was also named engineer of the Committee of Safety and, in November, began new duties that ranged from surveying to working on problems with arms and munitions manufacturing. He began making defensive surveys of the Delaware river, figuring out the best means to fortify it, with his meticulousness being observed by John Adams: "Rittenhouse is a mechanic; a mathematician, a philosopher, and an astronomer ... [he] is a tall slender man, plain, soft, modest, no remarkable depth or thoughtlessness in his face, yet cool, attentive, and clear."[45]

The burden of being in a war started to make itself felt around the city. Franklin bragged about the "great frugality and great industry" seen throughout Philadelphia, but for others less well-off, that frugality could be seen as hardship. When in this month, rumors abounded about a ball to be held at the New Tavern, with Martha Washington and Dorothy Hancock looking to attend, Sam Adams got word and went to try to persuade them not to go. A meeting was held, and

The Pennsylvania State House, now known as Independence Hall, housed the Second Continental Congress and was the scene of many internal political battles. (*The Historic Mansions and Buildings of Philadelphia*)

a delegation went and visited the ladies. All agreed that it would be best not to attend.[46]

Congress called for days of fasting, and plays, concerts, and horse races were banned in the city. By the end of 1775, the war started to get real for Philadelphia, as one editor/publisher wrote:

> Those whose leisure and abilities might lead them to a successful application to the muses now turn their attention to the rude preparations for war. Every heart and hand seems to be engaged in the interesting struggle for American liberty. Till this important point is settled the pen of the poet and the books of the learned must be in a great measure neglected. The arts and sciences are not cultivated but in the fruitful soil of peace.[47]

And Philadelphia began to change as a result, to meet the new challenges of a revolutionary war.

Conclusion: December 1775

There, as he looked out at December's early darkness, out at the lights of the London Coffee House next door, hearing the voices of the people passing by, he finished his writing. Working alone for the past three months, Thomas Paine poured all of himself into this manuscript, *Plain Truth*. Lessons and readings he called forth from secret reserves that surprised even him. Surprised everyone. And that would light a collective fire amongst the colonists. In no other spot, in no other city could these words have been written than in Philadelphia.

Paine had arrived in Philadelphia 12 months prior and had integrated himself quickly into the city's society. Born in Thetford, Norfolk, England, he had enjoyed a rather benign upbringing, having that precociousness found in many kids who turn into exceptional adults. His mother was an Anglican and his father a Quaker corset-maker. A pleasant if not humble childhood awaited Paine whose formal education ended at 13 when he began an apprenticeship with his father. He was a voracious reader though and educated himself by reading anything he could get his hands on.

After his apprenticeship ended, Paine tried his hand at such various professions as a corset-maker, sailor, and a teacher. But his heart was not in any of those, nor did they provide financially. He married Mary Lambert in 1759 but she died during childbirth along with the baby. All of which left Paine devastated and discontented, going through the motions of life for the next decade.

Beginning in 1762, he held a string of excise collector jobs that he was not

Portrait of Thomas Paine, editor of the *Pennsylvania Magazine* and writer of *Common Sense*, *Rights of Man*, and other works. (*The Many Sided Franklin*)

particularly good at, having been dismissed from one for not inspecting goods that he claimed to have. He remarried in 1771 to the daughter of a tobacconist. The following year he made his first forays into political activism by joining with other tax collectors in demanding better pay and working conditions from Parliament.

In 1772, he published his first political work, *The Case of the Officers of Excise*, a 12-page article making the argument for his fellow excise collectors. But his life imploded in 1774. He lost his excise job for leaving his post without permission. The tobacco shop went under. He had to sell most of his worldly possessions to avoid debtor's jail, and his wife left him. Cast adrift, he set his eye on America to offer some sort of salvation. He moved to London where he was put in contact with Franklin, who supplied him with a letter of introduction:

> The bearer, Mr. Thomas Paine, is very well recommended to me, as an ingenious, worthy young man. He goes to Pennsylvania with a view of settling there. I request you to give him your best advice and countenance, as he is quite a stranger there. If you can put him in a way of obtaining employment as a clerk, or assistant tutor in a school, or assistant surveyor, (of all which I think him very capable,) so that he may procure a subsistence at least, till he can make acquaintance and obtain a knowledge of the country.[1]

And in this lowest of lows, Thomas Paine set sail for America in October of 1774.

Paine somehow managed to arrive in America and Philadelphia in even more dire straits having contracted "ship fever" during the crossing which led him to be carried off the ship on a stretcher. It was November 30. After recuperating, he wasted no time ingratiating himself into the city's life. Browsing the selection of books at Robert Aitken's store, he struck up a conversation with the printer. Paine showed off some of his writings which impressed Aitken, who along with John Witherspoon was in the process of putting together a new magazine, *Pennsylvania Magazine*. Paine was offered the job of editor. Within just a few weeks in America, he already had a new career.

The first issue would come out at the end of January 1775. Paine introduced it: "I consider a magazine as a kind of beehive, which both allures the swarm, and provides room to store their sweets. Its division in cells, gives every bee a province of its own; and though they all produce honey, yet perhaps they differ in their taste for flowers, and extract with great dexterity from one than from another."[2] He used the magazine to publish a number of his own works, including scientific works, "Description of a New Electrical Machine", political essays, and poems, like "The Liberty Tree":

> IN a chariot of light, from the regions of day,
> The Goddess of Liberty came,
> Ten thousand celestials directed her way,
> And hither conducted the dame.
> A fair budding branch from the gardens above,
> Where millions with millions agree,

She brought in her hand as a pledge of her love,
And the plant she named Liberty Tree.
The celestial exotic stuck deep in the ground,
Like a native it flourished and bore;
The fame of its fruit drew the nations around,
To seek out this peaceable shore.
Unmindful of names or distinctions they came,
For freemen like brothers agree;
With one spirit endued, they one friendship pursued,
And their temple was Liberty Tree.
Beneath this fair tree, like the patriarchs of old,
Their bread in contentment they ate,
Unvexed with the troubles of silver or gold,
The cares of the grand and the great.
With timber and tar they Old England supplied,
And supported her power on the sea:
Her battles they fought, without getting a groat,
For the honor of Liberty Tree.
But hear, O ye swains ('tis a tale most profane),
How all the tyrannical powers,
Kings, Commons, and Lords, are uniting amain
To cut down this guardian of ours.
From the East to the West blow the trumpet to arms,
Thro' the land let the sound of it flee:
Let the far and the near all unite with a cheer,
In defense of our Liberty Tree.[3]

The *Pennsylvania Magazine* flourished under Paine's editorship, quickly building up its readership, while he made a name for himself in just a few short months. Paine along with publisher Witherspoon and Francis Hopkinson wrote half of the articles. He loved the challenge, remarking this was the "one kind of life I am fit for, and that is a thinking one, and, of course, a writing one."[4]

The year brought a flurry of writing from him where he was sending off articles not fit for the magazine to be published in the city's newspapers, such as his anti-slavery screed, "African Slavery in America." The magazine's success, going from the first issue selling 600 copies to having 1,500 subscribers in a few short months, bolstered Paine and he requested a raise, which the publishers denied. He began receiving some blowback from editing Witherspoon's work. The situation became untenable for Paine by the early fall, and he quit the magazine in September.

By then, though, he had bigger plans. He intended to produce a pamphlet calling for America's ultimate break with Great Britain and to provide an airtight argument for this ultimate split. Every work read; every idea consumed throughout his life went into his pamphlet. He laid out his liberal, republican beliefs, the stress on individual freedoms, whilst making an impassioned plea for a representative government that protected the citizens' life, liberty, and property.

Paine played things close to his vest: "I follow the rule … to consult nobody, nor to let anybody see what I write till it appears publicly."[5] Benjamin Rush got his hands on at least a few pages and suggested changing the name from *Plain Truth* to *Common Sense*. Rush also put Paine in contact with a sympathetic publisher, Robert Bell, who agreed to publish the pamphlet.

Common Sense came out on January 10, 1776, and promptly sold out in two weeks. It became a colonial best-seller: in the first few months of publication, 150,000 copies were distributed throughout the colonies. The demand was so high that bootleg copies were being printed and sold.

With the publication of *Common Sense*, the game had changed. For so long, even as lives were being lost on battlefields across North America, the hope of most white European Americans was to restore peace with the

Title page of the first edition of *Common Sense*, the most influential piece of writing that helped move the colonies toward declaring their independence. (New York Public Library)

Crown and be treated on the same footing as other British subjects. *Common Sense* showed Americans that they no longer needed to be subjects but were their own masters. Now the struggle became a matter of when independence would occur, not if.

For Philadelphia, the political change had been made permanent. A radical, revolutionary government would replace the Assembly that had stood for three-quarters of a century. The proprietorship dissolved, their lands confiscated. In a real sense all that came before built to this moment. A true sea change. Philadelphia had prepared itself for this momentous occasion.

Over the next years, the war would come to Philadelphia. Battles were fought on its outskirts at Brandywine and Germantown. Then came British occupation. And, finally, peace. The post-war years brought more change as city, state, and country figured out how to exist. Most of the same characters would still be active and take on familiar leadership roles but slowly made way for a new generation.

None of which could have happened if not for the structures, the institutions, and purpose set forth by those Philadelphians who from 1750 to 1775 built the city in their image. Benjamin Franklin and Robert Morris. Those enslaved like Olaudah Equiano and those trying to free them like Anthony Benezet. Elizabeth Graeme and Francis Hopkinson. William Smith and Joseph Galloway. John Dickinson and Charles Thomson. John Morgan and William Shippen, Jr. David Rittenhouse and Thomas Paine. All of them, and so many more exceptional individuals, were imbued with a shared enterprising spirit; an American one; a revolutionary one. It was the spirit of Philadelphia. And though they worked so hard and fought with one another, they had also fought for one another to build Philadelphia into being America's first great city.

Endnotes

Chapter 1

1 Commager, 20.
2 Oberholtzer, *The Literary History of Philadelphia*, 52–53.
3 Franklin, *The Autobiography of Benjamin Franklin*, 54–55.
4 Brands, *The First American*, 16–17.
5 Franklin, 57.
6 Franklin, 57.
7 Brands, 25.
8 Brands, 26–29.
9 "Silence Dogood, No. 5, 28 May 1722," *The Papers of Benjamin Franklin, Vol. 1, January 6, 1706 through December 31, 1734*, 18–21.
10 Brands, 34.
11 Morgan, *Benjamin Franklin*, 39–40.
12 Brands, 50–51.
13 Brands, 88–91.
14 Isaacson, *Benjamin Franklin*, 56.
15 Brands, 112–113.
16 Brands, 188–189.
17 Morgan, *Benjamin Franklin*, 11–14.
18 Morgan, 11–14.
19 Turner, "The Charity School, the Academy, and the College Fourth and Arch Streets," 179.
20 Brands, 244.
21 Morgan, *Benjamin Franklin*, 86–87.
22 Morgan, 102–103.
23 Brands, 338–339.
24 Brands, 354–355.
25 Brands, 356–357.
26 Brands, 360–363.
27 Isaacson, 224.
28 Morgan, *Benjamin Franklin*, 156–159.
29 "Benjamin Franklin to Lord Kames, February 21, 1769," *The Papers of Benjamin Franklin, Vol. 1, January 6, 1706 through December 31, 1734*, 18–21.
30 Morgan, *Benjamin Franklin*, 200–204.
31 Isaacson, 297.

Chapter 2

1 Oberholtzer, *Robert Morris*, 3–4.
2 Oberholtzer, 4.
3 Oberholtzer, 4.

4   Oberholtzer, 4.
5   Ver Steeg, *Robert Morris*, 3.
6   Ver Steeg, 4.
7   Ver Steeg, 4.
8   Ver Steeg, 5.
9   Oberholtzer, *Robert Morris*, 10–11.
10 Ver Steeg, 13.
11 Berg, "The Organization of Business in Colonial Philadelphia," 157.
12 Warner, 17.
13 Schlesinger, *The Colonial Merchants*, 77.
14 This entire process of the many different roles being performed by a merchant is demonstrated in Cathy Matson's "Putting the *Lydia* to Sea: The Material Economy of Shipping in Colonial Philadelphia."
15 Berg, "The Organization of Business in Colonial Philadelphia," 172.
16 The various duties performed by merchants and the overall impact they played on Philadelphia's economy are documented in a wide variety of books and articles like Harry D. Berg's "Economic Consequences of the French and Indian War for the Philadelphia Merchants" and "The Organization of Business in Colonial Philadelphia," Joseph E. Illick's *Colonial Pennsylvania: A History*, Jesse Lemisch, "Jack Tar in the Streets: Merchant Seamen in the Politics of Revolutionary America," Cathy Matson's "Putting the *Lydia* to Sea: The Material Economy of Shipping in Colonial Philadelphia" and *The Economy of Early America: Historical Perspectives & New Directions*, John J. McCusker's "Sources of Investment Capital in the Colonial Philadelphia Shipping Industry," Gary B. Nash's *First City: Philadelphia and the Forging of Historical Memory* and "Urban Wealth and Poverty in Pre-Revolutionary America," Edwin J. Perkins's *The Economy of Colonial America*, Jacob M. Price's "What Did Merchants Do? Reflections on British Overseas Trade, 1660–1790," Arthur M. Schlesinger's *The Colonial Merchants and the American Revolution, 1763–1776*, and Sam Bass Warner, Jr.'s *The Private City: Philadelphia in Three Periods of Its Growth*.
17 Perkins, *The Economy of Colonial America*, 10. Commager, 102.
18 Perkins, 12–13.
19 Wokeck, "German and Irish Immigration to Colonial Philadelphia," 132.
20 Smith, "Death and Life in a Colonial Immigrant City," 884–885.
21 Taken from multiple population figures and averaged out: Billy G. Smith, "Death and Life in a Colonial Immigrant City: A Demographic Analysis of Philadelphia," Susan Edith Klepp, "Philadelphia in Transition: A Demographic History of the City and Its Occupational Groups, 1720–1830," John K. Alexander, "The Philadelphia Numbers Game: An Analysis of Philadelphia's Eighteenth-Century Population," and Gary B. Nash and Billy G. Smith, "The Population of Eighteenth-Century Philadelphia." These numbers include Southwark and the Northern Liberties as they grew alongside Philadelphia and became the homes of many newly relocated peoples due to their cheaper rents and land. Workers of all sorts lived in these slum-like suburbs.
22 See above.
23 Descriptions of the lives and work of artisans can be found in Susan Edith Klepp, "Philadelphia in Transition: A Demographic History of the City and Its Occupational Groups, 1720–1830," Sharon V. Salinger, "Artisans, Journeymen, and the Transformation of Labor in Late Eighteenth-Century Philadelphia," Billy G. Smith, "The Family Lives of Laboring Philadelphians during the Late Eighteenth Century," and Harry D. Berg, "The Organization of Business in Colonial Philadelphia."
24 Philadelphia's diverse shipping industry and the occupations that supported it are chronicled in many different locations like Cathy Matson's "Putting the *Lydia* to Sea: The Material Economy of Shipping in Colonial Philadelphia," John J. McCusker's "Sources of Investment Capital in the Colonial Philadelphia Shipping Industry," Gary M. Walton's "A Quantitative Study of American Colonial Shipping: A Summary," and many of the above references.
25 Perkins, 35.
26 See above. The role that Philadelphia played in the larger Trans-Atlantic trade system is covered in a variety of sources such as Robin Pearson and David Richardson's "Social Capital, Institutional Innovation

and Atlantic Trade Before 1800," Jacob M. Price's "What Did Merchants Do? Reflections on British Overseas Trade, 1660–1790." Daniel Strum's "Institutional Choice in the Governance of the Early Atlantic Sugar Trade: Diasporas, Markets, and Courts," Cathy Matson's *The Economy of Early America: Historical Perspectives & New Directions*, and Edwin J. Perkins's *The Economy of Colonial America*.

27 Vickers, "The Northern Colonies," 237.
28 Vickers, "The Northern Colonies," 237.
29 These themes are thoroughly explored in K. Tawny Paul's "Credit and Ethnicity in the Urban Atlantic World: Scottish Associational Culture in Colonial Philadelphia."
30 See above.
31 See above.
32 See above.
33 McCusker, "Sources of Investment Capital," 147.
34 Perkins, 145.
35 Nash, "Up from the Bottom in Franklin's Philadelphia," 74–80.
36 Warner, *The Private City*, 7.
37 Perkins, 145. Warner, 7.
38 Warner, 19.
39 Warner, 68.
40 For a more in-depth look at the economic impact of the Seven Years' War see Harry D. Berg's "Economic Consequences of the French and Indian War for the Philadelphia Merchants."
41 See Gary B. Nash's "Poverty and Poor Relief in Pre-Revolutionary Philadelphia" for a detailed discussion of the nature of impoverishment in the city and the efforts made to combat it.
42 Williams, "The 'Industrious Poor'," 436.
43 Nash, "Poverty and Poor Relief," 8.
44 Berg, "Economic Consequences of the French and Indian War," 185–186.
45 Berg, 186
46 Berg, 187.
47 See above.
48 Berg, 188.
49 Berg, 189.
50 Berg, 190.
51 Johnson's "Fair Traders and Smugglers in Philadelphia, 1754–1763" provides a detailed look at the impact of smuggling on the Philadelphian economy during the Seven Years' War.
52 Nash, *First City*, 70.
53 Nash, "Poverty and Poor Relief," 15.
54 Nash, "Poverty and Poor Relief," 15.

Chapter 3

1   Equiano, *The Life of Olaudah Equiano*, 43–44.
2   Equiano, 47–48.
3   Equiano, 50–52.
4   Equiano, 110.
5   Equiano, 161.
6   Nash, "Slaves and Slaveowners in Colonial Philadelphia," 225–226.
7   Turner, "Slavery in Colonial Pennsylvania," 145.
8   Flanders and Mitchell, eds. *The Statues at Large of Pennsylvania from 1682 to 1801*, 59–60, 308.
9   Nash, *Forging Freedom*, 35.
10 Nash, "Slaves and Slaveowners in Colonial Philadelphia," 229.
11 Nash, *Forging Freedom*, 11.

12 Nash, *Forging Freedom*, 11.

13 Klepp, "Seasoning and Society," 477.

14 Klepp, "Seasoning and Society," 477.

15 Wax, "The Demand for Slave Labor in Colonial Pennsylvania," 343.

16 Brouwer, "The Negro as a Slave," 113.

17 Nash, "Slaves and Slaveowners in Colonial Philadelphia," 251.

18 Wax, "The Demand for Slave Labor in Colonial Pennsylvania," 334–335; Brouwer, 14.

19 A number of different researchers have delved into the different types of skills that enslaved people held throughout Philadelphia's history; see Merle Gerald Brouwer's "The Negro as a Slave and as a Free Black in Colonial Pennsylvania," Gary B. Nash's *Forging Freedom: The Formation of Philadelphia's Black Community, 1720–1840* and "Slaves and Slaveowners in Colonial Philadelphia," and Edward Raymond Turner's *The Negro in Pennsylvania: Slavery-Servitude-Freedom, 1639–1861.*

20 Wax, "The Demand for Slave Labor in Colonial Pennsylvania," 337.

21 Wax, "Preferences for Slaves in Colonial America," 376.

22 Wax, "Preferences for Slaves in Colonial America," 374.

23 Wax, "Preferences for Slaves in Colonial America," 398.

24 Wax, "Preferences for Slaves in Colonial America," 398.

25 Klepp, "Seasoning and Society," 478.

26 Klepp, 481–482.

27 Klepp, 486.

28 Saltar, "Fanny Saltar's Reminiscences," 189.

29 Klepp, "Seasoning and Society," 487.

30 Wax, "Negro Resistance to the Early American Slave Trade," 14–15.

31 Wax, "Negro Resistance to the Early American Slave Trade," 14–15.

32 Brouwer, 66, 311.

33 Phillips, *American Negro Slavery*, 112–113.

34 Nash, *Forging Freedom*, 13.

35 Soderland, "Black Women in Colonial Pennsylvania," 51.

36 Soderland, "Black Women in Colonial Pennsylvania," 51.

37 Soderland, "Black Women in Colonial Pennsylvania," 51.

38 Soderland, "Black Women in Colonial Pennsylvania," 60–61.

39 Salinger, *'To serve well and faithfully'*, 115–116.

40 Salinger, *'To serve well and faithfully'*, 115–116.

41 Salinger, *'To serve well and faithfully'*, 113–114.

42 Salinger, *'To serve well and faithfully'*, 152.

43 Nash, *Forging Freedom*, 38.

44 Nash, *Forging Freedom*, 38.

45 Jackson, *Let This Voice Be Heard*, 35–36.

46 Quaker attitudes towards enslavement and efforts to curtail it are discussed in Ira V. Brown's "Pennsylvania's Antislavery Pioneers, 1688–1776." Maurice Jackson's *Let This Voice Be Heard: Anthony Benezet, Father of Atlantic Abolitionism*, Edward Raymond Turner's "The Abolition of Slavery in Pennsylvania," and Darold D. Wax's "Quaker Merchants and the Slave Trade in Colonial Pennsylvania."

47 Bridenbaugh and Bridenbaugh, *Rebels and Gentlemen*, 254.

48 Jackson, 45.

49 Jackson, 105.

50 Jackson, 20.

51 Jackson, 22.

52 Bridenbaugh and Bridenbaugh, 254–255.

53 Jackson, 24.

54 Jackson, 109, 135.

Chapter 4

1   Lyons, *Sex Among the Rabble*, 1.
2   Nash, *First City*, 242.
3   Lyons, 64.
4   Wulf, 76.
5   Wulf, 108.
6   Shammas, "The Female Social Structure of Philadelphia in 1775," 77.
7   Sharon V. Salinger's "'Send No More Women': Female Servants in Eighteenth-Century Philadelphia" offers an in-depth look at the lives of female domestic servants in Colonial Philadelphia.
8   Warner, 19.
9   Nash, *First City*, 61.
10   Shammas, 78.
11   Isaac, "Ann Flower's Sketchbook," 143–144.
12   Isaac, 144. Ann Marsh was Philadelphia's best-known needlework teacher during this period.
13   Isaac, 144.
14   Ousterhout, *The Most Learned Woman in America*, 40.
15   Lyons, 18.
16   Lyons, 14.
17   Lyons, 18.
18   Lyons, 18.
19   Lyons, 55.
20   Lyons, 25.
21   Lyons, 45.
22   Lyons, 45–47.
23   Lyons, 32.
24   Lyons, 53.
25   Lyons, 54.
26   Wulf, 14.
27   Lyons, 24.
28   Lyons, 135.
29   Shammas, 83; Cleary, "'She will Be in the Shop'," 183, 189, 191.
30   Wulf, 123.
31   Shammas, 83.
32   Salinger, 30–31.
33   Salinger, 39.
34   Salinger, 36–37.
35   Salinger, 46–47.
36   Wulf, 126.
37   Lyons, 61.
38   Lyons, 68.
39   Lyons, 69; Brouwer, 114.
40   Lyons, 92.
41   Lyons, 105.
42   Lyons, 110.
43   Lyons, 106.
44   Lyons, 113.
45   Lyons, 37–42.
46   Lyons, 118–119.
47   Lyons, 121.
48   Lyons, 122.

49   Eve, "Extracts from the Journal of Miss Sarah Eve," 26.
50   Bridenbaugh and Bridenbaugh, 125.
51   Bridenbaugh and Bridenbaugh, 125.
52   Lyons, 137.
53   Lyons, 143.
54   Lyons, 152.
55   Lyons, 152–155.
56   Lyons, 164.
57   Lyons, 171.
58   Ousterhout, 38.
59   Ousterhout, 42.
60   Ousterhout, 44.
61   Ousterhout, 46–47.
62   Ousterhout, 53.
63   Ousterhout, 57.
64   Ousterhout, 67.
65   Ousterhout, 85.
66   Ousterhout, 85.
67   Ousterhout, 87.
68   Ousterhout, 102.
69   Ousterhout, examples on 106.
70   Ousterhout, 112.
71   Ousterhout, 115.
72   Ousterhout, 116.
73   Ousterhout, 122.
74   Ousterhout, 122–123.
75   Ousterhout, 134.
76   Ousterhout, 134.

Chapter 5

1   Bridenbaugh and Bridenbaugh, 83.
2   Thompson, "From the 'Most Ornamental'," 71–72.
3   Bridenbaugh and Bridenbaugh, 81.
4   Lively, "William Smith," 239.
5   Lively, 238.
6   Thompson, 54.
7   Thompson, 78–79.
8   Thompson, 96, 101, 119.
9   Franklin, "Observations Concerning the Increase of Mankind, 1751," *The Papers of Benjamin Franklin, Vol. 4, July 1, 1750 through June 30, 1753*, 225–234.
10   Thompson, 77, 81.
11   Thompson, 77, 81.
12   Lively, 240.
13   Smith, *A Brief State of the Province of Pennsylvania*, 52.
14   Byrnes, "The Pre-Revolutionary Career of Provost William Smith," 96.
15   Thompson, 152–153.
16   Byrnes, 101–102.
17   Lively, 245.
18   Byrnes, 110.
19   Lively, 253.

20   Lively, 128–129.
21   Lively, 254.
22   Buxbaum, "Benjamin Franklin and William Smith," 362.
23   Byrnes, 79.
24   Byrnes, 80. Buxbaum, 367.
25   Buxbaum, 379.
26   Norris, *The Early History of Medicine in Philadelphia*, 149.
27   Joseph Carson's *A History of the Medical Department of the University of Pennsylvania from Its Foundation in 1765* provides a comprehensive look at the early physicians of Philadelphia and their medical education background.
28   Bridenbaugh and Bridenbaugh, 300–301.
29   Hunter, 37; Bridenbaugh and Bridenbaugh, 273.
30   Bell, *John Morgan: Continental Doctor*, 106–107.
31   Corner, *William Shippen, Jr.*, 118.
32   Norris, 37.
33   Corner, 102.
34   Carson, *A History of the Medical Department*, 42.
35   Bridenbaugh and Bridenbaugh, 281; Norris, 44.
36   Bell, 110.
37   Carson, 46.
38   Carson, 46–47; Bridenbaugh and Bridenbaugh, 285.
39   Bridenbaugh and Bridenbaugh, 117–118.
40   Bell, 110–112.
41   Bell, 112.
42   Bell, 118.
43   Bell, 118, 120.
44   Bell, 124–125.
45   Bell, 132.
46   Carson, 57.
47   Carson, 70–71.
48   Bell, 156–157.
49   Bell, 158.
50   Bell, 143, 158.
51   Bell, 137.
52   Bridenbaugh and Bridenbaugh, 293.
53   Bell, 137.
54   Bell, 138.
55   Bell, 138–139.
56   Bridenbaugh and Bridenbaugh, 294–295.
57   Bell, 140–141.
58   Bell, 141–142.
59   Bell, 142.

Chapter 6

1   Bridenbaugh, "The Press and the Book," 8.
2   Oberholtzer, *The Literary History of Philadelphia*, 84; Bridenbaugh, 2.
3   Bridenbaugh, 5.
4   Bridenbaugh, 8, 13.
5   Oberholtzer, 48–49.
6   Oberholtzer, 89.

7   Oberholtzer, 95.
8   Oberholtzer, 64.
9   Oberholtzer, 72–73.
10 Pennington, *Nathaniel Evans: A Poet of Colonial America*, 14–15.
11 Bridenbaugh and Bridenbaugh, 107.
12 Sonneck, *Francis Hopkinson*, 9.
13 Sonneck, 9.
14 Hildeburn, "Francis Hopkinson," 315, 316, 318, 324.
15 Sonneck, *Francis Hopkinson*, 9.
16 Francis Hopkinson, *The Miscellaneous Essays and Occasional Writings*, 1–2.
17 Sonneck, *Francis Hopkinson*, 22, 40.
18 Sonneck, 1, 8, 11, 27.
19 Sonneck, 3.
20 Sonneck, 4, 31, 32, 45, 47.
21 Bridenbaugh, 6, 8.
22 Kintzel, "Vivaldi in Colonial America," 421.
23 Taricani, "Music in Colonial Philadelphia," 186–187.
24 Sonneck, *Francis Hopkinson*, 52–54, 57–58.
25 Sonneck, *Early Concert-Life in America*, 71–72.
26 Taricani, 193.
27 Taricani, 194.
28 Sonneck, *Francis Hopkinson*, 52–54, 57–58.
29 Sonneck, 18, 20, 50.
30 Quinn, "The Theatre and the Drama in Old Philadelphia," 313.
31 Zweers, "The Theatre in American Life," 17.
32 Brooks, "Against Vain Sports and Pastime," 168.
33 Brooks, 170.
34 Quinn, 313.
35 Quinn, 171.
36 Zweers, 313.
37 Brooks, 172.
38 Houchin, "The Struggle for Virtue," 173, 175.
39 Houchin, 172.
40 Quinn, 313–314.
41 Houchin, 176–177.
42 Coad, "Stage and Players in Eighteenth Century America," 205–206; Zweers, 33.
43 Zweers, 34.
44 Houchin, 178.
45 Houchin, 179.
46 Quinn, 314.
47 Quinn, 314.
48 Oberholtzer, 69.
49 Barton, *The Disappointment: or, The Force of Credulity*, Prologue.
50 Mickle, *Reminiscences of Old Gloucester*, 55.
51 Sonneck, *Francis Hopkinson*, 51.
52 Hindle, "Science and the American Revolution," 225.
53 Hindle, "Science and the American Revolution," 227.
54 Hindle, *The Pursuit of Science in Revolutionary America*, 79.
55 McLean, "John and William Bartram," 11.
56 "The Disownment of John Bartram," 16–17.
57 Darlington, *Memorials of John Bartram*, 46.
58 Darlington, 42.

59 Darlington, 52–53.
60 Darlington, 39.
61 Nash, "When We Were Young," 12–13.
62 McLean, 13.
63 Middleton, "John Bartram, Botanist," 191.
64 Middleton, 181–182; Peter Kalm, *Travels into North America*, 132.
65 Sparks, *Lives of Sir William Phips*, 310–311.
66 Rufus, "David Rittenhouse," 506–508.
67 Sparks, 313–314, 319.
68 Rufus, 509–510.
69 Babb and Rittenhouse, "David Rittenhouse," 194.
70 Hornor, 84.
71 "A Forgotten Masterpiece," 184.
72 Babb and Rittenhouse, 211.
73 Babb and Rittenhouse, 214.
74 Sheehan, "The Transit of Venus," 48.
75 Sheehan, 48
76 Sheehan, 51.
77 Babcock and Danson, "Locating Liberty," 340.
78 Smith et al., "Account of the Transit of Venus," 292.
79 Sparks, 349–350.
80 Smith et al., "Account of the Transit of Venus," 294.
81 Rufus, 511.
82 Smith et al., "Account of the Transit of Venus," 306.
83 Smith et al., "Account of the Transit of Venus," 294.
84 Smith et al., "Account of the Transit of Venus," 307.
85 Smith et al., "Account of the Transit of Venus," 309.
86 Smith et al., "Account of the Transit of Venus," 311.
87 Smith et al., "Account of the Transit of Venus," 314–315.
88 Rufus, 511.
89 Hindle, "Science and the American Revolution," 226.

Chapter 7

1   Baldwin, "Joseph Galloway, the Loyalist Politician," 168.
2   Deyerle, "'The Jaws of Proprietary Slavery'," 13.
3   Deyerle, 13–20.
4   Deyerle, 29.
5   Deyerle, 38.
6   Lively, "Toward 1756," 122.
7   Baldwin, "Joseph Galloway, the Loyalist Politician," 161, 163, 165.
8   Baldwin, 127.
9   Baldwin, 128.
10 Baldwin, 117.
11 Hutson, "The Campaign to Make Pennsylvania a Royal Province, 1764–1770, Part I," 430.
12 Hindle, "The March of the Paxton Boys," 462–463.
13 Hindle, "The March of the Paxton Boys," 463.
14 Hindle, "The March of the Paxton Boys," 465.
15 Hindle, "The March of the Paxton Boys," 473.
16 Hindle, "The March of the Paxton Boys," 474.
17 Hindle, *David Rittenhouse*, 22.

18   Hindle, "The March of the Paxton Boys," 479.
19   Hindle, "The March of the Paxton Boys," 475.
20   Hindle, "The March of the Paxton Boys," 476, 478.
21   Hindle, "The March of the Paxton Boys," 480.
22   Hindle, "The March of the Paxton Boys," 482.
23   Olson, "The Pamphlet War over the Paxton Boys," 31.
24   Olson, 32.
25   Olson, 46.
26   Olson, 47.
27   Hutson, "The Campaign to Make Pennsylvania a Royal Province, 1764–1770, Part I," 437.
28   Hutson, "The Campaign to Make Pennsylvania a Royal Province, 1764–1770, Part I," 438–439.
29   Bridenbaugh and Bridenbaugh, 36–38.
30   Deyerle, 83.
31   Deyerle, 443.
32   Deyerle, 452.
33   Deyerle, 453.
34   Baldwin, "Joseph Galloway, the Loyalist Politician," 259–260.
35   Bastian, "'To Secure the Approbation of the Worthy'," 2.
36   Calvert, "Liberty without Tumult," 237.
37   Bastian, 4.
38   Illick, *Colonial Pennsylvania*, 239.
39   Newcomb, "Effects of the Stamp Act," 260.
40   Newcomb, 260–261.
41   Newcomb, 262.
42   Newcomb, 262.
43   Newcomb, 263.
44   Hutson, "The Campaign to Make Pennsylvania a Royal Province, 1764–1770, Part II," 34–35.
45   Hutson, "The Campaign to Make Pennsylvania a Royal Province, 1764–1770, Part II," 35.
46   Hutson, "The Campaign to Make Pennsylvania a Royal Province, 1764–1770, Part II," 36.
47   Baldwin, "Joseph Galloway, the Loyalist Politician (Continued)," 289, 291.
48   Baldwin, "Joseph Galloway, the Loyalist Politician (Continued)," 265.
49   Baldwin, "Joseph Galloway, the Loyalist Politician (Continued)," 271.
50   Baldwin, "Joseph Galloway, the Loyalist Politician (Continued)," 266.
51   Baldwin, "Joseph Galloway, the Loyalist Politician (Continued)," 266.
52   Zimmerman, "Charles Thomson," 465.
53   Zimmerman, 465–466.
54   Harley, *The Life of Charles Thomson*, 47.
55   Harley, 49, 52.
56   Zimmerman, 467.
57   Harley, 63.
58   Zimmerman, 468.
59   Zimmerman, 471.
60   Zimmerman, 472.
61   Zimmerman, 475.
62   Zimmerman, 477.
63   Zimmerman, 479.
64   Deyerle, 7.
65   Hutson, "The Campaign to Make Pennsylvania a Royal Province, 1764–1770, Part II," 42–43.
66   Bastian, 6.
67   Dickinson, 138.
68   Hutson, "The Campaign to Make Pennsylvania a Royal Province, 1764–1770, Part II," 44.
69   Illick, 265–266.

70   Illick, 268. Nash, "When We Were Young," 26.
71   Harley, 68.
72   Ryerson, 40.
73   Harley, 71–72.
74   Ryerson, 41.
75   Ryerson, 41.
76   Ryerson, 41–42.
77   Ryerson, 42.
78   Ryerson, 62.
79   Zimmerman, 464.
80   Calhoon, "'I Have Deduced Your Rights'," 357.
81   Calhoon, 358.
82   Roney, 158–159.
83   Roney, 159.
84   York, 358, 360.
85   Calhoon, 360.
86   Calhoon, 361.
87   Calhoon, 356, 363, 373–375.
88   Calhoon, 376.
89   Bastian, 7.

Chapter 8

1   Ryerson, 102.
2   Marsh, "The First Session of the Second Continental Congress," 38.
3   "Manuscript Minutes of the American Philosophical Society for the Promotion of Useful Knowledge Meetings from 1744–1838," 95.
4   Hindle, *David Rittenhouse*, 83; Sparks, 364.
5   Hindle, 123.
6   Leder, *Dimensions of Change*, 145.
7   "From Benjamin Franklin to the Speaker of the Pennsylvania Assembly: a Circular Letter from Franklin, William Bollan, and Arthur Lee, 24 December 1774," *The Papers of Benjamin Franklin, Vol. 21, January 1, 1774, throughout March 22, 1775*, 398–399.
8   Galloway, *A candid examination of the mutual claims of Great-Britain*, 1–2.
9   Baldwin, "Joseph Galloway, the Loyalist Politician (Concluded)," 424, 426.
10   Brown, "Pennsylvania's Antislavery Pioneers, 1688–1776," 71.
11   Nash, *Forging Freedom*, 43.
12   Wax, "The Negro Slave Trade in Colonial Pennsylvania," 317; Brown, 73.
13   Jackson, *Let This Voice Be Heard*, 28.
14   Klepp, "Seasoning and Society" 496; Soderland, "Black Importation and Migration," 150.
15   Nash, *Forging Freedom*, 36.
16   Ryerson, *The Revolution is Now Begun*, 98–119.
17   Oberholtzer, *Robert Morris: Patriot and Financier*, 17.
18   Marsh, "A History of the First Session of the Second Continental Congress," 11–12.
19   Marsh, 117–118.
20   Marsh, 176.
21   Nicholson, "Sober Frugality and Siren Luxury," 105–106.
22   Marsh, "A History of the First Session of the Second Continental Congress, 223–224.
23   Marsh, 185.
24   Marsh, 167
25   Byrnes, 215.

26 Byrnes, 225.
27 Byrnes, 244.
28 Ryerson, 126.
29 McHenry, "The Life & Times of Dr. Robert Johnston," 11.
30 Calvert, "Liberty without Tumult," 238, 242.
31 Baldwin, "Joseph Galloway, the Loyalist Politician (concluded)," 432.
32 Calhoon, "I Have Deduced Your Rights," 378.
33 Ryerson, 5.
34 Williams, *Hurricane of Independence*, 132.
35 Williams, *Hurricane of Independence*, 133.
36 Ousterhout, 169–170.
37 Graydon, *Memoirs of a Life*, 123–124.
38 Graydon, 123.
39 Graydon, 132.
40 Graydon, 124.
41 Ryerson, 144.
42 Bell, *John Morgan: Continental Doctor*, 178–179.
43 Ver Steeg, 5.
44 Ver Steeg, 5.
45 Hindle, *David Rittenhouse*, 124.
46 Nicholson, 113.
47 Bell, "Some Aspects of the Social History of Pennsylvania," 292.

Conclusion

1 Benjamin Franklin, "From Benjamin Franklin to Richard Bache, 30 September 1774," *The Papers of Benjamin Franklin, Vol. 21, January 1, 1774, throughout March 22, 1775*, 325–326.
2 Paine, *The Life and Work of Thomas Paine*, 21.
3 Paine, "The Liberty Tree."
4 Nelson, "Thomas Paine and the Making of 'Common Sense'," 232.
5 Conway, *The Life of Thomas Paine*, 27.

Bibliography

"A Forgotten Masterpiece—The Rittenhouse Orrery—And Its Maker." *Scientific American* 97, no. 11 (September 14, 1907): 184. https://archive.org/details/ScientificAmerican1907v097n11/page/184/mode/2up.

Alexander, John K. "The Philadelphia Numbers Game: An Analysis of Philadelphia's Eighteenth-Century Population." *The Pennsylvania Magazine of History and Biography* 98, no. 3 (July 1974): 314–24. https://www.jstor.org/stable/20090869.

American Philosophical Society. *The Papers of Benjamin Franklin* Vol. 16. New Haven Conn: Yale University Press, 1959.

Babb, Maurice Jefferis, and Benjamin Rittenhouse. "David Rittenhouse." *The Pennsylvania Magazine of History and Biography* 56, no. 3 (1932): 193–224. https://journals.psu.edu/pmhb/article/view/28248.

Babcock, Todd M., and Edwin F. S. Danson. "Locating Liberty: The 1769 State House Observatory." *Proceedings of the American Philosophical Society* 163, no. 4 (December 2019): 339–63. https://www.jstor.org/stable/45380773.

Baldwin, Ernest H. "Joseph Galloway, the Loyalist Politician." *The Pennsylvania Magazine of History and Biography* 26, no. 2 (1902): 161–91. https://www.jstor.org/stable/20086024.

Baldwin, Ernest H. "Joseph Galloway, the Loyalist Politician (Concluded)." *The Pennsylvania Magazine of History and Biography* 26, no. 4 (1902): 417–42. https://www.jstor.org/stable/20086051.

Baldwin, Ernest H. "Joseph Galloway, the Loyalist Politician (Continued)." *The Pennsylvania Magazine of History and Biography* 26, no. 3 (1902): 289–321. https://www.jstor.org/stable/20086036.

Barone, Dennis. "An Introduction to William Smith and Rhetoric at the College of Philadelphia." *Proceedings of the American Philosophical Society* 134, no. 2 (June 1990): 111–60. https://www.jstor.org/stable/986842.

Barton, Andrew. *The Disappointment: or, The Force of Credulity.* New York: John Leacock, 1767. https://quod.lib.umich.edu/cgi/t/text/text-idx?c=evans;cc=evans;q1=clap;rgn=div1;view=toc;idno=N08267.0001.001;node=N08267.0001.001:3.

Bastian, Peter. "'To Secure the Approbation of the Worthy': The Political Journey of John Dickinson." *Australasian Journal of American Studies* 8, no. 1 (July 1989): 1–11. https://www.jstor.org/stable/41053518.

Bauman, Richard. "For the Reputation of Truth: Quaker Political Behavior in Pennsylvania, 1750–1800." Dissertation, University of Pennsylvania, 1968. http://ezproxy.apus.edu/login?qurl=https%3A%2F%2Fwww.proquest.com%2Fdissertations-theses%2Freputation-truth-quaker-political-behavior%2Fdocview%2F302325556%2Fse-2%3Faccountid%3D8289.

Bell, Jr., Whitfield J. "Astronomical Observatories of the American Philosophical Society, 1769–1843." *Proceedings of the American Philosophical Society* 108, no. 1 (February 28, 1964): 7–14. https://www.jstor.org/stable/985991.

Bell, Jr., Whitfield J. *John Morgan: Continental Doctor*. Philadelphia: University of Pennsylvania Press, 1965.

Bell, Jr., Whitfield J. "Some Aspects of the Social History of Pennsylvania, 1760–1790." *The Pennsylvania Magazine of History and Biography* 62, no. 3 (July 1938): 281–308. https://www.jstor.org/stable/20087125.

Benezet, Anthony. *A Caution to Great Britain and Her Colonies in a Short Representation of the Calamitous State of the Enslaved Negroes in the British Dominions*. Philadelphia: James Phillips, 1785. https://archive.org/details/bim_eighteenth-century_a-caution-to-great-brita_benezet-anthony_1767.

Benezet, Anthony. "Letters of Anthony Benezet." *The Journal of Negro History* 2, no. 1 (January 1917): 83–95. https://www.jstor.org/stable/2713478.

Benezet, Anthony. *Notes on the Slave Trade*. Philadelphia: Enoch Story, 1783. https://digital.library.temple.edu/digital/collection/p16002coll5/id/9835/.

Benezet, Anthony. *Observations On the Inslaving, Importing and Purchasing of Negroes*. Germantown: Christopher Sower, 1959. https://archive.org/details/bim_eighteenth-century_observations-on-the-insl_benezet-anthony_1760.

Benezet, Anthony. *A Short Account of That Part of Africa Inhabited by the Negroes*. Philadelphia, 1762. https://archive.org/details/bim_eighteenth-century_a-short-account-of-that-_1762.

Benezet, Anthony. *Some Historical Account of Guinea, Its Situation, Produce, and the General Disposition of Its Inhabitants*. London: J. Phillips, George Yard, 1788. https://archive.org/details/nby_231149.

Berg, Harry D. "Economic Consequences of the French and Indian War for the Philadelphia Merchants." *Pennsylvania History* 13, no. 3 (July 1946): 185–93. https://www.jstor.org/stable/27766716.

Berg, Harry D. "The Organization of Business in Colonial Philadelphia." *Pennsylvania History: A Journal of Mid-Atlantic Studies* 10, no. 3 (July 1943): 157–77. https://www.jstor.org/stable/27766564.

Berkin, Carol, and Susan Imbarrato Clair. "American Enlightenment." In *Encyclopedia of American Literature*, by Inc. Manly, 3rd ed. Facts On File, 2013.

Biddle, Owen, Joel Bailey, and Richard Thomas. "An Account of the Transit of Venus over the Sun, June 3d, 1769, as Observed near Cape Henlopen, on Delaware. By the Committee Appointed for That Observation." *Transactions of the American Philosophical Society* 1 (1771): 89–96. https://www.jstor.org/stable/1005005.

Bockelman, Wayne L., and Owen S. Ireland. "The Internal Revolution in Pennsylvania: An Ethnic-Religious Interpretation." *Pennsylvania History* 41, no. 2 (April 1974): 125–59. https://www.jstor.org/stable/27772195.

Brands, H. W. *The First American: The Life and Times of Benjamin Franklin*. New York: Doubleday, 2000.

Breen, T. H. "An Empire of Goods: The Anglicization of Colonial America, 1690–1776." *Journal of British Studies* 25, no. 4 (October 1986): 467–99. https://www.jstor.org/stable/175565.

Bridenbaugh, Carl. "The Press and the Book in Eighteenth Century Philadelphia." *The Pennsylvania Magazine of History and Biography* 65, no. 1 (January 1941): 1–30. https://www.jstor.org/stable/20087345.

Bridenbaugh, Carl and Jessica Bridenbaugh. *Rebels and Gentlemen: Philadelphia in the Age of Franklin*. New York: Hesperides, 1962.

Brobeck, Stephen. "Revolutionary Change in Colonial Philadelphia: The Brief Life of the Proprietary Gentry." *The William and Mary Quarterly* 33, no. 3 (July 1976): 410–34. https://doi.org/10.2307/1921541.

Brock, Leslie V. "The Colonial Currency, Prices, and Exchange Rates." *Essays in History* 35 (1992). https://journals.aperio.press/eh/article/id/1401/download/pdf/.

Brooks, Lynn Matluck. "A Decade of Brilliance: Dance Theater in Late-Eighteenth-Century Philadelphia." *Dance Chronicle* 12, no. 3 (1989): 333–65. https://www.jstor.org/stable/1567682.

Brooks, Lynn Matluck. "Against Vain Sports and Pastime: The Theater Dance in Philadelphia, 1724–90." *Dance Chronicle* 12, no. 2 (1989): 165–95. https://www.jstor.org/stable/1567770.

Brouwer, Merle Gerald. "The Negro as a Slave and as a Free Black in Colonial Pennsylvania." Dissertation, Wayne Street University, 1973. http://ezproxy.apus.edu/login?qurl=https%3A%2F%2Fwww. proquest.com%2Fdissertations-theses%2Fnegro-as-slave-free-black-colonial-pennsylvania%2F-docview%2F302711027%2Fse-2%3Faccountid%3D8289.

Brown, Ira V. "Pennsylvania's Antislavery Pioneers, 1688–1776." *Pennsylvania History: A Journal of Mid-Atlantic Studies,* no. 2 (April 1988): 59–77. https://www.jstor.org/stable/27773235.

Butzin, Peter A. "Politics, Presbyterians and the Paxton Riots, 1763–64." *Journal of Presbyterian History (1962–1985)* 51, no. 1 (Spring 1973): 70–84. https://www.jstor.org/stable/23327379.

Buxbaum, Melvin H. "Benjamin Franklin and William Smith Their School and Their Dispute." *Historical Magazine of the Protestant Episcopal Church* 39, no. 4 (December 1970): 361–82. https://www.jstor.org/stable/42974625.

Byrnes, Don Roy. "The Pre-Revolutionary Career of Provost William Smith, 1751–1780." Dissertation, Tulane University, 1969. http://ezproxy.apus.edu/login?qurl=https%3A%2F%2Fwww. proquest.com%2Fdissertations-theses%2Fpre-revolutionary-career-provost-william-smith%2F-docview%2F302478348%2Fse-2%3Faccountid%3D8289.

Cabeen, Francis Von A. "The Society of the Sons of Saint Tammany of Philadelphia." *The Pennsylvania Magazine of History and Biography* 25, no. 4 (1901): 433–51. https://www.jstor.org/stable/20085994.

Caldwell, Charles. *Extract from An Eulogium on William Shippen, M.D.* Philadelphia: J.H. Cunningham, 1818. https://archive.org/details/2545019R.nlm.nih.gov.

Calhoon, Robert M. "'I Have Deduced Your Rights': Joseph Galloway's Concept of His Role, 1774–1775." *Pennsylvania History: A Journal of Mid-Atlantic Studies* 35, no. 4 (October 1968): 356–78. https://www.jstor.org/stable/27771723.

Calvert, Jane E. "Letter to Farmers in Pennsylvania: John Dickinson Writes to the Paxton Boys." *The Pennsylvania Magazine of History and Biography* 136, no. 4 (October 2012): 475–77. https://www.jstor.org/stable/10.5215/pennmaghistbio.136.4.0475.

Calvert, Jane E. "Liberty without Tumult: Understanding the Politics of John Dickinson." *The Pennsylvania Magazine of History and Biography* 131, no. 3 (July 2007): 233–62. https://www.jstor.org/stable/20093948.

Caron, Nathalie, and Naomi Wulf. "American Enlightenments: Continuity and Renewal." *The Journal of American History* 99, no. 4 (March 2013): 1072–91. https://www.jstor.org/stable/44307504.

Carraher, Sarah Sally. "The Body Politic: Splitting Gender Medically in Eighteenth-Century Philadelphia." Thesis, Louisiana State University, 2006. digitalcommons.lsu.edu/gradschool_theses/2665.

Carson, Joseph. *A History of the Medical Department of the University of Pennsylvania from Its Foundation in 1765.* Philadelphia: Lindsay and Blakiston, 1869. https://archive.org/details/historyofmedical00cars.

Chang, Ha-Joon. "Institutions and Economic Development: Theory, Policy and History." *Journal of Institutional Economics* 7, no. 4 (2011): 473–98. https://doi.org/10.1017/S1744137410000378.

Clark, Dennis. "A Pattern of Urban Growth: Residential Development and Church Location in Philadelphia." *Records of the American Catholic Historical Society of Philadelphia* 82, no. 3 (September 1971): 159–70. https://www.jstor.org/stable/44210774.

Cleary, Patricia. "'She Will Be in the Shop': Women's Sphere of Trade in Eighteenth-Century Philadelphia and New York." *The Pennsylvania Magazine of History and Biography* 119, no. 3 (July 1995): 181–202. https://www.jstor.org/stable/20092959.

Coad, Oral Sumner. "Stage and Players in Eighteenth Century America." *The Journal of English and Germanic Philology* 19, no. 2 (April 1920): 201–23. https://www.jstor.org/stable/pdf/27700999.pdf.

Coclanis, Peter A. "Review: In Retrospect: McCusker and Menard's 'Economy of British America.'" *Reviews in American History* 30, no. 2 (June 2002): 183–97. https://www.jstor.org/stable/30031266.

Commanger, Henry Steel. *The Empire of Reason: How Europe Imagined and America Realized the Enlightenment*. Garden City, NY: Anchor Press, 1977.

Conway, Moncure Daniel. *The Life of Thomas Paine: With a History of His Literary, Political, and Religious Career in America, France, and England*. England: Watts & Co., 1909.

Corner, Betsy Copping. *William Shippen, Jr.: Pioneer in American Medical Education*. Philadelphia: American Philosophical Society, 1951. https://archive.org/details/williamshippenjr0000bets.

Coss, Stephen. "What Led Benjamin Franklin to Live Estranged From His Wife for Nearly Two Decades?" *Smithsonian Magazine*, September 2017. https://www.smithsonianmag.com/history/benjamin-franklin-estranged-wife-nearly-two-decades-180964400/.

Darlington, William. *Memorials of John Bartram and Humphrey Marshall with Notices of Their Botanical Contemporaries*. Philadelphia: Lindsay and Blakiston, 1849. https://archive.org/details/memorialsofjoh00darl.

Deyerle, Steven. "'The Jaws of Proprietary Slavery': The Pennsylvania Assembly's Conflict With the Penns, 1754–1768." Thesis, Liberty University, 2013. http://ezproxy.apus.edu/login?qurl=https%3A%2F%2Fwww.proquest.com%2Fdissertations-theses%2Fjaws-proprietary-slavery-pennsylvania-assemblys%2Fdocview%2F1353352961%2Fse-2%3Faccountid%3D8289.

Dickinson, John. *Letters from a Farmer in Pennsylvania, to the Inhabitants of the British Colonies*. New York: The Outlook Company, 1903. https://archive.org/details/lettersfromfarme0000john/page/n13/mode/2up.

Dickson, William. "Account of Anthony Benezet of Philadelphia, a Zealous Advocate for the Abolition of the Slave Trade. Extracted from Clarkson's Interesting History of the Abolition of the African Slave Trade." *The Belfast Monthly Magazine* 4, no. 19 (February 28, 1810): 117–23. https://www.jstor.org/stable/30073662.

"The Disownment of John Bartram." *Bulletin of Friends Historical Association* 17, no. 1 (Spring 1928): 16–22. https://www.jstor.org/stable/41943725.

Ditz, Toby L. "Shipwrecked; or, Masculinity Imperiled: Mercantile Representation of Failure and the Gendered Self in Eighteenth-Century Philadelphia." *The Journal of American History* 81, no. 1 (June 1994): 51–80. https://www.jstor.org/stable/2080993.

Dixon, John M. "Henry F. May and the Revival of the American Enlightenment: Problems and Possibilities for Intellectual and Social History." *The William and Mary Quarterly* 71, no. 2 (April 2014): 255–80. https://www.jstor.org/stable/10.5309/willmaryquar.71.2.0255.

Egnal, Marc. *New World Economies: The Growth of the Thirteen Colonies and Early Canada*. Oxford: Oxford University Press, 1998.

Ellis, Joseph. "Habits of Mind and an American Enlightenment." *American Quarterly*, An American Enlightenment, 28, no. 2 (Summer 1976): 150–64. https://www.jstor.org/stable/2712347.

Engels, Jeremy. "'Equipped for Murder': The Paxton Boys and 'the Spirit of Killing All Indians' in Pennsylvania, 1763–1764." *Rhetoric and Public Affairs* 8, no. 3 (Fall 2005): 355–81. https://www.jstor.org/stable/41939988.

Engerman, Stanley L., and Robert E. Gallman. *The Cambridge Economic History of the United States*. Vol. 1. Cambridge: Cambridge University Press, 1996.

Equiano, Olaudah. *The Life of Olaudah Equiano, or Gustavus Vassa, The African*. Boston: Isaac Knapp, 1837. https://archive.org/details/2340a9ec-1c61-405b-a2df-84933b022d45.

Eve, Sarah. "Extracts from the Journal of Miss Sarah Eve," *The Pennsylvania Magazine of History and Biography* 5, no. 1 (1881): 19–36. https://www.jstor.org/stable/20084486.

Fatherly, Sarah E. "'The Sweet Recourse of Reason': Elite Women's Education in Colonial Philadelphia." *The Pennsylvania Magazine of History and Biography* 128, no. 3 (July 2004): 229–56. https://www.jstor.org/stable/20093721.

Ferling, John E. "Joseph Galloway: A Reassessment of the Motivations of a Pennsylvania Loyalist." *Pennsylvania History: A Journal of Mid-Atlantic Studies* 39, no. 2 (April 1972): 163–86. https://www.jstor.org/stable/27772014.

Fernandez-Sacco, Ellen. "Framing 'The Indian': The Visual Culture of Conquest in the Museums of Pierre Eugene Du Simitiere and Charles Willson Peale, 1779–96." *Social Identities* 8, no. 4 (2002): 571–618. https://doi.org/10.1080/1350463022000068389.

Flanders, Henry and James T. Mitchell, eds. *The Statutes at Large of Pennsylvania from 1682 to 1801*, Harrisburg: William Stanley Ray, 1915.

Florea, Silvia. "Lessons From the Heart and Hearth of Colonial Philadelphia: Reflections on Education, As Reflected in Colonial Era Correspondence to Wives." *Americana: E-Journal of American Studies in Hungary* VI, no. 2 (Fall 2010). https://web.archive.org/web/20160309140113/https://americanaejournal.hu/vol6no2/florea.

Franklin, Benjamin. *The Autobiography of Benjamin Franklin*. New Haven: Yale University Press, 2003.

Franklin, Benjamin, Verner W. Crane, and N. N. "Benjamin Franklin on Slavery and American Liberties." *The Pennsylvania Magazine of History and Biography* 62, no. 1 (January 1938): 1–11. https://www.jstor.org/stable/20087083.

Galloway, Joseph. *A candid examination of the mutual claims of Great-Britain, and the Colonies, with a plan of accommodation on constitutional principles*. New York: Research Reprints, 1970.

Geiser, Karl Frederick. "Redemptioners and Indentured Servants in the Colony and Commonwealth of Pennsylvania." *Yale Review* X, no. 2 (August 1901). https://archive.org/details/redemptionersind00geis/page/n3/mode/2up.

Gleason, J. Philip. "A Scurrilous Colonial Election and Franklin's Reputation." *The William and Mary Quarterly* 18, no. 1 (January 1961): 68–84. https://www.jstor.org/stable/1922808.

Golovin, Anne Castrodale. "Daniel Trotter: Eighteenth-Century Philadelphia Cabinetmaker." *Winterthur Portfolia* 6 (1970): 151–84. https://www.jstor.org/stable/1180528.

Graydon, Alexander. *Memoirs of a Life, Chiefly Passed in Pennsylvania within the Last Sixty Years*. Edinburgh: William Blackwood and T. Cadell, 1822.

Green, Stuart A. "Notes and Documents: Repeal of the Stamp Act: The Merchants' and Manufacturers' Testimonies." *The Pennsylvania Magazine of History and Biography* 128, no. 2 (April 2004): 179–97. https://www.jstor.org/stable/20093704.

Greenhouse, Linda. "Dinner with Ben Franklin: The Origins of the American Philosophical Society." *Proceedings of the American Philosophical Society* 163, no. 1 (March 2019): 1–9. https://www.jstor.org/stable/45222117.

Greeson, Jennifer. "American Enlightenment: The New World and Modern Western Thought." *American Literary History*, The Second Book Project, 25, no. 1 (Spring 2013): 6–17. https://www.jstor.org/stable/23358467.

Harley, Lewis R. *The Life of Charles Thomson*. Philadelphia: George W. Jacobs & Co., 1900. https://archive.org/details/lifecharlesthom00thomgoog.

Harris, P. M. G. "The Demographic Development of Colonial Philadelphia in Some Comparative Perspective." *Proceedings of the American Philosophical Society* 133, no. 2 (June 1989): 262–304. https://www.jstor.org/stable/987055.

Haulman. "Fashion and the Culture Wars of Revolutionary Philadelphia." *The William and Mary Quarterly* 62, no. 4 (October 2005): 625–62. https://www.jstor.org/stable/3491443.

Heavner, Robert O. "Indentured Servitude: The Philadelphia Market, 1771–1773." *The Journal of Economic History* 38, no. 3 (September 1978): 701–13. https://www.jstor.org/stable/2119476.

Henry, Frederick P., and James M. Anders. *Standard History of the Medical Profession of Philadelphia*. Chicago: Goodspeed Broters, 1897.

Henry Steele Commager. *The Empire of Reason: How Europe Imagined and America Realized the Enlightenment*. Garden City, NY: Anchor Press, 1977. https://hdl.handle.net/2027/heb00820.0001.001.

Higgins, Padhraig. "Down but Not Out in Late Eighteenth-Century Philadelphia." *American Journal of Irish Studies* 15 (2019): 47–70. https://www.jstor.org/stable/26859681.

Hildeburn, Charles R. "Francis Hopkinson." *The Pennsylvania Magazine of History and Biography* 2, no. 3 (1878): 314–24. https://www.jstor.org/stable/20084353.

Hindle, Brooke. *David Rittenhouse*. Princeton, New Jersey: Princeton University Press, 1964.

Hindle, Brooke. "The March of the Paxton Boys." *The William and Mary Quarterly* 3, no. 4 (October 1946): 461–86. https://www.jstor.org/stable/1921899.

Hindle, Brooke. *The Pursuit of Science in Revolutionary America, 1735–1789*. Chapel Hill: University of North Carolina Press, 1956.

Hindle, Brooke. "The Rise of the American Philosophical Society, 1766–1787." Dissertation, University of Pennsylvania, 1949. http://ezproxy.apus.edu/login?qurl=https%3A%2F%2Fwww.proquest.com%2Fdissertations-theses%2Frise-american-philosophical-society-1766-1787%2F-docview%2F301863413%2Fse-2%3Faccountid%3D8289.

Hindle, Brooke. "Science and the American Revolution." *The Journal of General Education* 28, no. 3 (Fall 1976): 223–36. https://www.jstor.org/stable/27796579.

Hobbs, Christopher. "The Medical Botany of John Bartram." *Pharmacy in History* 33, no. 4 (1991): 181–89. https://www.jstor.org/stable/41112512.

Hoffer, Peter C. "Law and Liberty: In the Matter of Provost William Smith of Philadelphia, 1758." *The William and Mary Quarterly* 38, no. 4 (October 1981): 681–701. https://www.jstor.org/stable/1918910.

Hopkinson, Francis. *The Miscellaneous Essays and Occasional Writings of Francis Hopkinson, Esq., Vol. I*. Philadelphia: T. Dobson, 1792.

Hoppes, Ronald R. *The Most Important Clock in America: The David Rittenhouse Astronomical Musical Clock at Drexel University*. Philadelphia: American Philosophical Society, 2009.

Hornick, Nancy Slocum. "Anthony Benezet and the Africans' School: Toward a Theory of Full Equality." *The Pennsylvania Magazine of History and Biography* 99, no. 4 (October 1975): 399–421. https://www.jstor.org/stable/20091000.

Hornor, Jr., William Macpherson. "The Famous Rittenhouse Orrery Case Made by the Philadelphia Chippendale, John Folwell." *Bulletin of the Pennsylvania Museum* 27, no. 145 (January 1932): 81–90. https://www.jstor.org/stable/3794625.

Houchin, John H. "The Struggle for Virtue: Professional Theater in 18th Century Philadelphia." *Theatre History Studies* 19 (1999): 167–88. http://ezproxy.apus.edu/login?qurl=https%3A%2F%2Fwww.proquest.com%2Fscholarly-journals%2Fstruggle-virtue-professional-theatre-18th-century%2F-docview%2F2156700%2Fse-2%3Faccountid%3D8289.

Howell, William Huntting. "A More Perfect Copy: David Rittenhouse and the Reproduction of Republican Virtue." *The William and Mary Quarterly* 64, no. 4 (October 2007): 757–90. https://www.jstor.org/stable/25096749.

Hunter, Robert J. "The Origin of the Philadelphia General Hospital." *The Pennsylvania Magazine of History and Biography* 57, no. 1 (1933): 32–57. https://www.jstor.org/stable/20086821.

Hutson, James H. "Benjamin Franklin and William Smith More Light on an Old Philadelphia Quarrel." *The Pennsylvania Magazine of History and Biography* 93, no. 1 (January 1969): 109–13. https://www.jstor.org/stable/20090263.

Hutson, James H. "The Campaign to Make Pennsylvania a Royal Province, 1764–1770, Part I." *The Pennsylvania Magazine of History and Biography* 94, no. 4 (October 1970): 427–63. https://www.jstor.org/stable/20090474.

Hutson, James H. "The Campaign to Make Pennsylvania a Royal Province, 1764–1770, Part II." *The Pennsylvania Magazine of History and Biography* 95, no. 1 (January 1971): 28–49. https://www.jstor.org/stable/20090508.

Iachini, Gian Domenico. "Pierre Eugene Du Simitiere and the First American National Museum." *RSA Journal* 23 (2012): 131–59. https://archive.org/details/domenicodusimitiere.

Illick, Joseph E. *Colonial Pennsylvania: A History*. New York: Charles Scribner's Sons, 1976.

Irvin, Benjamin H. "Tar, Feathers, and the Enemies of American Liberties, 1768–1776." *The New England Quarterly* 76, no. 2 (June 2003): 197–238. https://www.jstor.org/stable/1559903.

Isaac, Amanda. "Ann Flower's Sketchbook: Drawing, Needlework, and Women's Artistry in Colonial Philadelphia." *Winterthur Portfolio* 41, no. 2/3 (Summer/Autumn 2007): 141–60. https://www.jstor.org/stable/10.1086/518919.

Jackson, Maurice. *Let This Voice Be Heard: Anthony Benezet, Father of Atlantic Abolitionism*. Philadelphia: University of Pennsylvania Press, 2010.

Jacobson, David L. "John Dickinson's Fight Against Royal Government, 1764." *The William and Mary Quarterly* 19, no. 1 (January 1962): 64–85. https://www.jstor.org/stable/1919958.

Johnson, Victor L. "Fair Traders and Smugglers in Philadelphia, 1754–1763." *The Pennsylvania Magazine of History and Biography* 83, no. 2 (April 1959): 125–49. https://www.jstor.org/stable/20089178.

Jones, Alice Hanson. *Wealth of a Nation To Be*. New York: Columbia University Press, 1980.

Juhnke, William E. "Benjamin Franklin's View of the Negro and Slavery." *Pennsylvania History: A Journal of Mid-Atlantic Studies* 41, no. 4 (October 1974): 374–88. https://www.jstor.org/stable/27772233

Kalm, Peter. *Travels into North America*. Warrington: William Eyres, 1770. https://archive.org/details/travelsintonorth01kalm_2/page/132/mode

Kellery, Jr., Joseph J. *Pennsylvania: The Colonial Years, 1681–1776*. New York: Doubleday & Co., Inc., 1980.

Kintzel, Robert. "Vivaldi in Colonial America: The Cases of Francis Hopkinson, Peter Pelham and Thomas Jefferson." *Early Music* 42, no. 3 (August 2014): 421–33. https://www.jstor.org/stable/43307085.

Klepp, Susan Edith. "Lost, Hidden, Obstructed, and Repressed: Contraceptive and Abortive Technology in the Early Delaware Valley." In *Early American Technology: Making and Doing Things from the Colonial Era to 1850*, 68–113. Chapel Hill: University of North Carolina Press, 1994. https://ebookcentral.proquest.com/lib/apus/detail.action?docID=4322193.

Klepp, Susan Edith. "Philadelphia in Transition: A Demographic History of the City and Its Occupational Groups, 1720–1830." Dissertation, University of Pennsylvania, 1980. http://ezproxy.apus.edu/login?qurl=https%3A%2F%2Fwww.proquest.com%2Fdissertations-theses%2Fphiladelphia-transition-demographic-history-city%2Fdocview%2F303073448%2Fse-2%3Faccountid%3D8289.

Klepp, Susan Edith. "Seasoning and Society: Racial Differences in Mortality in Eighteenth-Century Philadelphia." *The William and Mary Quarterly* 51, no. 3 (July 1994): 473–506. https://www.jstor.org/stable/2947439.

Koch, Adrienne. "Pragmatic Wisdom and the American Enlightenment." *The William and Mary Quarterly* 18, no. 3 (July 1961): 313–29. https://www.jstor.org/stable/1921168.

Labaree, Leonard W., ed. *The Papers of Benjamin Franklin, Vol. 1, January 6, 1706 through December 31, 1734*. New Haven: Yale University Press, 1959.

Leder, Lawrence H. *Dimensions of Change; Problems and Issues of American Colonial History*. Minneapolis: Burgess Publishing Co., 1972.

Leff, Linda Ringer. "Seven Women Diarists of Eighteenth-Century Philadelphia." Dissertation, Oklahoma State University, 1987. https://shareok.org/bitstream/handle/11244/14344/Thesis-1987D-L493s.pdf?sequence=1&isAllowed=y.

Lemisch, Jesse. "Jack Tar in the Streets: Merchant Seamen in the Politics of Revolutionary America." *The William and Mary Quarterly* 25, no. 3 (July 1968): 371–407. https://www.jstor.org/stable/1921773.

Levey, Martin. "The First American Museum of Natural History." *Isis* 42, no. 1 (April 1951): 10–12. https://www.jstor.org/stable/226659.

Lincoln, Charles H. *The Revolutionary Movement in Pennsylvania, 1760–1776.* Phil: Ginn & Co., 1901.

Lively, Bruce Richard. "Toward 1756: The Political Genesis of Joseph Galloway." *Pennsylvania History: A Journal of Mid-Atlantic Studies* 45, no. 2 (April 1978): 117–38. https://www.jstor.org/stable/27772506.

Lively, Bruce Richard. "William Smith, The College and Academy of Philadelphia and Pennsylvania Politics 1753–1758." *Historical Magazine of the Protestant Episcopal Church* 38, no. 3 (September 1969): 237–58. https://www.jstor.org/stable/43748489.

Lloyd, Jr., William H. "The Courts of Pennsylvania in the Eighteenth Century Prior to the Revolution." *University of Pennsylvania Law Review and American Law Register* 56, no. 1 (January 1908): 28–51. https://www.jstor.org/stable/3313511.

Lundin, Robert Ashley. "A History of the Second Session of the Second Continental Congress." Dissertation, University of Southern California, 1942. http://ezproxy.apus.edu/login?qurl=https%3A%2F%2F-www.proquest.com%2Fdissertations-theses%2Fhistory-second-session-continental-congress%2F-docview%2F1642732268%2Fse-2%3Faccountid%3D8289.

Lyons, Clara A. "Mapping an Atlantic Sexual Culture: Homoeroticism in Eighteenth-Century Philadelphia." In *Long Before Stonewall: Histories of Same-Sex Sexuality in Early America*, 164–203. New York: New York University Press, 2007. https://ebookcentral.proquest.com/lib/apus/detail.action?docID=865438.

Lyons, Clara A. *Sex Among the Rabble: An Intimate History of Gender and Power in the Age of Revolution, Philadelphia, 1730–1830.* Chapel Hill: University of North Carolina Press, 2006.

Mader, Rodney. "Elizabeth Graeme Fergusson's 'The Deserted Wife.'" *The Pennsylvania Magazine of History and Biography* 135, no. 2 (2011): 151–90. https://doi.org/10.5215/pennmaghistbio.135.2.0151.

Main, Gloria L. "Women on the Edge: Life at Street Level in the Early Republic." *Journal of the Early Republic* 32, no. 3 (Fall 2012): 331–47. https://www.jstor.org/stable/23315158.

Manges, Frances May. "Women Shopkeepers, Tavernkeepers, and Artisans in Colonial Philadelphia." Dissertation, University of Pennsylvania, 1958. http://ezproxy.apus.edu/login?qurl=https%3A%2F%2Fwww.proquest.com%2Fdissertations-theses%2Fwomen-shopkeep-ers-tavernkeepers-artisans-colonial%2Fdocview%2F301940876%2Fse-2%3Faccountid%3D8289.

"Manuscript Minutes of the American Philosophical Society for the Promotion of Useful Knowledge Meetings from 1744–1838." *Proceedings of the American Philosophical Society* 22, no. 119 (July 1885): 94–98. https://www.biodiversitylibrary.org/item/86411#page/9/mode/1up.

Marsh, Esbon R. "The First Session of the Second Continental Congress." *The Historian*, no. 2 (Spring 1941): 181–94. https://www.jstor.org/stable/24435926.

Marsh, Esbon R. "A History of the First Session of the Second Continental Congress, May 10 to August 1, 1775." Dissertation, University of Southern California, 1940. http://ezproxy.apus.edu/login?qurl=https%3A%2F%2Fwww.proquest.com%2Fdissertations-theses%2Fhistory-first-ses-sion-second-continental-congress%2Fdocview%2F1646485558%2Fse-2%3Faccountid%3D8289.

Maskelyne, Nevil. "A Letter from Revd. Nevil Maskelyne, B.D.F.R.S. Astronomer Royal, to Rev. William Smith, D.D. Provost of the College of Philadelphia, Giving Some Account of the Hudson's Bay and Other Northern Observations of the Transit of Venus." *Transactions of the American Philosophical Society* 1 (1771): 1–4. https://www.jstor.org/stable/1005010.

Matson, Cathy. *The Economy of Early America: Historical Perspectives & New Directions.* State College, PA: Penn State Press, 2006.

Matson, Cathy. "Putting the *Lydia* to Sea: The Material Economy of Shipping in Colonial Philadelphia." *The William and Mary Quarterly* 74, no. 2 (April 2017): 303–32. https://www.jstor.org/stable/10.5309/willmaryquar.74.2.0303.

May, Henry Farnham. *The Enlightenment in America.* New York: Oxford University Press, 1976. https://hdl.handle.net/2027/heb00282.0001.001.

McCreary, Nancy H. "Pennsylvania Literature of the Colonial Period." *The Pennsylvania Magazine of History and Biography* 52, no. 4 (1928): 289–316. https://www.jstor.org/stable/20086681.

McCusker, John J. "Sources of Investment Capital in the Colonial Philadelphia Shipping Industry." *The Journal of Economic History* 32, no. 1 (March 1972): 146–57. https://www.jstor.org/stable/2117181.

McHenry, Justin. "The Life & Times of Dr. Robert Johnston." *Journal of the Franklin County Historical Society* 29 (201): 7–30.

McLean, Elizabeth P. "John and William Bartram: Their Importance to Botany and Horticulture." *Bartonia*, no. 57 (1992): 10–27. https://www.jstor.org/stable/44898392.

McMahon, Lucia. "'So Truly Afflicting and Distressing to Me His Sorrowing Mother': Expressions of Maternal Grief in Eighteenth-Century Philadelphia." *Journal of the Early Republic* 32 (Spring 2012): 27–60. https://www.jstor.org/stable/41478746.

McMahon, Michael. "'Publick Service' versus 'Mans Properties': Dock Creek and the Origins of Urban Technology in Eighteenth-Century Philadelphia." In *Early American Technology: Making and Doing Things from the Colonial Era to 1850*, 114–47. Chapel Hill: University of North Carolina Press, 1994. https://ebookcentral.proquest.com/lib/apus/detail.action?docID=4322193.

Merritt, Jane T. "Tea Trade, Consumption, and the Republican Paradox in Prerevolutionary Philadelphia." *The Pennsylvania Magazine of History and Biography* 128, no. 2 (April 2004): 117–48. https://www.jstor.org/stable/20093702.

Meyer, D. H. "The Uniqueness of the American Enlightenment." *American Quarterly*, An American Enlightenment, 28, no. 2 (Summer 1976): 165–86. https://www.jstor.org/stable/2712348.

Michaels, Blake J. "I Humbly Request the Favour of Your Votes: Political Discourse and Campaigning in Philadelphia Print, 1719–1776." Thesis, Lehigh University, 2017. http://ezproxy.apus.edu/login?qurl=https%3A%2F%2Fwww.proquest.com%2Fdissertations-theses%2Fi-humbly-request-favour-your-votes-political%2Fdocview%2F1892854876%2Fse-2%3Faccountid%3D8289.

Mickle, Isaac. *Reminiscences of Old Gloucester.* Philadelphia: Townsend Ward, 1845. https://archive.org/details/reminiscencesofo01mick/page/n7/mode/2up.

Middleton, William Shainline. "John Bartram, Botanist." *The Scientific Monthly* 21, no. 2 (August 1925): 191–216. https://www.jstor.org/stable/7513.

Mittleberger, Gotlieb. *Gottlieb Mittelberger's Journey to Pennsylvania.* Translated by Carl Theo Eben. Philadelphia: Joseph Y. Jeanes, 1898. https://archive.org/details/gottliebmittelbe00mitte.

Morgan, Edmund S. *Benjamin Franklin.* New Haven: Yale University Press, 2002.

Morgan, John. *A Discourse Upon the Institution of Medical Schools in America.* Philadelphia: William Bradford, 1765. https://archive.org/details/discourseuponins0000unse.

Morgan, John. *The Journal of Dr. John Morgan of Philadelphia.* Philadelphia: J. B. Lippincott Co., 1907. https://archive.org/details/journalofdrjohnm00morg.

Nash, Gary B. *First City: Philadelphia and the Forging of Historical Memory.* Philadelphia: University of Pennsylvania Press, 2002.

Nash, Gary B. *Forging Freedom: The Formation of Philadelphia's Black Community, 1720–1840.* Cambridge, MA: Harvard University Press, 1988.

Nash, Gary B. "Franklin and Slavery." *Proceedings of the American Philosophical Society* 150, no. 4 (December 2006): 618–35. https://www.jstor.org/stable/4599029.

Nash, Gary B. "Poverty and Poor Relief in Pre-Revolutionary Philadelphia." *The William and Mary Quarterly* 33, no. 1 (January 1976). https://www.jstor.org/stable/1921691.

Nash, Gary B. "Reverberations of Haiti in the American North: Black Saint Dominguans in Philadelphia." *Pennsylvania History: A Journal of Mid-Atlantic Studies* 65 (1998): 44–73. https://www.jstor.org/stable/27774161.

Nash, Gary B. "Slaves and Slaveowners in Colonial Philadelphia." *The William and Mary Quarterly* 30, no. 2 (April 1973): 223–56. https://www.jstor.org/stable/1925149.

Nash, Gary B. "The Transformation of Urban Politics, 1700–1765." *The Journal of American History* 60, no. 3 (December 1973): 605–32. https://www.jstor.org/stable/1917681.

Nash, Gary B. "Up from the Bottom in Franklin's Philadelphia." *Past & Present* 77 (November 1977): 57–83. https://www.jstor.org/stable/650387.

Nash, Gary B. "Urban Wealth and Poverty in Pre-Revolutionary America." *The Journal of Interdisciplinary History* 6, no. 4 (Spring 1976): 545–84. https://www.jstor.org/stable/202532.

Nash, Gary B. "When We Were Young: The American Philosophical Society in the 18th Century." *Proceedings of the American Philosophical Society* 163, no. 1 (March 2019): 10–50. https://www.jstor.org/stable/45222118.

Nash, Gary B., and Billy G. Smith. "The Population of Eighteenth-Century Philadelphia." *Pennsylvania Magazine of History and Biography* 99 (1975): 362–68. https://journals.psu.edu/pmhb/article/view/43167.

Nelson, Craig. "Thomas Paine and the Making of 'Common Sense.'" *New England Review* 27, no. 3 (2006): 228–50. https://www.jstor.org/stable/40244868.

Neptune, H. Reuben. "Throwin' Scholarly Shade: Eric Williams in the New Histories of Capitalism and Slavery." *Journal of the Early Republic* 39 (Summer 2019): 299–326. http://ezproxy.apus.edu/login?qurl=https%3A%2F%2Fwww.proquest.com%2Fscholarly-journals%2Fthrowin-scholar-ly-shade-eric-williams-new%2Fdocview%2F2632238961%2Fse-2%3Faccountid%3D8289.

Newcomb, Benjamin H. "Effects of the Stamp Act on Colonial Pennsylvania Politics." *The William and Mary Quarterly* 23, no. 2 (April 1966): 257–72. https://www.jstor.org/stable/1922510.

Newman, Simon P. "Benjamin Franklin and the Leather-Apron Men: The Politics of Class in Eighteenth-Century Philadelphia." *Journal of American Studies* 43, no. 2 (2009): 161–75. https://www.jstor.org/stable/40464376.

Nicholson, Wendy Anne. "Sober Frugality and Siren Luxury: The Transformation of Elite Culture in Philadelphia, 1750–1800." (Dissertation, University of California at Berkeley. 1994.)

Norris, George W. *The Early History of Medicine in Philadelphia*. Philadelphia: Collins Printing House, 1886. https://archive.org/details/earlyhistoryofme00norr.

Oberholtzer, Ellis Paxton. *The Literary History of Philadelphia*. Philadelphia: George W. Jacobs & Co., 1906. https://archive.org/details/literaryhistofphil00oberrich.

Oberholtzer, Ellis Paxton. *Robert Morris: Patriot and Financier*. New York: Burt Franklin, 1903. https://archive.org/details/robertmorrispat01obergoog.

Olson, Alison. "The Pamphlet War over the Paxton Boys." *The Pennsylvania Magazine of History and Biography* 123, no. 1/2 (April 1999): 31–55. https://www.jstor.org/stable/20093260.

O'Neal, Debra M. "Mistresses & Maids: The Transformation of Women's Domestic Labor and Household Relations in Late Eighteenth-Century Philadelphia." Dissertation, University of California, Riverside, 1994. http://ezproxy.apus.edu/login?qurl=https%3A%2F%2Fwww.proquest.com%2Fdissertations-theses%2Fmistresses-maids-transformation-womens-domestic%2F-docview%2F304094938%2Fse-2%3Faccountid%3D8289.

Orosz, Joel J. *Curators and Culture: The Museum Movement in America, 1740–1870*. Tuscaloosa: University of Alabama, 1990.

Orosz, Joel J. *The Eagle That Is Forgotten*. Wolfeboro, NH: Bowers and Merena Galleries, Inc., 1988. https://archive.org/details/eaglethatisforgo0000joel.

Ousterhout, Anne M. *The Most Learned Woman in America: A Life of Elizabeth Graeme Fergusson*. State College, PA: Penn State Press, 2004.

Pacholl, Keith. "'Let Both Sexes Be Carefully Instructed': Educating Youth in Colonial Philadelphia." In *Children in Colonial America*, 301–20. New York: New York University Press, 2006. https://ebookcentral.proquest.com/lib/apus/reader.action?docID=2081605&ppg=206.

Paine, Thomas. "The Liberty Tree." July 1775. Thomaspaine.org. Accessed February 19, 2024. https://thomaspaine.org/works/essays/poetry/liberty-tree.html.

Paine, Thomas. *The Life and Work of Thomas Paine, Vol. 2*. New Rochelle, New York: Thomas Paine National Historical Association, 1925.

Paul, K. Tawny. "Credit and Ethnicity in the Urban Atlantic World: Scottish Associational Culture in Colonial Philadelphia." *Early American Studies* 13, no. 3 (Summer 2015): 661–91. https://www.jstor.org/stable/24474860.

Pearson, Robin, and David Richardson. "Social Capital, Institutional Innovation and Atlantic Trade Before 1800." *Business History* 50, no. 6 (November 2008): 765–80. https://www.tandfonline.com/doi/full/10.1080/00076790802420336.

Pennington, Edgar Legare. *Nathaniel Evans: A Poet of Colonial America*. Ocala: Taylor Printing Company, 1935. https://archive.org/details/nathanielevanspo00penn/page/n17/mode/2up?view=theater.

Perkins, Edwin J. *The Economy of Colonial America*. New York: Columbia University Press, 1980. https://archive.org/details/economyofcolonia0000perk/page/n5/mode/2up?view=theater.

Phillips, Ulrich Bonnell. *American Negro Slavery: A Survey of the Supply, Employment and Control of Negro Labor as Determined by the Plantation Regime*. Baton Rouge: Louisiana State University Press, 1966.

Plummer, Wilbur C. "Consumer Credit in Colonial Philadelphia." *The Pennsylvania Magazine of History and Biography* 66, no. 4 (October 1942): 385–409. https://www.jstor.org/stable/20087527.

Pollock, Thomas Clark. "Rowe's Tamerlane and The Prince of Parthia." *American Literature* 6, no. 2 (May 1934): 158–62. https://www.jstor.org/stable/2919793.

Potts, William John, and Pierre Eugene Du Simitiere. "Du Simitiere, Artist, Antiquary, and Naturalist, Projector of the First American Museum, with Some Extracts from His Note-Book." *The Pennsylvania Magazine of History and Biography* 13, no. 3 (October 1889): 341–75. https://www.jstor.org/stable/20083331.

Price, Jacob M. "What Did Merchants Do? Reflections on British Overseas Trade, 1660–1790." *The Journal of Economic History* 49, no. 2 (June 1989): 267–84. https://www.jstor.org/stable/2124062.

Quinn, Arthur Hobson. "The Theatre and the Drama in Old Philadelphia." *Transactions of the American Philosophical Society* 43, no. 1 (1953): 313–17. https://www.jstor.org/stable/1005685.

Rankin, Hugh F. *The Theater in Colonial American*. Chapel Hill: University of North Carolina Press, 1965.

Reid-Maroney, Nina Ruth. "Theology and Science in Philadelphia's Enlightenment, 1740–1800." Thesis, University of Toronto, 1992. http://ezproxy.apus.edu/login?qurl=https%3A%2F%2Fwww.proquest.com%2Fdissertations-theses%2Ftheology-science-philadelphias-enlightenment-1740%2F-docview%2F304024711%2Fse-2%3Faccountid%3D8289.

Riddell, William Renwick. "Pre-Revolutionary Pennsylvania and the Slave Trade." *The Pennsylvania Magazine of History and Biography* 52, no. 1 (1928): 1–28. https://www.jstor.org/stable/20086656.

Ridner, Judith. "Unmasking the Paxton Boys: The Material Culture of the Pamphlet War." *Early American Studies* 14, no. 2 (Spring 2016): 348–76. https://www.jstor.org/stable/earlamerstud.14.2.348.

Rittenhouse, David, and William Smith. "A Description of an Orrery, Executed on a New Plan." *Transactions of the American Philosophical Society* 1 (January 1, 1769): 1–3. https://www.jstor.org/stable/1005000.

"The Rittenhouse Orrery." *The Princeton University Library Chronicle* 12, no. 3 (Spring 1951): 121–25. https://www.jstor.org/stable/i26401767.

Rodgers, Glen M. "Benjamin Franklin and the Universality of Science." *The Pennsylvania Magazine of History and Biography* 85, no. 1 (January 1961): 50–69. https://www.jstor.org/stable/20089360.

Rolater, Frederick Strickland. "Charles Thomson: Secretary of the Continental Congresses, 1774–1789." Thesis, University of Southern California, 1963. http://ezproxy.apus.edu/login?qurl=https%3A%2F%2Fwww.proquest.com%2Fdissertations-theses%2Fcharles-thomson-secretary-continental-congresses%2Fdocview%2F1642055329%2Fse-2%3Faccountid%3D8289.

Roney, Jessica Choppin. *Governed by a Spirit of Opposition: The Origins of American Political Practice in Colonial Philadelphia*. Baltimore: Johns Hopkins University Press, 2014.

Rufus, W. Carl. "David Rittenhouse—Pioneer American Astronomer." *The Scientific Monthly* 26, no. 6 (June 1928): 506–13. https://archive.org/details/sim_scientific-monthly_1928-06_26_6.

Ryerson, Richard Alan. *The Revolution Is Now Begun: The Radical Committees of Philadelphia, 1765–1776*. Philadelphia: University of Pennsylvania Press, 2012.

Sahle, Esther. "Law and Gospel Order: Resolving Commercial Disputes in Colonial Philadelphia." *Continuity and Change* 35 (2020): 281–310. https://doi.org/10.1017/S0268416020000259.

Salinger, Sharon V. "Artisans, Journeymen, and the Transformation of Labor in Late Eighteenth-Century Philadelphia." *The William and Mary Quarterly* 40, no. 1 (January 1983): 62–84. https://www.jstor.org/stable/1919528.

Salinger, Sharon V. "'Send No More Women': Female Servants in Eighteenth-Century Philadelphia." *The Pennsylvania Magazine of History and Biography* 107, no. 1 (January 1983): 29–48. https://www.jstor.org/stable/20091738.

Salinger, Sharon V., and Charles Wetherall. "Wealth and Renting in Prerevolutionary Philadelphia." *The Journal of American History* 71, no. 4 (March 1985): 826–40. https://www.jstor.org/stable/1888506.

Saltar, Fanny. "Fanny Saltar's Reminiscences of Colonial Days in Philadelphia." *The Pennsylvania Magazine of History and Biography* 40, no. 2 (1916): 187–98. https://www.jstor.org/stable/20086261.

Scharf, J. Thomas, and Thompson Westcott. *History of Philadelphia, 1609–1884*. Vol. I. Philadelphia: L. H. Everts & Co., 1884. https://archive.org/details/historyofphilade01scha.

Schlesinger, Arthur M. *The Colonial Merchants and the American Revolution, 1763–1776*. New York: Frederick Ungar Publishing Col, 1964.

Schlesinger, Arthur M. "The Colonial Newspapers and the Stamp Act." *The New England Quarterly* 8, no. 1 (March 1935): 63–83. https://www.jstor.org/stable/359430.

Shammas, Carole. "The Female Social Structure of Philadelphia in 1775." *The Pennsylvania Magazine of History and Biography* 107, no. 1 (January 1983): 69–83. https://www.jstor.org/stable/20091740.

Sheehan, William. "The Transit of Venus: Tales from the 18th Century." *Sky & Telescope*, February 2004, 46–54. https://search-ebscohost-com.ezproxy1.apus.edu/login.aspx?direct=true&AuthType=ip&db=sch&AN=12085060&site=ehost-live&scope=site.

Shelling, Richard I. "William Sturgeon, Catechist to the Negroes of Philadelphia and Assistant Rector of Christ Church, 1747–1766." *Historical Magazine of the Protestant Episcopal Church* 8, no. 4 (December 1939): 388–401. https://www.jstor.org/stable/42968345.

Shepherd, James. "A Balance of Payments for the Thirteen Colonies, 1768–1772: A Summary." *The Journal of Economic History* 25, no. 4 (December 1965): 691–95. https://www.jstor.org/stable/2116140.

Shippen, Nancy. *Nancy Shippen Her Journal Book*. Philadelphia: J. B. Lippincott Co., 1935. https://archive.org/details/nancyshippenherj006968mbp.

Skemp, Sheila L. "Benjamin Franklin, Patriot, and William Franklin, Loyalist." *Pennsylvania History: A Journal of Mid-Atlantic Studies* 65, no. 1 (Winter 1998): 35–45. https://www.jstor.org/stable/27774078.

Skemp, Sheila L. "William Franklin: His Father's Son." *The Pennsylvania Magazine of History and Biography* 109, no. 2 (April 1985): 145–78. https://www.jstor.org/stable/20091919.

Smith, Billy G. "Death and Life in a Colonial Immigrant City: A Demographic Analysis of Philadelphia." *The Journal of Economic History* 37, no. 4 (December 1977): 863–89. https://www.jstor.org/stable/2119346.

Smith, Billy G. "The Family Lives of Laboring Philadelphians during the Late Eighteenth Century." *Proceedings of the American Philosophical Society*, Symposium on the Demographic History of the Philadelphia Region, 1600–1860, 133, no. 2 (June 1989): 328–32. https://www.jstor.org/stable/987058.

Smith, Billy G. "Inequality in Late Colonial Philadelphia: A Note on Its Nature and Growth." *The William and Mary Quarterly* 41, no. 4 (October 1984): 629–45. https://www.jstor.org/stable/1919157.

Smith, William. *A Brief State of the Province of Pennsylvania*. New York: Joseph Sabin, 1865. https://archive.org/details/briefstateofprov00smit/page/n8/mode/1up.

Smith, William, John Lukens, David Rittenhouse, and Owen Biddle. "Account of the Transit of Mercury, Observed at Norriton, in Pennsylvania, Nov. 9, 1769 Agreeable to an Appointment of the American Philosophical Society Held at Philadelphia, for Promoting Useful Knowledge." *Philosophical Transactions* 60 (January 1, 1770): 504–7. https://www.jstor.org/stable/105914.

Smith, William, John Lukens, David Rittenhouse, and John Sellers. "Account of the Transit of Venus Over the Sun's Disk, as Observered at Norriton, in the County of Philadelphia, and Province of Pennsylvania, June 3, 1769." *Philosophical Transactions* 59 (1769): 289–326. https://www.jstor.org/stable/105839.

Snyder, Mark R. "The Education of Indentured Servants in Colonial America." *The Journal of Technology Studies* 33, no. 1/2 (Winter/Spring 2007): 65–72. https://www.jstor.org/stable/43604120.

Soderland, Jean R. "Black Importation and Migration into Southeastern Pennsylvania, 1682–1810." *Proceedings of the American Philosophical Society* 133, no. 2 (June 1989): 144–53. https://www.jstor.org/stable/987045.

Soderland, Jean R. "Black Women in Colonial Pennsylvania." *The Pennsylvania Magazine of History and Biography* 107, no. 1 (January 1983): 49–68. https://www.jstor.org/stable/20091739.

Soderland, Jean R. "Conscience, Interest, and Power: The Development of Quaker Opposition to Slavery in the Delaware Valley, 1688–1780." Dissertation, Temple University, 1981. http://ezproxy.apus.edu/login?qurl=https%3A%2F%2Fwww.proquest.com%2Fdissertations-theses%2Fconscience-interest-power-development-quaker%2Fdocview%2F303253306%2Fse-2%3Faccountid%3D8289.

Soderland, Jean R. "Women in Eighteenth-Century Pennsylvania: Toward a Model of Diversity." *The Pennsylvania Magazine of History and Biography* 115, no. 2 (April 1991): 163–83. https://www.jstor.org/stable/20092603.

Sonneck, O. G. *Early Concert-Life in America, 1731–1800*. Leipzig: Breitkopf & Hartel, 1907. https://archive.org/details/earlyconcertlife0000sonn.

Sonneck, O. G. *Francis Hopkinson: The First American Poet-Composer, 1737–1791 and James Lyon: Patriot, Preacher, Psalmodist, 1735–1794*. Washington, DC: H. L. McQueen, 1905.

Sonneck, O. G. "Francis Hopkinson: The First American Poet-Composer and Our Musical Life in Colonial Times." Address presented at the Pennsylvania Society of the Colonial Dames of America, Historical Society of Pennsylvania, November 12, 1919. https://archive.org/details/cu31924018493761/mode/1up.

Sparks, Jared. *Lives of Sir William Phips, Israel Putnam, Lucretia Maria Davidson, and David Rittenhouse.* Vol. VII. The Library of American Biography. Boston: Hilliard, Gray, and Co., 1837. https://archive.org/details/livessirwilliam00unkngoog.

Stavisky, Leonard Price. "Negro Craftsmanship in Early America." *The American Historical Review* 54, no. 2 (January 1949): 315–25. https://www.jstor.org/stable/1845390.

Strum, Daniel. "Institutional Choice in the Governance of the Early Atlantic Sugar Trade: Diasporas, Markets, and Courts." *Economic History Review* 72, no. 4 (2019): 1202–28. https://search-ebscohost-com.ezproxy2.apus.edu/login.aspx?direct=true&AuthType=ip& db=bth&AN=139102783&site=ehost-live&scope=site.

Sullivan, Aaron. "'That Charity Which Begins at Home': Ethnic Societies and Benevolence in Eighteenth-Century Philadelphia." *The Pennsylvania Magazine of History and Biography* 134, no. 4 (October 2010): 305–37. https://www.jstor.org/stable/10.5215/pennmaghistbio.134.4.0305.

Taricani, Jo Ann. "Music in Colonial Philadelphia: Some New Documents." *The Musical Quarterly* 65, no. 2 (April 1979): 185–99. https://www.jstor.org/stable/741702.

Thompson, Peter. *Rum, Punch, and Revolution: Taverngoing and Public Life in Eighteenth-Century Philadelphia.* Philadelphia: University of Pennsylvania Press, 1998.

Thompson, Ryan K. "From the 'Most Ornamental' to the 'Most Useful': Educational Experiments in Philadelphia, 1682–1836." Dissertation, University of Delaware, 2013. http://ezproxy.apus.edu/login?qurl=https%3A%2F%2Fwww.proquest.com%2Fdissertations-theses%2Fmost-ornamental-useful-educational-experiments%2Fdocview%2F1443846520%2Fse-2%3Faccountid%3D8289.

Tiedemann, Joseph S. "Interconnected Communities: The Middle Colonies on the Eve of the American Revolution." *Pennsylvania History: A Journal of Mid-Atlantic Studies* 76, no. 1 (Winter 2009): 1–41. https://www.jstor.org/stable/27778871.

Tiedemann, Joseph S. "A Tumultuous People: The Rage for Liberty and the Ambiance of Violence in the Middle Colonies in the Years Preceding the American Revolution." *Pennsylvania History: A Journal of Mid-Atlantic Studies* 77, no. 4 (Autumn 2010): 387–431. https://www.jstor.org/stable/10.5325/pennhistory.77.4.0387.

Tinkcom, Margaret B. "Southwark, a River Community: Its Shape and Substance." *Proceedings of the American Philosophical Society* 114, no. 4 (August 20, 1970): 327–42. https://www.jstor.org/stable/985956.

Turner, Edward Raymond. "The Abolition of Slavery in Pennsylvania." *The Pennsylvania Magazine of History and Biography* 36, no. 2 (1912): 129–42. https://www.jstor.org/stable/20085586.

Turner, Edward Raymond. *The Negro in Pennsylvania: Slavery-Servitude-Freedom, 1639–1861.* Washington: The American Historical Society, 1911. https://archive.org/details/DKC0107.

Turner, Edward Raymond. "Slavery in Colonial Pennsylvania." *The Pennsylvania Magazine of History and Biography* 35, no. 2 (1911): 141–51. https://www.jstor.org/stable/20085542.

Turner, William L. "The Charity School, the Academy, and the College Fourth and Arch Streets." *Transactions of the American Philosophical Society* 43, no. 1 (1953): 179–86. https://doi.org/10.2307/1005670.

Vaughan, Alden T. "Frontier Banditti and the Indians: The Paxton Boys' Legacy, 1763–1775." *Pennsylvania History: A Journal of Mid-Atlantic Studies* 51, no. 1 (January 1984): 1–29. https://www.jstor.org/stable/27772947.

Vaux, Roberts. *Memoirs of The Life of Anthony Benezet.* Philadelphia: W. Alexander, 1817. https://archive.org/details/memoirslifeanth00benegoog.

Ver Steeg, Clarence L. *Robert Morris: Revolutionary Financier.* New York: Octagon Books, 1972.

Vickers, Daniel. "The Northern Colonies: Economy and Society, 1600–1775". In *The Cambridge Economic History of the United States, The Colonial Era*, Vol. 1. Cambridge: Cambridge University Press, 1996. https://doi.org/10.1017/CHOL9780521394420.006.

Wall, Richard. "Woman Alone in English Society." *Annales de Demographie Historique*, 1981, 303–17. https://www.jstor.org/stable/44384667.

Walton, Gary M. "A Quantitative Study of American Colonial Shipping: A Summary." *The Journal of Economic History* 26, no. 4 (December 1966): 595–98. https://www.jstor.org/stable/2115916.

Warner, Jr., Sam Bass. *The Private City: Philadelphia in Three Periods of Its Growth*. Philadelphia: University of Pennsylvania Press, 1968.

Wax, Darold D. "'A People of Beastly Living': Europe, Africa and the Atlantic Slave Trade." *Phylon* 41, no. 1 (1980): 12–24. https://www.jstor.org/stable/274664.

Wax, Darold D. "Africans on the Delaware: The Pennsylvania Slave Trade, 1759–1765." *Pennsylvania History: A Journal of Mid-Atlantic Studies* 50, no. 1 (January 1983): 38–49. https://www.jstor.org/stable/27772875.

Wax, Darold D. "The Demand for Slave Labor in Colonial Pennsylvania." *Pennsylvania History: A Journal of Mid-Atlantic Studies* 34, no. 4 (October 1967): 331–45. https://www.jstor.org/stable/27770523.

Wax, Darold D. "A Philadelphia Surgeon on a Slaving Voyage to Africa, 1749–1751." *The Pennsylvania Magazine of History and Biography* 92, no. 4 (October 1968): 465–93. https://www.jstor.org/stable/20090230.

Wax, Darold D. "Negro Import Duties in Colonial Pennsylvania." *The Pennsylvania Magazine of History and Biography* 97, no. 1 (January 1973): 22–44. https://www.jstor.org/stable/20090706.

Wax, Darold D. "The Negro Slave Trade in Colonial Pennsylvania." Dissertation, University of Washington, 1962. http://ezproxy.apus.edu/login?qurl=https%3A%2F%2Fwww.proquest.com%2Fdissertations-theses%2Fnegro-slave-trade-colonial-pennsylvania%2Fdocview%2F288009883%2Fse-2%3Faccountid%3D8289.

Wax, Darold D. "Negro Resistance to the Early American Slave Trade." *The Journal of Negro History* 51, no. 1 (January 1966): 1–15. https://www.jstor.org/stable/2716373.

Wax, Darold D. "Preferences for Slaves in Colonial America." *The Journal of Negro History* 58, no. 4 (October 1973): 371–401. https://www.jstor.org/stable/2716746.

Wax, Darold D. "Quaker Merchants and the Slave Trade in Colonial Pennsylvania." *The Pennsylvania Magazine of History and Biography* 86, no. 2 (April 1962): 143–59. https://www.jstor.org/stable/20089497.

Wax, Darold D. "Robert Ellis, Philadelphia Merchant and Slave Trader." *The Pennsylvania Magazine of History and Biography* 88, no. 1 (January 1964): 52–69. https://www.jstor.org/stable/20089673.

West, Francis D. "John Bartram and the American Philosophical Society." *Pennsylvania History: A Journal of Mid-Atlantic Studies* 23, no. 4 (October 1956): 463–66. https://www.jstor.org/stable/27769686.

West, Francis D. "John Bartram: Geologist." *Bulletin of Friends Historical Association* 47, no. 1 (Spring 1958): 35–38. https://www.jstor.org/stable/41944656.

Willcox, William B., ed. *The Papers of Benjamin Franklin, Vol. 21, January 1, 1774, throughout March 22, 1775*. New Haven: Yale University Press, 1978.

Williams, Tony. *Hurricane of Independence: The Untold Story of the Deadly Storm at the Deciding of the American Revolution*. Naperville, Illinois: Sourcebooks, Inc., 2008.

Williams, W. H. "The 'Industrious Poor' and the Founding of the Pennsylvania Hospital." *The Pennsylvania Magazine of History and Biography* 97 (October 1973): 431–43. https://www.jstor.org/stable/20090788.

Wistar, Caspar. *Eulogium on Doctor William Shippen*. Philadelphia: Thomas Dobson and Son, 1818. https://archive.org/details/2578005R.nlm.nih.gov.

Wokeck, Marianne S. "German and Irish Immigration to Colonial Philadelphia." *Proceedings of the American Philosophical Society*, Symposium on the Demographic History of the Philadelphia Region, 1600–1860, 133, no. 2 (June 1989): 128–43. https://www.jstor.org/stable/987044.

Woolf, Henry Bosley. "Thomas Godfrey: Eighteenth-Century Chaucerian." *American Literature* 12, no. 4 (January 1941): 486–90. https://www.jstor.org/stable/2920569.

Wulf, Karin. *Not All Wives: Women of Colonial Philadelphia*. Philadelphia: University of Philadelphia Press, 2005.

York, Neil L. "The First Continental Congress and the Problem of American Rights." *The Pennsylvania Magazine of History and Biography* 122, no. 4 (October 1998): 353–83. https://www.jstor.org/stable/20093242.

Zimmerman, John J. "Charles Thomson, 'The Sam Adams of Philadelphia.'" *The Mississippi Valley Historical Review* 45, no. 3 (December 1958): 464–80. https://www.jstor.org/stable/1889321.

Zweers, John Underhill. "The Theatre in American Life, 1750–1800." Thesis, University of Southern California, 1958. https://impa.usc.edu/asset-management/2A3BF16RVIH7?-FR_=1&W=726&H=714.